MARTYRS

FROM ST STEPHEN TO JOHN TUNG

MARTYRS

FROM ST STEPHEN TO JOHN TUNG

by

Donald Attwater

SHEED & WARD : LONDON

First Published 1958
by Sheed & Ward Ltd.
33 Maiden Lane, London W.C.2

NIHIL OBSTAT:
Thomas J. McHugh
Censor librorum

IMPRIMATUR:
Jerome D. Hannan
✠ *Bishop of Scranton*

June 25, 1957.

Printed in Great Britain by
Lowe & Brydone (Printers) Ltd., London, N.W.10

CONTENTS

Contents

INTRODUCTION

Of the saints named in the canon of the Mass according to the Roman rite, in the prayers *Communicantes* and *Nobis quoque peccatoribus*, all, except the Blessed Virgin Mary and St John, were martyrs. This is an evidence of the great antiquity of this eucharistic prayer, for it is a reminiscence of those early days of the Church when the words "martyr" and "saint," in the meanings that they bear today, were practically synonymous. "Christ is in the martyr," wrote Tertullian (d. *c*.225), present and suffering in him, and others wrote in the same sense. According to the Canons of Hippolytus, the simple fact of confessing the faith in the court of the persecutors qualified a man, were he set free, for ordination to the priesthood, even were he a slave. Those in prison for confessing Christ's name, "martyrs designate" (again the expression is Tertullian's), were regarded with the greatest reverence by the faithful; and it was recognized that the intervention of these confessors could soften the rigour of the Church's discipline in respect of those who had weakened and then repented.*

The whole great business of the *cultus* of the saints in the public worship of the Christian Church originated in the veneration given to martyrs, and firstly at the place where they had suffered and been buried, whence it often spread to other places and even to the whole Church. The first extant record of the annual commemoration of a martyr's passion goes back to St Polycarp at Smyrna, in the second half of

* Christian veneration for the confessors was so well known that Lucian of Samosata (d *c*.180), wrote a satire on the subject, the *Death of Peregrinus*.

the second century.* At the heart of the observance was the celebration of the holy Mysteries, during which the martyr's name was pronounced with honour, and the atmosphere of the whole celebration was not funereal but wholly joyous and triumphant. The Mysteries came to be often celebrated over the tomb of a martyr (to this day the relics of saints sealed into every altar-stone and Eastern *antimension* must include those of at least one martyr), and the body itself was at first jealously guarded at its original place of burial: the ancient Roman list of martyrs' feasts, the *Depositio martyrum*, gives not only the dates but also the relevant cemeteries, where the faithful would meet. The honorific translation of a martyr's remains was a Greek innovation (the first recorded instance is of St Babylas at Antioch, *c*.353), and so was the severance of parts of a dead body as relics.† Associated in some way with this regard for the martyrs' mortal remains was the widespread custom of being buried as near as possible to a martyr's tomb.

From very early times it was customary for Christians to call on their dead, especially their close relatives, for their prayers in Heaven; there is plenty of evidence for this in the catacombs. This soon spread to martyrs in particular, superseding the former practice, and then to saints in general; invocations of martyrs were written on the walls near their resting-places, and elsewhere, and many of these scribblings are still there to be read, in Rome and other places: *e.g.*, *Paule et Petre petite pro Victore*, "Paul and Peter, intercede for Victor" (Rome, *c*.275). Nearly a century earlier the Alexandrian martyr Potamiaena promised a kind soldier to speak for him when she came into God's presence.‡ Calling oneself

* It was, and is, called the martyr's *natalis*. According to Father Delehaye, the word simply had the sense of anniversary, the idea of "birthday into the heavenly life" being a later reflection.

† At first this proceeding would have evoked horror, some Christians still regard it with strong disfavour.

‡ As Father Delehaye points out, the practice of invoking the saints depends on belief in their ability to hear and intercede, and not the other way round.

by a martyr's name, in the first place as an expression of reverence towards him or her, was a usage that soon became established. St Dionysius of Alexandria (d.265) tells us that Peter and Paul were favourite names in his day; and the very word "martyr," in the forms Martyrius, Martyria, became popular from the fourth century throughout the Roman empire, east and west. As may easily be imagined, all this development did not take place without abuse and excess among the faithful. Already in the early years of the third century, Tertullian had to rebuke Christians who attributed to the martyrs power that belongs to God alone, nor was he the last who had to protest.*

Not till later on (even in the case of our Lady St Mary herself) were such honours, anniversaries, invocation, dedications, commemorative services, gradually extended to outstandingly holy people who had, nevertheless, not been called on to give their lives for Christ. This development of public veneration did not get into its stride until after the later fourth century, and then with varying degrees of speed and intensity in different places and at different times.

In its origins the word "martyr" simply means a witness; and it is significant that all other saints are called "confessors" (in its non-technical sense the term applies equally to women): for confessor means exactly the same thing, a witness, and the term was originally applied to those Christians who were notable sufferers for their faith, but short of death. The profession of the Christian religion is not anybody's private affair. In virtue of his baptism every Christian is called to be a witness to Christ, in an infinity of possible ways; but of all those ways, none is more final and decisive, none more effective and fruitful, than the willing giving up of life itself;

---

* Cf. below, p. 21, St Augustine and the Passion of St Perpetua and St Felicity. On the origin and development of the *cultus* of the martyrs, see H. Delehaye, *Les origines du culte des martyrs* (Brussels, 1933), chs.i-iv, on which most of the above depends. For a remarkable example of superstition about St Peter's tomb, see p. 118 of Delehaye's work.

martyrdom is the highest point of the spiritual priesthood of holiness. "The martyrs' blood is the seed of Christians" are words that were written at a time when martyrdom might be any Christian's lot at almost any moment.*

For the first three hundred years of Christian history, till the Peace of the Church in A.D. 313, the faithful everywhere lived in an atmosphere of witness by blood. It was the age of the classical Ten Persecutions at the hands of Roman emperors. Those persecutions did not go on continuously and without intermission; even when they were operative their intensity varied at times and in places: but the possibility, often the probability, of being called to die for the name of the Lord Christ was never far away; when there was no official persecution in force, there were still sporadic outbreaks of hatred and violence. The martyrs of those days from Nero to Diocletian have always had a special place of honour and reverence in the mind and heart of the Church.

But when what is sometimes called the Era of the Martyrs came to an end, the era of the martyrs did not come to an end: it never has done, and doubtless never will till the end of time. During the fourth century a new and terrible phenomenon was seen the persecution of Christians among themselves. The heresy of Arius, with the complication of political factors, brought about the oppression and death on behalf of the true faith of many, especially in North Africa under the Arian Vandals in the early fifth century. This horror among brothers in Christ was to recur at intervals, in various differing circumstances, for centuries to come in country after country. Contemporaneously in Persia, under the Sassanian kings, there was persecution of Christians which was at times the proportionately fiercest and bloodiest known in the Church's history. Then came Islam, breaking into the Christian homelands: the followers of Mohammed wiped out the

---

* Two centuries after Tertullian, St John Chrysostom said in a sermon that "the blood of martyrs is to the churches what water is to a garden."

Church in North Africa and Nubia, nearly so in Egypt and Syria, and watered the soil of Spain with Christian blood. Later on the Moslem Timur Leng did the same in Persia and Mesopotamia on the scale of massacre. Twice in the eighth and ninth centuries Moslems could look on approvingly while Christian emperors at Constantinople slew their orthodox subjects in the name of a false Iconoclasm. All this time, and continuing on into the later middle ages, there were the sporadic martyrdoms of Christian missionaries in foreign lands, from the two English Hewalds in Germany to the Franciscans among the Moors and elsewhere.

In the sixteenth century came the internecine strife of Catholic and Protestant, when in Great Britain and Ireland particularly the Catholic Church was defended by the blood of many martyrs. But at the same time there began a missionary activity such as had not been seen for centuries. The gospel was carried to the peoples of the Americas, to Japan, to China, and to new parts of India, and everywhere the roots of the young churches were watered with blood. But in time one of the oldest of the churches was to undergo a time of special trial: the Revolution failed to destroy the Church in France, and martyrdoms contributed to her saving. Then came the great missionary revival of the nineteenth century, and again many in China and Indo-China, in Korea and Central Africa, hereditary Christians and neophytes and missionaries, were slaughtered for their faith.

In our own time we have seen a recrudescence of something approximating to conditions in the earliest ages, when in some countries the very profession of Christianity, "not the investigation of a charge, but the confession of the Name," as Tertullian put it, is officially looked on as a deliberate separation from the "ideological" solidarity of one's country;* to

---

* Father J. P. Thoonen writes in *Black Martyrs* (p. 281): "Notwithstanding the divergence of time and place and other circumstances there is a sinister affinity between the Central African potentate doing to death his Christian subjects as the supposed enemies of his tiny state, and the Roman emperors putting to the

this action the state may attach direct or indirect penalties, and in any case by varying methods seeks to destroy the society of the Christian faithful, the Church. In Mexico and Spain for a time Christians, especially clergy, suffered the murderous barbarities of revolutionary violence; in those countries that have come under a communist regime since 1939, from Czechoslovakia to China, persecution is endemic, open or concealed. The U.S.S.R., whose practical policy has been somewhat modified, especially since 1943, is the pattern. There have been martyrs in most or all of these lands, though none of them have yet been formally recognized as such by the Church. And here a point must be made that is not always appreciated. During the cruellest and most direct phases of the Soviet persecution in Russia, the main object of the campaign and the overwhelmingly most numerous sufferers were the members of the Russian Orthodox Church. Numerically speaking, the Catholic victims were insignificant, for the simple reason that between 1917 and 1939 Catholics in the Soviet Union were a tiny and localized minority.

"We must obey God rather than men," said Peter and the Apostles once for all (Acts 5: 29), and conflict between the Church and temporal authorities is recurrent in history. In face of attempts by the civil power to coerce the consciences of its citizens, Christian witness has been consistent: "Give honour to Caesar as Caesar, but fear to God," said St Donata before her judges in Proconsular Africa in the second century; "It is more in accord with true wisdom to obey the eternal King in Heaven than an earthly ruler," said St Jonan in Persia in the fourth; "The king's good servant, but God's first," said St Thomas More in England in the sixteenth; "We sincerely obey the Soviet authority in lawful things, but we look on it

---

sword the early followers of Jesus Christ on the pretext of hostility to their mighty empire. *Both presumed to lay unrestricted claim to the minds and hearts of their subjects . . .*" (emphasis added.) Mr Christopher Dawson has pointed out that it was this "totalitarianism," rather than the worship of Jupiter, Mars and the rest, that made the Roman Empire antichristian.

as God's punishment for our sins," said Father Leonid Feodorov in Russia in the twentieth. Although one loyalty is eternal and the other a passing thing of time, there is still a conflict, sometimes a very painful conflict, of loyalties. And this collision and mingling of sacred and secular does not fail to produce delicate problems of motive in the persecutor and of innocence of illegitimate provocation in the persecuted. Voluntary endurance of death is not alone sufficient to constitute martyrdom; there must be on the other side some element of *odium fidei*, hatred of the faith, or of some truth or virtue essential to the Christian religion. Instances of these problems are several times referred to in the pages that follow.

There was consciousness from very early times that what actually constitutes martyrdom is a serious consideration. To "rush on martyrdom" by giving oneself up was looked on with disapproval—there is an instance in the Martyrdom of Polycarp; and the Martyrs of Lyons rejected this title for themselves as long as they were still among the living. But in days before such questions were authoritatively resolved, and when a "process" of canonization was still in the distant future, popular devotion led local ecclesiastical authorities to allow the name and honours of a martyr to not a few people who, whatever their personal virtue, can hardly be considered entitled to that name. (Some of them are still to be found commemorated in current liturgical books or mentioned in the Roman Martyrology.) Such, for example, were princes slain in battle against the heathen, among whom the fame of the English St Oswald spread half across Europe (St Edmund of the East Angles was another); princes, too, who were murdered for dynastic or personal reasons, of whom England again provides two examples, St Ethelbert of the East Angles and St Edward the Martyr (and perhaps St Kenelm); men of holy repute who were murdered for motives of robbery, especially if the criminals were heathen men, like St Donnan on the Isle of Eigg and St Meinrad at Einsiedeln; victims of revenge (St Helen of Skovde), and so on. For a considerable period any unjust putting to death patiently accepted was liable to be construed as martyrdom, especially if wonders were reported at the victim's grave, as in the case of St Godeleva, murdered by order of her husband. A particularly interesting example is that of the young Varangian Russian princes, St Boris and St Gleb, whose immemorial *cultus* as martyrs was confirmed by the Holy See in 1724; they were killed, refusing to resist, at the instigation of their half-brother for reasons of personal ambition.

But such cases as these, and others like them, are outside the main stream of the Church's tradition of martyrdom. In the present book will be found a representative selection, from all eras and many countries, of narratives of how individual persons fulfilled that tradition. Towards the end will be found a few examples of contemporaries; to these the name of martyr is given without any intention of anticipating the Church's decision in their regard. Some such could hardly be omitted, for "if ancient examples of faith, which both witness to God's grace and give strength to men and women, were therefore set out in writing so that by the reading and remembering of them God might be glorified and men strengthened, ought not new examples also to be set forth for the attainment of the same ends?" (*The Passion of St Perpetua and St Felicity*, 1). For all of them it is equally true that "They asked for life and God gave it them, and they shared it with their neighbours, and then went away to him, wholly victorious. Having always loved peace and ever commended it to us, they went in peace to God; to their Mother [the Church] they left no sorrow, to their brethren they left no strife or disagreement, but rather joy and quietness and concord and love" (*The Martyrs of Lyons*, ii, 7).

ST STEPHEN

AT JERUSALEM, *C.* A.D. 34

St Stephen was one of the first seven deacons of the Church, and she honours him as The Protomartyr, that is, the first martyr to give his life for the Lord Jesus Christ. Nothing is known about him except what St Luke relates in the Acts of the Apostles; but that includes the reply he made when he was charged before the Jewish council, and a short account of his martyrdom by stoning. In its simplicity and straightforwardness that first written account of the "acts" and passion of a martyr provided a prototype or pattern for all such sacred writings; but in ages that were to come that model was not always, indeed, so far as surviving records go, not often, given heed to. St Luke wrote as follows.

Now in these days, when the disciples were multiplying in number, complaint was made by the Grecian Jews against the Hebrews that their widows were being overlooked in the daily ministration. So the Twelve summoned the multitude of the disciples and said, "It is not seemly that we should forsake the word of God and minister at tables. Look ye out from among you, brethren, seven men of good repute, full of the Spirit and of wisdom, whom ye shall appoint to this duty; but we shall devote ourselves to prayer and to the ministry of the word."

And the saying pleased the whole multitude; and they chose Stephen, a man full of faith and the Holy Spirit, and Philip and Prochorus and Nicanor and Timon and Parmenas and Nicolas, a proselyte from Antioch. These they set before the apostles, who after prayer laid their hands upon them. . . .

Now Stephen, full of grace and power, was working great signs and wonders among the people. But there rose up some from the synagogue called that of the Freedmen, and from the synagogues of the Cyrenaeans and Alexandrians, and of those from Cilicia and Asia, disputing with Stephen; and they were not able to resist the wisdom and the Spirit wherewith he spoke. Then they suborned some men to say, "We have heard him speaking blasphemous words against Moses and against God."

And they stirred up the people and the elders and the scribes, and they came upon him and seized him, and took him before the council. And they brought forward false witnesses, who said, "This man ceaseth not to speak words against this holy place and the Law; for we have heard him say that this Jesus of Nazareth will destroy this place and will change the customs handed down to us by Moses."

Then all who were sitting in the council gazed at him, and they saw his face to be as the face of an angel. And the high priest said, "Are these things so?" But he replied: "Brethren and fathers, hear me. . . ."

Stephen then at some length set forth God's dealings with Israel, in answer to the accusations made against him as a Christian, intimating at the same time that the worship of God was not wholly bound up with the Temple at Jerusalem. He showed Israel's complete dependence upon God, and how they had always been a pilgrim-people, from Abraham in Mesopotamia onwards; Moses had been commanded to set up a tabernacle, and had foretold a Prophet whom God would raise up, but they would not listen to Moses, and fell into idolatry; that Solomon had built the Temple, yet the Most High does not dwell in houses made by hands. He ended with a sharp rebuke to his hearers that they, like their forefathers before them, resisted the Holy Spirit.

"Stiff of neck, uncircumcised of heart and ear, ye always resist the Holy Spirit; as did your fathers, so do ye. Which of the prophets did not your fathers persecute? And they killed those who proclaimed beforehand the coming of the Just One, of whom now ye are become the betrayers and murderers, ye who have received the Law promulgated by angels, and have not kept it."

Now upon hearing these things they were cut to the heart, and gnashed their teeth at him. And being full of the Holy Spirit, he gazed at the heavens and saw the glory of God, and Jesus standing at the right hand of God; and he said, "Behold, I see the heavens opened, and the Son of man standing on the right hand of God."

But they cried out with a loud voice, and stopped their ears, and with one accord rushed upon him; and they cast him out of the city and stoned him. And the witnesses laid down their garments at the feet of a young man called Saul. And while they were stoning Stephen, he prayed and said, "Lord Jesus, receive my spirit." And falling upon his knees, he cried out with a loud voice, "Lord, lay not this sin to their charge."

And after saying this he fell asleep. And Saul was consenting to his death.

Now that day there broke out a great persecution of the church in Jerusalem; and all except the apostles were scattered over Judaea and Samaria. Stephen some religious men buried, and made a great lamentation over him. But Saul was devastating the church, entering into house after house, dragging away men and women and committing them to prison. They therefore who were scattered abroad went about preaching the word of the gospel. . . .

ST POLYCARP

AT SMYRNA, *C.* A.D. 155

About the year 107 there suffered at Rome one of the most famous of the very early martyrs, St Ignatius, bishop of Antioch, called "the God-bearer." Of his actual martyrdom only legendary particulars survive; but in the course of his long journey under arrest from Antioch to Rome, Ignatius wrote seven letters which have come down to us and they afford precious evidence about Christianity in his time. They also tell us something in passing of his own sufferings: for instance, the squad of soldiers in charge of him were like ten wild beasts, who reacted to courtesy by behaving more badly. Six of these letters were addressed to churches, but the seventh was a personal letter to the young bishop of Smyrna, Polycarp, who was asked to write on behalf of Ignatius to those Asian churches with which he had not had time to communicate.

This Polycarp had been a personal disciple of the apostle St John, and half a century after the martyrdom of St Ignatius he too gave his life for Christ. Polycarp is of special interest, both because the account of his end is the earliest full and genuine account, after St Stephen, of a martyrdom that has survived, and because the first known annual festival of a martyr is that of St Polycarp, beginning at once after his death. It is generally said that this took place, at Smyrna, on February 23 in 155 or 156, but there has been much discussion about the exact year. After it had happened an account of their bishop's triumph was sent by "the church of God which dwells in Smyrna to the church of God which dwells in Philomelium, and to all the dwelling-places of the holy universal Church everywhere." It is this letter to which we owe the details of St Polycarp's passion.

After the courageous death of one Germanicus, who did what St Ignatius in his letter to the Roman Christians had said he would do, namely, encourage the beasts in the arena to attack him, several Smyrniot Christians voluntarily gave themselves up. The leader among them, a Phrygian named Quintus, allowed himself to be persuaded to apostatize, "wherefore," says the letter, "we do not commend those who give themselves up, for this is not the teaching of the Gospel." Bishop Polycarp would neither surrender himself nor go into hiding, but he was persuaded to retire quietly with a few friends to a small farm near the city. Here he passed the time in prayer for his flock and for all churches everywhere; and he had a vision in which he saw his pillow on fire, so that he told his friends "I must be burnt alive." He then moved to another farm, and here one of his servants, under torture, betrayed him.

When the sheriff, who was named Herod, arrived with his

men, Polycarp was resting in an upstairs room. He refused to
slip away; "God's will be done," he said and went down to the
police, who were in an inordinate hurry to take the old man.
As it was about supper time, Polycarp directed that a meal
be given them, and asked that he be allowed time to pray,
which was granted. "And he stood and prayed aloud, so filled
with God's grace that for two hours he could not cease; he
remembered all who had ever had contact with him, high and
low, well-known or obscure, and the whole Church throughout the world. Those who heard him were astonished, and
some were sorry they had come out against such a godly old
man."

His prayer ended, Polycarp was mounted on a donkey and
taken into the city, where the officer Herod and his father,
Niketas, transferred him to their own carriage. They sat with
him and tried to talk him over. "What harm is there," they
asked, "in calling Caesar 'Lord' and offering incense, thus saving your life?" and so forth. At first Polycarp was silent, but
when they persisted he replied, "I am not going to follow your
advice." This irritated them, and when the carriage stopped
they hustled Polycarp out so quickly that he scraped his shin;
but he took no notice of this, and walked quickly into the
stadium, where a great uproar was going on at the news that
Polycarp was taken.

As he entered, he and the Christians with him heard a voice
from Heaven that said, "Be strong, Polycarp, and play the
man!" He was led to the proconsul, who tried to persuade
him to recant: "Consider your age," he said, "Swear by
Caesar's *genius*.* Repent, and say 'Away with the atheists.'"
And Polycarp looked steadfastly around him, indicated the
crowd of lawless heathen by a wave of the hand and, turning
his eyes to Heaven, said, "Away with the atheists!"

Again the proconsul urged him: "Take the oath, and I will
set you free; curse Christ."—"I have served him for eighty-six

* In Roman religion a man's *genius* or *fortuna* was a sort of guardian
spirit.

years and he has done me no wrong," was the reply. "How can I blaspheme my King and my Saviour?" The proconsul persisted: "Swear by Caesar's *genius*." Polycarp answered: "If you vainly suppose that I will swear by Caesar's *genius*, as you call it, and pretend not to know what I am, listen to a plain statement: I am a Christian. If you want to know what the Christian religion is, fix a time and give me your attention."

THE PROCONSUL: "It is the people you have to convince."

POLYCARP: "I should find you worthy to be reasoned with, for we are taught to give due honour, when it can be done without harm, to authorities and powers ordained by God. But I do not feel called on to justify myself before these people."

THE PROCONSUL: "I have fierce beasts at my disposal, and you shall be thrown to them if you do not repent."

POLYCARP: "Bring them in, for we may not change from better to worse. But to change from wickedness to righteousness is good."

THE PROCONSUL: "If you despise the beasts, I will have you burnt unless you repent."

POLYCARP: "You threaten me with a fire that burns for a time and is soon put out, for you know nothing of the fire of the judgement to come and of the everlasting punishment which awaits evildoers. What are you waiting for? Do what you will."

The proconsul was surprised by Polycarp's appearance and demeanour, and he sent a herald to announce three times about the stadium that "Polycarp has confessed that he is a Christian." Whereupon the crowd of heathens and Jews shouted out in a rage, "He is the teacher of Asia . . . the father of the Christians . . . the man who destroys our gods . . . he teaches people not to sacrifice or worship!" Then they called on the president, Philip, to let a lion loose on Polycarp, but he replied that he could not lawfully do this, as he had closed the animal combat. "Burn him then!" the mob roared back with one voice. At once people ran in from all sides with fuel collected from workshops and baths, Jews showing themselves particularly active.

When the fire was ready, Polycarp removed his clothes and tried to take off his shoes, not without difficulty, for the faithful had always been anxious to do this for him, seeking the privilege of touching his flesh—so much was he honoured for the goodness of his life. When he was about to be nailed to the stake he asked that this should not be done, for "he who strengthens me to endure the fire will enable me to remain unmoved at the stake without the help of your nails."* So they simply bound him, with his hands behind, "a goodly ram from the sacrificial flock, an acceptable whole burnt-offering to God."

Then Polycarp looked up to Heaven and said: "Lord God Almighty, Father of your beloved and blessed Child, Jesus Christ, through whom we have learned to know you, the God of angels and of powers, of all creation and of the whole family of the righteous who live before you!—I bless you, for that you have brought me to this day and hour, that I may share with the martyrs in the cup of your Christ for resurrection to everlasting life of soul and body in the immortality of the Holy Spirit. May I today be accepted among them before you as an abounding and acceptable sacrifice, as you, the God of truth, have made ready and foreshown and brought about. Wherefore I praise and bless and glorify you for all things, through the eternal high-priest in Heaven, Jesus Christ, your well-beloved Child, through whom be glory to you with him and the Holy Spirit, now and for ever. Amen."

When he had thus made his offering and finished his prayer with Amen, light was set to the pyre and a great flame blazed up. And then a wonderful thing was seen. "The fire made a sort of arch, like a ship's sail filled with the wind, and it was like a wall round the martyr's body, within which Polycarp looked, not like burning flesh, but like bread in the oven or

* Cf. note to St Pionius on page 32.

gold and silver being refined in a furnace. And we smelled a sweet fragrance, like incense or some other precious spice."

When it was seen that the fire did not consume his body, the executioner was ordered to stab Polycarp with a dagger, and when this was done there was such a gush of blood that the fire was quenched. Everybody marvelled that there should be such a difference between unbelievers and the elect—"those elect of whom the wonderful Polycarp was indeed one, he who in our time was an apostolic and prophetic teacher and bishop of the universal Church in Smyrna. Every word that he said was and shall be fulfilled."

The authorities, under pressure from the local Jews, were anxious that the martyr's body should not come into the hands of the Christians, and Niketas, father of the sheriff Herod, asked the proconsul not to give it up, "lest they leave the man who was crucified and begin to worship this man." The letter comments that "They do not know that we can never forsake Christ, who suffered for the salvation of those who are being saved throughout the world, the sinless One for sinners, nor can we worship any other. For we worship him as Son of God, while we love the martyrs as his followers and imitators . . . ." So Polycarp's dead body was burnt, but the faithful were able to gather up the ashes and put them in a fitting place. "And there the Lord will enable us to assemble so far as we can, and joyfully to celebrate the birthday of his martyrdom, in memory of those who have already fought the good fight and to strengthen and train others to follow them."

"Glory, honour, might and majesty for ever and ever be to him who is able by his grace and bounty to bring us all to his kingdom in Heaven through his only begotten Child, Jesus Christ. Greet all the saints. Those who are with us, and Everistus, the writer of this letter, with all his household, salute you."

ST JUSTIN
and His Companions
AT ROME, C. A.D. 165

St Justin, known both as "the Philosopher" and "the Martyr," was born in Samaria but was probably of Greek origin. He was an ardent student of philosophy, and came by way of Platonism to Christianity soon after the year 132. He acted on his own words, "It is our duty to make our teaching known," by speech and writing, and he is the first Christian apologist of whose works notable parts survive. Justin remained a layman. During a second visit to Rome, about the year 165, he was denounced as a Christian, and suffered martyrdom with five other men and a woman. When they were brought before the prefect of Rome, Rusticus by name, the following dialogues ensued.

RUSTICUS: "Submit to the gods and obey the emperors."

JUSTIN: "Obedience to the commands of our Saviour Jesus Christ is not a matter for reproach or condemnation."

RUSTICUS: "What teaching do you follow?"

JUSTIN: "I have studied all in turn, but have given my adhesion to the teaching of the Christians, however displeasing it may be to those who follow error."

RUSTICUS: "And that is the learning that pleases you, you foolish man?"

JUSTIN: "Yes; I follow Christian teaching because it is true."

RUSTICUS: "What is this teaching?"

JUSTIN: "Christians religiously believe in one God, who exists from all time, creator and maker of all things, seen and unseen; and we believe in the Lord Jesus Christ, the Son of God, whose coming the prophets foretold, to be the announcer of salvation to mankind and the master of those who should truly follow him. I am but a man, and what I can say in relation to his infinite Godhead is worth little. I appeal to the power of prophecy, which aforetime has proclaimed him whom I have just called the Son of God. I know that from the beginning the prophets foretold that he would come to men."

RUSTICUS: "Where do you people meet?"

JUSTIN: "Wherever we are able to. Do you suppose we all meet in the same place? Not at all. The God of the Christians is not confined in this or that place; he is invisible and is everywhere in Heaven and earth, and his faithful people worship and glorify him in any place."

RUSTICUS: "Tell me, then, where *you* meet and assemble your followers."

JUSTIN: "I stay in the house of one Martin, near Timothy's baths. This is my second visit to Rome, and I have never used any other meeting-place. Whoever wanted could find me there, and there I imparted the word of truth to him."

RUSTICUS: "Let us come to the point. You are a Christian?"

JUSTIN: "Yes, I am a Christian."

The prefect then turned to Chariton and asked if he too were a Christian, to which he replied, "By God's will, I am." Then Charito was asked, and she replied, "By God's grace, I am." Another prisoner, Evelpistus, who was a slave of the imperial household, replied that "Christ has set me free, and by his grace I share the hope of these others." Hierax also said he worshipped the same God. Rusticus asked the accused whether it was Justin who had converted them, to which Hierax answered "I was a Christian before, and always shall be." Then a man called Paeon stood up in court and declared, "I too am a Christian."

RUSTICUS: "Who taught you?"

PAEON: "I received this good religion from my parents."

EVELPISTUS: "I listened gladly to what Justin said, but I also was taught Christianity by my parents."

RUSTICUS: "Where are your parents?"

EVELPISTUS: "In Cappadocia."

RUSTICUS, to Hierax: "Where do your parents live?"

HIERAX: "Christ is our real father, and our mother is our faith in him. My earthly parents are dead; I was carried off from Iconium in Phrygia before coming here."

After the prisoner Liberian had added his confession to those of the rest, Rusticus turned to Justin and said, "Listen! You are said to be a learned man and you think that you know the truth—if I have you beaten and beheaded, do you believe that you will then go up into Heaven?"

JUSTIN: "If I endure to the end I hope to have God's gifts; for I know that his free gift awaits those who do so, even to the consummation of the world."

RUSTICUS: "So you think that you will go up to Heaven and there receive certain rewards?"

JUSTIN: "I do not think it, I know it. I have no doubt at all."

RUSTICUS: "To the point, then:—Agree among yourselves, and sacrifice to the gods together."

JUSTIN: "No right-minded man forsakes truth for falsehood."

RUSTICUS: "If you do not do as you are told, you will be punished unmercifully."

JUSTIN: "If we are punished for the sake of the Lord Jesus Christ we hope to be saved, for that will be our salvation and the ground of our confidence before a more awe-inspiring judgement-seat—that of our Lord and Saviour, where the whole world shall be judged."

And the rest spoke in like manner: "Do what you will. We are Christians, and we do not sacrifice to idols." Whereupon the prefect sentenced them: "Let those who will not sacrifice to the gods and obey the emperor's orders be scourged, and taken away to be put to death in accordance with the law."

Glorifying God, the holy martyrs went out to the place of execution and were beheaded, thus fulfilling their witness by confession of their Saviour. Some of the faithful took their bodies by stealth and laid them in a fitting place, sustained by the grace of the Lord Jesus Christ, to whom be glory for ever and ever. Amen.

ST CARPUS, ST PAPYLUS and ST AGATHONICE

AT PERGAMOS, *C.* A.D. 170 OR 250

Carpus was bishop at Gurdos in Lydia, in Asia Minor, and Papylus was a deacon of Thyateira; of Agathonice nothing is known but her martyrdom. It is not certain whether these martyrs suffered in the persecution of Marcus Aurelius or of Decius; but the surviving account of their passion is reliable.

The proconsul being in residence at Pergamos, Christ's blessed martyrs Carpus and Papylus were brought before him. When he had taken his seat on the bench, he asked Carpus his name.

CARPUS: "My first and finest name is Christian; if you want to know my name in the world, it is Carpus."

PROCONSUL: "You are certainly aware of the imperial command that the gods who rule the world must be worshipped. I therefore advise you to come forward and sacrifice."

CARPUS: "I am a Christian. I worship Christ, the Son of God, who in these latter times came to save us and has delivered us from the Evil One's deceits. I do not offer sacrifice to such idols as these."

PROCONSUL: "Sacrifice to the gods, both of you, and make an end of this nonsense."

CARPUS: "Gods that have not made Heaven and earth shall perish." [Cf. Jeremiah 10: 11.]

PROCONSUL: "You must sacrifice; the emperor orders it."

CARPUS: "The living do not sacrifice to the dead."

PROCONSUL: "Do you mean to say the gods are dead?"

CARPUS: "Do you want to hear the answer? They cannot die, for they were never alive."

PROCONSUL: "I have put up with your idle talk and so enabled you to blaspheme the gods and our rulers. Lest you go further, sacrifice! What do you say?"

CARPUS: "I cannot. I have never sacrificed to idols."

The proconsul ordered him to be strung up and his flesh to be torn [with small metal claws]. Carpus cried out, "I am a Christian!" but after a time the torture rendered him speechless. The proconsul then turned to Papylus and asked, "Are you a town-councillor?"

PAPYLUS: "I am a citizen."

PROCONSUL: "Of what city?"

PAPYLUS: "Of Thyateira."

PROCONSUL: "Have you any children?"

PAPYLUS: "Yes, many."

A BYSTANDER: "He means that some of the Christians are his children according to his religion."

PROCONSUL: "Why do you lie, saying that you have children?"

PAPYLUS: "I am speaking the truth, not lying. I have children in God everywhere."

PROCONSUL: "Will you sacrifice, or tell me why not?"

PAPYLUS: "I have served God from my youth up and I have never offered sacrifice to idols. I am a Christian, and you will get no other answer, for I could not give you a finer or better one."

Papylus was then strung up and tortured thrice with two instruments at once. But he made no sound, withstanding the Enemy's fury like the noble athlete* that he was. Seeing that nothing would shake their constancy, the proconsul sentenced them both to be burnt alive; whereupon the blessed ones walked quickly to the amphitheatre, the sooner to be quit of this world.

Papylus was fastened to a stake first, and it was set up; as the flames reached him, he prayed and peacefully gave up his

---

* A common epithet for one who contended in martyrdom. Cf., for example, the Breviary hymn, "Athleta Christi nobilis."

soul. While Carpus was being fastened he smiled at his executioners, and an astonished bystander asked him what he was
laughing at. "I saw the glory of the Lord and was glad," he replied.* To a soldier who was piling up the faggots he said,
"We were born of the same mother Eve and we have the same
flesh as you; but we must bear all things and look to truth's
judgement-seat." As the fire reached him, he prayed aloud:
"Blessed art thou, Lord Jesus Christ, Son of God, for having
allowed me, a sinner, to have this part with thee." And when
he had said these words he died.

Then the God-fearing Agathonice was brought before the
proconsul and, being ordered to sacrifice to the gods, she refused. She was urged to have thought for her children, but
she answered, "They have God, and he will look after them."
Threats did not move her, and she too was condemned to be
burnt. When she took off her outer clothes the spectators were
struck by her beauty, and there were murmurs of, "A cruel
sentence! An unjust condemnation!" As the fire was lit,
Agathonice exclaimed, "Help me, Lord Jesus Christ, for I
must bear this for you!" Three times she prayed thus, and
then died.

So was she perfected with the saints; and the Christians took
their bodies secretly and treasured them, to the glory of Christ
and the praise of his martyrs, for to him glory and power belong, to the Father, to the Son and to the Holy Spirit, now,
always and for ever. Amen.

* According to another version, these words were spoken by
Papylus.

ST BLANDINA

AT LYONS, A.D. 177

The letter from the churches of Lyons and Vienne to the churches of Asia and Phrygia, recounting the sufferings of their martyrs under the Emperor Marcus Aurelius, is one of the most precious documents of Christian antiquity; its text has been preserved in the pages of Eusebius. The martyrs suffered on various dates in the summer of 177 (this is the generally accepted year, though it has been questioned). The names of forty-eight of them have come down to us, of whom the letter gives some particulars of ten, with the ninety-year-old bishop of Lyons, St Pothinus, at their head. The following account of the slave-girl St Blandina is extracted from the letter.

It is impossible to tell in writing how great was the tribulation here, the fury of the heathen against the saints, and all that the blessed martyrs underwent. The Enemy came upon us with all his strength, an earnest of what he shall do hereafter. He did everything, training his servants against the servants of God: not only were we excluded from houses and baths and markets, but we were forbidden to show ourselves anywhere. . . . The martyrs first of all suffered general indignities, insults, blows, stone-throwing, plundering, everything in fact that an infuriated mob does to those it hates. Then they were officially brought into the forum and questioned in front of the people; they confessed their faith, and were put in gaol till they could be brought before the governor, who was showing the utmost cruelty. . . .

Orders had been given for mass-arrests, and this included some of our servants who were not Christians. These, prompted by the Devil and the soldiers, and afraid of being tortured, falsely accused us of eating human flesh like Thyestes and committing incest like Oedipus, and of other abominations which we cannot name or even believe that people ever do.

B

When these reports got about everybody was furious against us, including some who had so far been friendly, who now rounded on us. The saying of the Lord was fulfilled, that the time should come when "whoever killeth you will think that he doth a service to God." Thenceforward the holy martyrs suffered torments beyond description, Satan doing his worst to try and make them speak some blasphemous slander.

The fury of the mob and the governor fell most heavily on Sanctus, a deacon from Vienne, on Maturus, newly baptized but a fine fighter, on Attalus, a native of Pergamos who had always been a pillar and support of our church, and on Blandina. In her, Christ showed that things that appear weak, mean and contemptible to men are esteemed of glorious worth by God, because of their love of him, which is manifested in power and not in outward show. We were all afraid, and her mistress in this world (who was herself among the martyrs) particularly was fearful, lest Blandina should through physical weakness not be able to make her confession boldly. But she was so filled with power that even those who in relays tortured her from morning to night got tired, and admitted they could do nothing with her. They were astonished that she still lived, so torn and broken was her body; they claimed that any one of the tortures inflicted was sufficient to kill her. But Blandina, noble athlete that she was, renewed her strength by confessing her faith, and found solace, peace and relief from her agony in repeating the words "I am a Christian, and nothing vile is done among us." . . .

The martyrs were put to death in various ways. They offered up to the Father a single wreath, but it was plaited of divers colours and flowers of all kinds; for it was fitting that these noble athletes should suffer a varied conflict and win a great victory, that they might receive the final crown of everlasting life. So a special day was set apart for the spectacle of those of our brethren who were to be faced with wild beasts, and Maturus, Sanctus, Blandina and Attalus were brought to the amphitheatre. . . . Blandina was hung from a stake, food for the beasts to be let loose on her. Her fervent prayers, and the sight of her hanging as if crucified, strengthened the others in their combat: for in the person of their sister they saw Him who was crucified for them, an assurance to those who believed that every one who suffers for Christ's glory has fellowship with the living God for evermore. But none of the beasts touched Blandina, so she was taken down from the stake and put back into prison, to await another contest. . . .

Then, on the last day of the contests, Blandina was again brought into the amphitheatre, with a boy named Ponticus who was only about fifteen. Day after day they had been compelled to watch the torture of the rest, and their enemies tried to make them swear by the idols; but they refused and rejected them, so that the mob was furious, having no pity for the age of the boy or respect for the sex of the woman. They were subjected to every terrifying torment in turn, and attempts were made again and again to induce them to swear; but all to no purpose. Ponticus, encouraged, as the heathen could see, by the words and example of his sister, nobly endured every torment, and at last yielded up his spirit to God.

Last of all, the blessed Blandina, like a mother of high degree who has encouraged her children and sent them ahead victorious to the King, hastened to join them—rejoicing and triumphing at her departure as if she had been called to a marriage-feast instead of to be thrown to wild beasts. After the whips, after the beasts, after the fire, she was put at last in a net and thrown to a bull. When she had been tossed about for a long time, upheld by her hope and faith and communing with Christ so that she no longer knew what was happening to her, she too was offered up. The heathen themselves declared they had never known a woman show such endurance.

[But the people were not satisfied, and they wreaked their savagery on the dead bodies of the saints.] After being subjected to all kinds of outrage for a week, the bodies were burnt and the ashes cast in the river Rhône, so that no trace of them should be left. The heathen thought that by so doing they

could circumvent God and prevent any resurrection of the
martyrs. . . .

These martyrs were very thorough in their following of the
example of Christ, he who, "though he was by nature God,
did not consider being equal to God a thing to be clung to":
for, though they had reached such a height of glory, though
they had borne witness to their faith, not once or twice but
often, though they bore the burns and scars of their previous
contendings, yet they would not in life call themselves martyrs or allow us so to call them; if any one did so, in speech or
in writing, he was sharply rebuked. Gladly did they relinquish
the name of martyr to Christ, the true and faithful witness,
first born of the risen dead and sovereign of the life of God;
and of the martyrs who had gone before them they said, "They
indeed are now martyrs. . . ." They humbled themselves under
the mighty hand which has now exalted them so highly. To
all they gave reasons for their faith, but none did they condemn; they loosed all, but bound none; and they prayed for
those who treated them cruelly, as did the perfect martyr,
Stephen: "Lord, lay not this sin to their charge!" And if he
prayed for those who stoned him, how much the more must
he have prayed for the brethren. . . . They asked for life, and
God gave it them: they shared it with their neighbours, and
then went away to him, wholly victorious. Having always
loved peace and ever commended it to us, they went in peace
to God; to their Mother* they left no sorrow, to their brethren they left no strife or disagreement, but rather joy and
quietness and concord and love. . . .

* i.e., the Church. Elsewhere in the letter the Church is referred to
as the Virgin Mother.

THE MARTYRS OF SCILLIUM

AT CARTHAGE, A.D. 180

Scillium was a place in what is now called Tunisia, and the acts of the twelve martyrs, seven men and five women, from there who suffered at Carthage on July 17 in the year 180 are the earliest concerning any martyrs of the Church in Africa.

When Praesens was consul for the second time, with Condian, on the 16th of the kalends of August [180], Speratus, Nartzalus and Cittinus, with Donata, Secunda and Vestia, were brought up for trial in court at Carthage. The proconsul, Saturninus, said to them: "If you will come to a better frame of mind you may receive clemency from our master the emperor." To which Speratus answered: "We have done no harm to any man, nor have we lent ourselves to any wickedness. We have spoken ill of nobody, but given thanks when mistreated, for we hold our emperor in honour."

SATURNINUS: "We also are religious people, and our religion is a simple one: we swear by the *genius* of our master the emperor and pray for his safety. You must do the same."

SPERATUS: "If you will give me a fair hearing, I will show you the religious mystery of true simplicity."

SATURNINUS: "I will not listen to anything against our sacred rites. Rather is it for you to swear by our master the emperor's *genius*."

SPERATUS: "I do not recognize an empire of this world. Rather do I serve the God whom no man has seen, whom no man is able to see. I have not stolen, and if I engage in trade I pay the duties, because I recognize my master, the King of kings and ruler of all peoples."

SATURNINUS, to the others: "Give up these beliefs."

SPERATUS: "That we should do murder or bear false witness, that is the evil belief."

SATURNINUS: "Do not share this lunacy."

CITTINUS: "We have no-one to fear except the Lord our God who is in Heaven."

DONATA: 'We give to Caesar the honour that is due to Caesar, but we fear God alone."

VESTIA: "I am a Christian."

SECUNDA: "So am I, and I want to be nothing else."

SATURNINUS, to Speratus: "Are you still resolved to remain a Christian?"

Speratus replied that he was, and all the other prisoners agreed. "Will you take time to think about it?" asked the proconsul.

SPERATUS: "There is nothing to think about when what is right is so clear."

SATURNINUS: "What have you got in your case?"

SPERATUS: "The Books, and the letters of a righteous man called Paul."

SATURNINUS: "I offer you a remand of thirty days, to reconsider the matter."

To this Speratus, and the rest with him, only repeated that he was a Christian. Thereupon Saturninus read out the sentence from his record: "Whereas Speratus, Nartzalus, Cittinus, Donata, Vestia, Secunda and the others have confessed that they live according to the religion of the Christians, and, when the opportunity was given them of returning to Roman customs, continued in their obstinacy, we order that they be put to death by the sword."

"Thanks be to God!" exclaimed Speratus; and Nartzalus added, "This day we are martyrs in Heaven. Thanks be to God!"

The proconsul ordered a herald to announce that orders had been given that Speratus, Nartzalus, Cittinus, Veturius, Felix, Aquilinus, Laetantius, Januaria, Generosa, Vestia, Donata and

Secunda be forthwith executed. And they all said, "Thanks be to God."

And so they together received the crown of martyrdom, and reign with the Father and the Son and the Holy Spirit for ever and ever. Amen.

ST PERPETUA
and ST FELICITY
with Their Companions

AT CARTHAGE, A.D. 203

The document called the Passion of St Perpetua and St Felicity may probably be accounted the most famous martyr-narrative of the early ages of Christianity. St Augustine has recorded that in his day is was publicly read on the martyrs' anniversary in the churches of North Africa (and was sometimes regarded with even an excessive reverence); and still, seventeen hundred years later, it is treasured, for its religious beauty, for its historical interest, and for the circumstances of its composition. St Perpetua and St Felicity are named in the canon of the Roman Mass (though some hold that the Felicity there referred to is the martyr whose feast-day is November 23).

This group of martyrs was six in number: Vibia Perpetua, a young married woman of noble family, with a baby son; Felicity, a slave-girl, who was with child, and her fellow slave Revocatus; and three other men, Secundulus, Saturninus and Saturus. At the time of their arrest under a decree of Septimius Severus, the first five were catechumens, while Saturus, who voluntarily joined the others in prison, seems to have been their teacher in the faith.

After a short introduction by an unknown hand, the first part of the written Passion claims to be related by St Perpetua herself; there is then a shorter passage attributed to St Saturus, and the narrative is

completed anonymously. It seems to be generally held that the at-
tributions to Perpetua and Saturus are genuine; while not a few scholars
favour the view that the rest of the document was written by Tertul-
lian, the great theological writer who was living in Carthage at the
time of the martyrdom. This took place on March 7 in the year 203.
These martyrs suffered at games held in honour of Geta Caesar,
younger son of that Emperor Septimius Severus who died at York
in the year 211.

The accused were at first held together in a sort of "house arrest," and Perpetua tells us she was much troubled by the importunities of her father, who was not a Christian, so that she felt relieved when he left her. During this time the catechumens received baptism, and a few days later they were removed to the common prison. Here they suffered much from the bad conditions and rough treatment by the guards, till two deacons bribed the gaoler to give them a respite in a better part of the prison. Perpetua was very worried about her baby, till eventually she got leave to have him with her: "I at once felt better and my trouble and anxiety left me; the prison seemed a palace, so that I would rather have been there than anywhere else."

One of Perpetua's brothers, a catechumen, suggested she should ask God for a sign about what was to happen. She prayed accordingly, and received the first of four visions. She seemed to see a narrow ladder reaching up to Heaven, all set about with dangerous barbs, and at its foot a threatening dragon lying. Up this ladder went Saturus, and at the top he turned and called, "Perpetua, I am waiting for you; but mind the dragon does not bite you."—"In the name of Jesus Christ, it shall not hurt me," she replied, and put her foot on the dragon's head, using it as the first rung. She climbed the ladder and came into a large garden, where a tall, white-haired Man sat, dressed like a shepherd and milking sheep, and thousands of white-robed people stood around. When the man looked up and saw Perpetua he said, "You are welcome, child." He beckoned her to him and gave her a morsel from the curd of the milk in her joined hands and she ate it, and all those standing by said "Amen." Then Perpetua awoke, still seeming to eat something sweet. "And I at once told my brother, and we understood that there was suffering to come, and we began to have no hope in this world."

A few days after, Perpetua had another visit from her father, who fell at her feet, "calling me, not daughter, but lady," imploring her in the name of her family* and his own grey hairs not to bring sorrow upon them all by her resolution. "And I grieved for him, for he alone of all my kindred would not find any cause for happiness in my passion. And I comforted him, saying, 'What happens will be as God pleases, for you must know that we do not stand in our own power but in his.'" Sadly he went away.

Later the prisoners were without warning taken from table to be tried, before a big crowd. Each confessed his faith, and when it came to Perpetua's turn there was her father, standing by the bench with her little son, and he besought her to have pity on the child and to sacrifice. The procurator, Hilarion, added his voice: "Spare your father's grey hairs; spare your boy's tender years. Offer sacrifice for the emperor's welfare." And Perpetua answered that she would not. "Are you a Christian?" asked Hilarion, and she said that she was. Her father still tried to move her, so that the procurator ordered him to be removed, and he was struck with a staff. "And I sorrowed for my father as though I had myself been struck, grieving at the unhappiness of his old age." . . .

Hilarion passed sentence, condemning them all to the beasts, and they returned cheerfully to their prison. Perpetua sent a message to her father, asking for the return of her baby, but this he refused. "And God so willed it that the child no longer sought my breasts, nor did they become inflamed, so that I might not be troubled by anxiety for the baby and by discomfort in my breasts."

Shortly after, while at prayer, Perpetua suddenly remem-

* No mention is anywhere made of Perpetua's husband. She was perhaps a widow.

*B**

bered her brother Dinocrates, who had died of a horrible skin disease at the age of seven. She set herself to pray for him, and that same night had a second dream. She saw Dinocrates come out of some dark place, feverish and thirsty, his face still diseased. There was a bowl full of water, from which he tried to drink, but he could not because the rim of the bowl was too high above him. Perpetua then awoke, but she prayed for her brother every day, until she was taken with the others to another prison, where they had to spend a day confined in the stocks. During that time she again seemed to see Dinocrates, now cleansed and well; the bowl was as low as his middle, and by it was a never-failing golden cup of water, from which he drank. "And when he had had enough, he left the water and began to play happily as children do."*

Perpetua's fourth vision took place on the day before the prisoners were to contend in the arena. In it the deacon Pomponius led her by rough and broken ways to the amphitheatre, and there left her, standing in the arena, with a large crowd looking on. "I knew that I was condemned to the beasts, and so I was surprised that none was let loose on me. And there came out to fight with me an evil-looking Egyptian and his helpers; there also came good-looking young men to be my aids and helpers. And I was stripped, and I was turned into a man. And my helpers began to rub me down with oil, as is usual before a contest; and I saw that Egyptian opposite me rolling in the dust. And there came forth a Man so tall that he reached above the top of the amphitheatre; he was wearing an open gown, between the stripes of which could be seen a purple tunic, and his shoes were curiously wrought in gold and silver; he carried a rod like a trainer's staff and a green branch on which were golden apples. He called for silence, and said: 'If the Egyptian overcomes this woman he shall slay her with the sword; if she overcomes him, she shall receive this branch.' And he withdrew.

* This dream is interpreted variously. It is by no means certain that it refers to Purgatory.

"Then the Egyptian and I closed and began to struggle together. He tried to catch hold of my feet, but I kicked him in the face with my heels. And I was lifted into the air, and I set myself to smiting him like one who is not held down to earth. But when I saw that things were going slowly, I locked together the fingers of my two hands and caught hold of his head, and he fell on his face and I trod on his head. And the people began to shout and my helpers to sing. And I went up to the trainer and received the branch; he kissed me, and said, 'Peace be with you, daughter.' And I moved in triumph towards the Gate of Life.* And I awoke, understanding that I should fight, not with beasts, but with the Devil.

"So much of me up to the day before the games; of what happened then let him write who will."

The tale is then taken up by Saturus, who relates the vision seen by him, writing it down, we are told, with his own hand.

It seemed to him that their passion was over, and that the martyrs were being conducted by four angels towards the east, "not on our backs looking upward, but as though moving up a gentle slope." Passing beyond the world below, they saw a great light, and Saturus said to Perpetua, "This is what the Lord promised us; his promise is fulfilled." And they came to a great open space like a flower-garden, whose trees were tall as cypresses and whose leaves "sang without ceasing." Here they were welcomed by four other angels, and were set down and proceeded on foot, till they met Jocundus, Saturninus and Artaxius, who had been burned alive in the same persecution, and Quintus, who had died in prison. They inquired of them after other martyrs, but the angels said, "Come, first go in and greet the Lord."

"And we drew nigh to a place whose walls seemed all of light, and at the door stood four angels who clothed us in white raiment. And we went in, hearing voices like one voice singing endlessly 'Holy, Holy, Holy!' And we saw sitting

---

* The *porta sanavivaria*, through which victorious gladiators left the arena.

there One like a man, youthful of face but with hair like snow, whose feet we saw not. On his right hand and on his left were four elders, and behind them stood many other elders. And going in we stood in wonder before the throne; and the four angels raised us up, and we kissed him, and he passed his hand over our faces.* And the elders said to us, 'Stand up,' and we stood and gave the kiss of peace. And they said to us, 'Go and play.' I said to Perpetua, 'You have what you wanted'; and she replied, 'Thanks be to God for it; I was merry in the flesh, and am now merrier still.' "

Then they withdrew, and outside the door found the bishop Optatus and Aspasius, a presbyter and teacher, standing sadly apart. They knelt at the martyrs' feet, saying, "Make peace between us, because you went forth and left us thus." And the martyrs answered, "Are not you our father, and you our presbyter? Why then should you kneel before us?" They embraced them, and Perpetua began to talk with Optatus and Aspasius in Greek, apart under a rose-tree. And angels said to the two, "Let these others go and refresh themselves; if you have any disagreements among yourselves, forgive one another." They were put to shame, and the angels said to Optatus, "Correct your people, for they come to you like men returning from the games and quarrelling about the various sides." The martyrs began to recognize other martyrs and brethren there, and an inexpressible fragrance took hold of them. Then, full of joy, Saturus awoke.

The third writer now tells us that the slave-girl Felicity, meanwhile, being eight months gone with child, was very disturbed lest she should be kept back, since it was against the law for a pregnant woman to be brought up for punishment; she was afraid she would have to suffer later, in company with common criminals. So her fellows prayed that they might all be kept together, and immediately, three days before the games, Felicity was brought to bed. It was a difficult labour,

* A reference to Apocalypse 7:17: "And God shall wipe away all tears from their eyes."

and a warder jeered at her: "You are groaning now. What will you do when you are thrown to the beasts, which you did not care about when you refused to sacrifice?" And Felicity answered: "Now I myself suffer what I am suffering; but then there will be Another in me who will suffer for me, because I am to suffer for him." She gave birth to a girl, whom a sister adopted.

The commandant had been warned that magic might be used to spirit away the Christian prisoners, and Perpetua protested to him against the consequent restrictions and ill-treatment. "Why do you not let us have some comfort," she asked, "seeing that we are the most noble Caesar's most noble victims, chosen to fight on his festival day? Is it discreditable to you that we should look strong and healthy when we appear?" The commandant stammered and blushed, and gave orders that they should be better treated and allowed to receive visitors. On the eve of the games, instead of the usual last feast of the condemned, they held a love-feast, so far as they could. Inquisitive people gathered to see what was going on, and the Christians warned them of God's judgement and made light of their curiosity. "Won't you see enough of us tomorrow?" asked Saturus. "Why do you like to gaze on those you hate? You are friends today and foes tomorrow. Still, take a good look so that you will recognize us again." The crowd broke up, wondering; and many of them believed.

The day of triumph dawned and the martyrs, with gay and gallant looks, were led to the amphitheatre. "Perpetua brought up the rear with shining steps, true bride of Christ and darling of God, her piercing gaze abashing all eyes. Felicity, too, rejoicing to come from blood to blood, from the midwife to the gladiator, to be washed after child-bearing in a second baptism." At the gate it was sought to dress the men as priests of Saturn, the women as priestesses of Ceres, but Perpetua would have none of it. "That our freedom might be seen by all men, we came here of our own free will," she declared. "We pledged our lives to do nothing of this sort. And you agreed."

The commandant acknowledged the justice of her plea, and
they entered the arena in their ordinary clothes. Perpetua was
singing, as if she already trod down the Egyptian's head.
Revocatus, Saturninus and Saturus* uttered warnings of retribution to the onlookers; and when they saw the procurator
Hilarion they pointed to him and exclaimed, "You judge us,
God will judge you!" The infuriated people called for them
to run the gauntlet of gladiators' whips, and the martyrs gave
thanks for this share in the Lord's sufferings.

Saturninus had always hoped he would be exposed to several
beasts, and so it came about; he, with Revocatus, was confronted by a leopard and then mauled by a bear. Saturus had
a particular dread of bears, and counted on being killed by a
leopard. But he was tied to a boar, which turned on the keeper
and gored him so that he afterwards died, while Saturus was
only dragged about, unharmed; and a bear refused to attack
him.

For the women the keepers had a savage cow ready, an
unusual animal, chosen in mockery of their sex. They were
stripped and wrapped in nets, and when they were thus
brought out the people were shocked at the sight, the one a
graceful girl, the other fresh from childbirth with milk dripping from her breasts. So they were brought back and clothed
in loose gowns. First Perpetua was tossed. She sat up and
drew her torn tunic about her, being more mindful of shame
than of pain; and then she tidied her tumbled hair, for it was
not seemly that a martyr should suffer with hair dishevelled,
lest she should appear to mourn in her glory. Then she got
up and went to help Felicity, who had been knocked down,
and they were both called back to the *Sanavivaria* gate. Perpetua, "so lost was she in the Spirit and in ecstasy," looked
around and to everyone's astonishment asked when they were
to be thrown to the cow. Only her bruises and torn dress
persuaded her that it had already happened. Then she turned
to her brother and another catechumen and said to them,

* Secundulus had died, or perhaps was executed, in prison.

"Stand fast in the faith and love one another. And do not let what we suffer be a stumbling-block to you."

At another gate Saturus was encouraging Pudens.* "As I expected and foretold, I have so far felt nothing of the beasts. And now, believe with all your heart. Watch: I shall go out there, and with one bite of the leopard all will be over." It happened accordingly, and Saturus was so covered with blood that the people testified to his second baptism with shouts of "Well washed! Well washed!" (And indeed he who was thus washed was well cleansed.) Then Saturus bade farewell to Pudens: "Be mindful of the faith and of me," he said, "and do not let these things disturb you, but be strong in them." Then he drew a ring from Pudens' finger, dipped it in his blood, and gave it him back as a pledge and keepsake. Dying, he was cast among those whose throats were to be pierced.

When the people clamoured that these should be brought forward so that their murderous eyes might see the last stroke, the martyrs got up of their own accord and went to the place; but first they kissed one another, that their martyrdom might be perfected with the rite of peace. The others received the sword without sound or stir: Saturus was the first to breathe out his spirit, for he had been the first to go up the ladder, and now as then he awaited Perpetua. The first stroke pierced her neck between the bones, so that she shrieked with the pain of it; but when the unpractised gladiator's hand still wavered, she herself guided the sword to her throat. "Perhaps so great a woman, feared by the unclean spirit, could not have been slain unless she so willed it."

"Valiant and blessed martyrs, truly called and chosen to the glory of our Lord Jesus Christ! Whoever magnifies and honours and reverences that glory ought to read these examples also for the building together of the Church, for they are not of less worth than those that went before: thus these new

---

* Pudens was a soldier, adjutant at the military prison, where he had befriended the martyrs. He was now converted, and in due course himself suffered martyrdom.

examples of power too may testify that one and the same Holy Spirit is working to this day, with the Father, God Almighty, and with his Son, Jesus Christ our Lord, to whom belong splendour and endless power for ever and ever. Amen."

ST PIONIUS

AT SMYRNA. A.D. 250

St. Pionius, whose feast is kept by the Christians of Smyrna to this day, was a priest of that city. He was an eloquent and well-educated man, unmarried, travelled, and very high-spirited, being disinclined to suffer knaves or fools gladly. Probably in the persecution under Decius, his arrest (of which he had been forewarned in a dream) took place immediately after the Christians had celebrated the anniversary of St Polycarp's martyrdom (February 23), and with him were taken a freedwoman named Sabina and another man, Asclepiades.

Arrived at the market-place, the three were invited to sacrifice to the gods, whereupon Pionius addressed the people present at some length. He had heard, he said, that they made fun of Christians who forsook their faith; he would, then, remind those of them who were Greeks of Homer's opinion of people who boasted over dying men, and those who were Jews of Moses' command to help an enemy whose donkey had fallen beneath its burden. He warned them of God's judgement, a foreshadowing of which he had himself seen at the Dead Sea; and he ended by quoting the words of the three young men to King Nebuchadnezzar: "We will not worship your gods, nor adore the golden statue which you have set up." When he had finished, there was some heckling, in which

Pionius held his own, and when he was asked at least to visit
the temple of the Nemeses he answered, "It will not do your
gods any good for us to go there." "Take my advice and
come," said the official who had captured him. "I wish," replied Pionius, "that you all would take my advice, and become
Christians." This was greeted with laughter and jeers, and
someone remarked that they could not be persuaded to be
burned alive. To which Pionius retorted, "It is much worse to
burn after you are dead." Sabina laughed at this, and someone
in the crowd said to her, "You laugh, do you?" "Yes, thank
God," she replied. "We are Christians, and all who believe in
God will laugh happily in the joy to come." There was a
shout of, "You will be taken to a brothel!" "That," she said,
"is in God's hands."

The official examination followed the usual lines. When it
was the turn of Asclepiades, he said he worshipped Jesus
Christ. He was asked if this was a different god, and he replied, "No, it is the same God as the others have confessed."
As they were taken through the crowd to prison, there were
again threats and jeers, and again Pionius dealt with them
with a quick wit. Some time after they were visited by two
officials and a detachment of police. "Your bishop, Eudaemon,
has sacrificed," they were told. "You must come and do the
same." Pionius asked for their authority from the proconsul to
remove them from prison. At that, one of the officials, shouting "I am a magistrate," seized Pionius and they were all
marched off; Pionius threw himself to the ground and strug-
gled so violently that it took six men to overpower him.

At the temple, there was the apostate bishop still standing
by the altar. In his presence the three Christians remained firm.
A rhetor urged Pionius to discard his worthless ideas. "Is that
the wisdom you learn?" demanded Pionius. "The people of
Athens did not treat Socrates like this—nowadays everyone is
an Anytus or a Meletus. Do you look on Socrates, Aristides,
Anaxarchus and their like as men of worthless ideas because

they were given to philosophy and justice and endurance?"*
An official told Pionius not to be so noisy. "Don't you be so
violent," retorted Pionius. "Light a fire and we will walk
into it." Sacrificial garlands were put on their heads, and they
tore them off, and the priest carrying the sacrificial food
hovered nervously in the background, afraid to approach to
tender it to them. Eventually he ate it himself, amid the grins
of the crowd. At length, seeing that they could not be moved,
the three Christians were returned to jail.

When the proconsul, Quintilian, returned to Smyrna,
Pionius was again interrogated as before. Quintilian asked the
priest why he looked up at the sky. "I do not lift my eyes to
the sky, but to Him who made it and all that is in it," was the
reply. "Who made it?" asked Quintilian. Pionius said that
he could not answer that. "I will tell you," said Quintilian.
"God made it—that is, the heavenly Zeus, king of the gods."
That was clever of the proconsul, but Pionius could not be
caught that way. So he was tortured, his flesh being torn with
hooks. When asked why he was so bent on death he replied,
"I am not bent on death, but on life." The proconsul had been
patiently persistent, but now he had had enough. "You," he
said, "are like one of those men who would rather face the
wild beasts than pay a small debt. As you are determined to
die you shall be burnt." And he wrote down the sentence.

Pionius was executed in the public stadium. When he had
been fastened to the stake and the nails driven in, the presiding officer said, "Change your mind now, and the nails shall
be drawn."† "I welcome death quickly," answered the martyr,
"so that I may rise again the sooner." He closed his eyes in
prayer; then, as the flames leaped up, he opened them again
and happily exclaimed "Amen!" With the words "Lord, re-

---

* Anytus and Meletus were the accusers of Socrates. Anaxarchus
was a philosopher and friend of Alexander the Great; he was put to
death by Nikokreon.

† It appears that nails were not driven through the hands in this
form of execution; they secured the iron bands to the stake.

ceive my soul," he gave up his spirit "into the hands of the Father, who has promised that he will look after all blood that is unjustly shed and every soul that is unjustly condemned."

There suffered with Pionius another priest, one Metrodore, who was an adherent of the Marcionite sect; "but," says the writer of the *acta*, "both of them were looking towards the east."* It is not known what happened to Sabina and Asclepiades.

ST LAWRENCE

AT ROME, A.D. 258

Except that they certainly existed and were martyrs, what has come down to us about some of the most famous early martyrs varies from the rather unreliable to the wholly fictitious: such, for example, are in their various degrees the stories of St Agnes, St Christopher, St George, St Lucy, St Sebastian. One of the most outstanding of these cases is that of the greatly venerated Roman martyr, St Lawrence. Scholars are still not wholly in agreement about how much credence can be given to the various particulars of him given by St Ambrose, the poet Prudentius and others, so that Lawrence cannot be spoken of with the certainty that attaches to the martyrs whose passions are related above. The most coherent account is that given by Prudentius (d. c. 410) in his Peristephanon, ii, a hymn in honour of the martyr's passion: the particulars given in this "hymn" are followed in the narrative below.

* The writer probably meant no more than a statement of physical fact (he has just referred to Pionius as being on the right hand), but the words may be given a more significant meaning. There are several references in these "acts" to Catholics and the Catholic Church in distinction from Christians belonging to separated bodies.

When the bishop of Rome, Sixtus, was dying on the cross,[*]
he saw his deacon Lawrence standing in tears close by. "Weep
no more at my departure," he said; "I go before you,
brother; you will follow me in three days' time." And so it
happened. This Lawrence was at the head of the seven
deacons of Rome, and in this capacity was responsible for the
safeguarding of charitable and other funds. Hearing of this,
the prefect of the city sent for Lawrence and said to him:
"You Christians complain that our cruelty towards you goes
beyond all bounds. I am not like that: I am gently asking you
to do something which you should be ready to do. It is known
that you use cups of silver and candlesticks of gold in your
worship, that the brethren sell family property and give the
proceeds to the church. Fetch out these treasures, then, from
their hiding-places: the emperor has need of them. I am told
your rule is to render to each man his due. Caesar's stamp is
on your coins, so give to Caesar what is his: that is fair enough.
Your God mints no coinage; he gave only teaching to his followers. Live up to the teaching that you praise so much. Hand
your treasure over gracefully, and find your wealth in words."

"I do not deny that our church is rich," answered Lawrence
quietly, "no man in the world is richer, not even the emperor.
I will bring forth all God's precious treasure. Only give me
three days, that I may make an inventory."

Delightedly the prefect agreed, and in due course Lawrence
took him to the church. On opening the door, it was found to
be full of people, the sick and diseased, the lame, the halt and
the blind, the poor and unfortunate, beneficiaries of the
Church's charity whom the deacon had collected from every
corner of the city. The prefect started back and rounded
angrily on him. "But why are you angry?" asked Lawrence,
and proceeded to discourse to him on the vanity and harm-
fulness of earthly riches when here were men and women,

[*] Thus Prudentius. Pope St Sixtus II was in fact beheaded, on 6
August 258, a victim of the persecution of Valerian. He, like Lawrence,
is named in the canon of the Mass.

indigent and disease-ridden, yet children of light, whose destiny was to shine in glory with their Father in Heaven; but those who appeared great in this world were inwardly rotting with corruption. "Here are the gold coins I promised you, shining jewels, too, that adorn Christ's temple. These are the Church's necklace, these her gems, these her wealth; take them to adorn the city of Romulus, to enrich the emperor, and yourself too."

The prefect was furious. "You mock me and make a laughing-stock of me with your foolery," he raged. "Christians say they long for a martyr's death. So you shall die—but slowly, by inches, over a slow fire. Then we shall see if you say that my fire-god Vulcan is nothing." So Lawrence was stripped and bound to an iron grating, beneath which a fire was kindled. To the Christian bystanders his face appeared to shine with a heavenly light, and his suffering flesh to give off a sweet smell; but the heathen neither saw the light nor perceived the fragrance, but only an offence. "Thus is God an everlasting fire, for Christ it is who is true fire, filling the righteous with light and burning the evil."

When one side had been charred away, Lawrence said, "This part of my body has been burned enough; turn me round, and see your Vulcan's work." The prefect ordered this to be done, and Lawrence said, "It is cooked enough. Eat, and try whether it be nicer raw or roasted."* Prudentius then puts into Lawrence's mouth a long and allusive prayer for the conversion of Rome to Christ, ending on a note of prophecy: "I foresee there will one day be an emperor who will serve God and will not suffer Rome to follow abominations. . . . Then at last her marbles will shine bright, cleansed from all blood, and her bronze statues—idols now—will then be innocent."

As he ended his prayer, Lawrence's spirit left its fleshly house, and his dead body was carried to burial on the

---

* This famous incident has been much discussed. The balance of learned opinion seems to be against its authenticity.

shoulders of senators, whom the martyr's constancy had persuaded to follow Christ. According to Prudentius, Lawrence's
martyrdom marked the beginning of the end of paganism in
Rome: "The holy martyr's death was in truth the death of
the temples." He refers to veneration of the martyr at his
burial-place,* and the poem ends with an appeal for Lawrence's
advocacy in Heaven: "Listen to a country poet confessing
his misdeeds and his inward sins . . . In your kindness, hear
the entreaty of Prudentius. . . ."

ST CYPRIAN

AT CARTHAGE, A.D. 258

*St Cyprian, bishop of Carthage, who was brought up in paganism
and became a Christian in middle life, was a striking figure in the
Western church of the third century, as a bishop, an ecclesiastical
writer and a martyr. His written works include many letters, a famous
treatise on the unity of the Church and an exhortation to martyrdom. (See the Appendix herein, p. 216.) St Cyprian is named in the
canon of the Roman Mass, which is the more notable because he had
a serious disagreement with Pope St Stephen I on the subject of
baptism ministered by heretics and schismatics; this was apparently
still not composed when the pope died, and in the following year,
258, St Cyprian was one of the first victims of the persecution of the
Emperor Valerian.*

*In the document called the Passion of Cyprian, Father Hippolyte
Delehaye, s.j. recognizes three separate elements, connected into a con-
tinuous narrative by an editor: namely, a report from official sources
of the bishop's first trial, another of the second trial, and a brief
account of the martyrdom. This document runs as follows. The*

* In the cemetery of Cyriaca *in agro Verano* on the Via Tiburtina,
where the basilica of St Lawrence-outside-the-Walls now stands.

mutual courtesy between bishop and proconsul shown therein is noticeable, and Cyprian is treated with a considerateness amounting to deference.

When the Emperor Valerian was consul for the fourth time and the Emperor Gallienus for the third, on the 3rd of the kalends of September [257], the proconsul at Carthage, Paternus, said to the bishop Cyprian in the audience-chamber: "The most sacred emperors Valerian and Gallienus have been pleased to send me a letter in which they enjoin that those who do not follow the Roman religion shall observe those rites. I have therefore been making inquiries about yourself. What have you to say?"

CYPRIAN: "I am a Christian and a bishop. I recognize no god but the one true God, who made heaven and earth and sea and all that is in them. We Christians serve this God; day and night we pray to him, for ourselves, for all men and for the good estate of the emperors themselves."

PATERNUS: "Are you determined to continue in this way?"

CYPRIAN: "A good will which acknowledges God cannot be deflected."

PATERNUS: "Will you then, in accordance with the decree of Valerian and Gallienus, go into exile at Curubis?"

CYPRIAN: "I will do so."

PATERNUS: "The emperors have been pleased to write to me about priests, as well as about bishops. I should therefore like to know from you who are the priests living in this city."

CYPRIAN: "There is a wise provision in your laws that forbids informers. I cannot divulge their names. But they can be found in their towns."

PATERNUS: "I will have search made for them here today."

CYPRIAN: "Our discipline does not allow anyone to give himself up voluntarily, and to do so is contrary to your principles; so they cannot surrender themselves. But if you look for them you will find them."

PATERNUS: "I will find them. The emperors have also forbidden any assemblies of people anywhere, and also access to the cemeteries. For disregard of this salutary ordinance the penalty is death."

CYPRIAN: "You will do your duty."

Paternus then gave instructions for Cyprian's exile, which lasted long enough for Aspasius Paternus to be succeeded as proconsul by Galerius Maximus; he recalled the bishop in order to bring him to trial.

When the holy God-chosen martyr Cyprian had come back from Curubis whither he had been banished, he remained in his own gardens in accordance with official orders; from day to day he expected to be sent for, as had been shown him in a vision. Eventually, without warning, on the ides of September [258], Tuscus and Bassus being consuls, two officers came to him: one was the proconsul's equerry and the other marshal of his guard. They took Cyprian in a carriage to the Villa Sexti, where Galerius Maximus was staying for his health. Here the bishop was remanded for twenty-four hours.

Thereupon the blessed Cyprian went to stay at the house of one of the proconsular officers. This house was in Saturn Street, between the temple of Venus and the temple of Public Welfare, and thither all the Christian brethren flocked. When Cyprian learned this, he gave instructions that care should be taken of the young women, because the crowd was lingering in the street in front of the officer's house. On the morning of the next day, many people assembled at the Villa Sexti by order of Galerius Maximus, who then had Cyprian brought before him in the hall called Sauciolum. He then asked the bishop if he were Thascius Cyprianus.

CYPRIAN: "I am."

MAXIMUS: "And you are the father [*papa*, 'pope'] of people who hold sacrilegious opinions?"

CYPRIAN: "Yes."

MAXIMUS: "The most sacred emperors command you to sacrifice."

CYPRIAN: "I will not do so."

MAXIMUS: "Take thought for yourself."

CYPRIAN: "Carry out your duty. When a thing is so clear there is no need to think about it."

The proconsul consulted his assessors. He then pronounced sentence, very reluctantly, as follows: "You have long lived an irreligious life; you have gathered round you many members of a wicked association; you have set yourself up against the Roman gods and their religion; and you have rejected the call of our pious and most sacred emperors, the *Augusti* Valerian and Gallienus and the most noble *Caesar* Valerian, to the observance of their rites. Accordingly, since you are found guilty of being the author and leader of most shameful crimes, you shall be made an example to those whom you have associated with yourself in wickedness; the law must be vindicated in your blood." (Here he read from his tablets.) "We order that Thascius Cyprianus be put to death by the sword." And Cyprian answered, "Thanks be to God!"

When they heard this sentence, the assembled brethren cried out, "Let us too be beheaded with him!" and amid a tumult the crowd went along with him to the place of execution. Cyrian was taken to the field of Sextus, where people had climbed into trees to get a better view. He took off his cloak and knelt down, bowing in prayer to the Lord. Then he took off his tunic, handing it to his deacons, and stood up in his linen undergarment to wait for the executioner; on his arrival Cyprian directed that twenty-five gold coins be given him. The brethren spread linen cloths on the ground around their bishop,* and he blindfolded himself, but he could not tie the ends of the handkerchief and a priest and a subdeacon, both named Julian, did it for him. Thus did blessed Cyprian suffer.

His body was laid in a place near by, to satisfy the curiosity of the heathen. From thence it was taken by night and carried by the light of torches and with prayers and much triumphing, to the graveyard of Macrobius Candidian the procurator,

---

* Doubtless that they might be soaked with the martyr's blood and carried away as relics.

which is on the road to Mappalia, near the ponds. A few days later the proconsul Galerius Maximus died.

The most blessed martyr Cyprian suffered on the 18th of the ides of October, under the emperors Valerian and Gallienus in the reign of our Lord Jesus Christ, to whom be honour and glory for ever and ever. Amen.

ST FRUCTUOSUS

AT TARRAGONA, A.D. 259

St. Fructuosus was bishop of Tarragona in Spain, and with his two deacons was martyred by fire on January 21 in the year 259.

It was on a Sunday, the 17th of the kalends of February [259], during the reign of Valerian and Gallienus and when Aemilian and Bassus were consuls, that the bishop Fructuosus was arrested, together with his deacons, Augurius and Eulogius. The bishop was going to bed when six officers arrived, and when he heard them he came out in his slippers. They told him that he and his deacons were wanted by the governor. "Very well," said Fructuosus. "But if I may I will first put on my shoes." They were kept in prison for several days, during which time the bishop baptized a man named Rogatian, and on the Wednesday they observed the usual fast. On the following Friday they were brought up for trial. The governor, Aemilian, first asked Fructuosus whether he had heard what the emperors had ordered.

FRUCTUOSUS: "I do not know what they have ordered. But whatever it is, I am a Christian."

AEMILIAN: "They have ordered that the gods are to be worshipped."

FRUCTUOSUS: "I worship one God, who made heaven and earth and the sea and all that is in them."

AEMILIAN: "Do you know that there are gods?"

FRUCTUOSUS: "I know nothing of the sort."

AEMILIAN: "I will make you know shortly. If the gods are not worshipped and the countenances of the emperors not respected, who are left to be obeyed and feared and worshipped? (To Augurius) Do not take any notice of what Fructuosus says."

AUGURIUS: "I worship the almighty God."

AEMILIAN, to Eulogius: "Do you worship Fructuosus too?"

EULOGIUS: "I do not. I worship Him whom Fructuosus worships."

AEMILIAN, to Fructuosus: "Are you a bishop?"

FRUCTUOSUS: "I am."

AEMILIAN: "You mean you have been."

And thereupon the governor sentenced all three to be burnt alive.

While they were being taken to the amphitheatre people commiserated with the bishop, for he was beloved by all; but the Christians rejoiced rather than mourned. When some offered the martyrs wine, Fructuosus refused it, saying it was not yet time for them to break their fast. At the amphitheatre, his reader, Augustalis, asked to be allowed to undo the bishop's shoes. "Not so, my son," replied Fructuosus, "I will do it myself, being unafraid and joyful and secure in the Lord's promise." Another Christian seized his hand, beseeching his prayers. Fructuosus answered him in a loud voice that everyone could hear: "I am bound to pray for the whole universal Church spread over the world from the east to the west." Officers had been posted to prevent any demonstration, but the bishop was able to say in the hearing of all his flock, "You will not be left without a shepherd for long, nor will the Lord's love and promise fail you, either here or hereafter."

When, then, Fructuosus had comforted the brethren, the martyrs entered on the way of salvation, happy in their very sufferings, for theirs was the fruit of the holy Scriptures according to promise. For they were like Ananias, Azarias and Misael * and in them also the divine Trinity might be seen: to each as he stood amid the flames the Father was present, the Son gave aid, and the Holy Sprirt walked in the midst of the fire. When the bonds that held their hands were burnt through, having in mind the divine prayer and their custom, and being joyful in the certainty that they would rise again, they fell on their knees and stretched out their arms in symbol of the Lord's victory, praying to him till they gave up their souls.

Nor were the Lord's marvellous doings afterwards lacking. Heaven was opened to the eyes of two of the brethren, Babylas and Mygdonius, who belonged to the governor's household, his daughter being their mistress in this world. To her they showed Fructuosus and his deacons going up crowned into Heaven. And they said to Aemilian, "Come and see how those men whom you condemned have been taken to Heaven and to their hope." Aemilian came; but he was not accounted worthy to see what they saw.

The brethren, sheep without a shepherd, were very sorrowful: not, indeed, that they were sorry for Fructuosus, but they missed him, remembering his faith and that of his deacons. On the following night they hastened to the amphitheatre, taking wine to quench the smouldering bodies. Then each collected what he could of their ashes, and claimed them for himself. And again our Lord and Saviour sent wonders to increase the faith of those that believed and to be a sign to his little ones. During his life in this world the martyred Fructuosus had promised bodily resurrection in our Lord and Saviour through God's mercy, and now it was for him to confirm what he had taught. And so he appeared to the

* Cf. Daniel 3:19-24.

brethren, and told them that what each had taken of the ashes should be at once restored, and all buried together in one place.

ST MARIAN and ST JAMES

AT LAMBESA IN AFRICA, A.D. 259

These two martyrs, of whom Marian (Marianus) was an ordained reader and James a deacon, were also victims of the persecution of Valerian. An account of their passion was written, at their own request, for the information and encouragement of their brethren in faith, by an anonymous writer who knew them personally extremely well and for a time shared their imprisonment. Here the story is retold from the original, somewhat shortened in respect of the author's reflections, but retaining the first person of the narrative.

We were travelling together into Numidia when we came to a place called Muguae, on the outskirts of Cirta, a city where persecution was then raging. Having been led into that district at just that time, Marian and James were convinced that Christ called them to the crown of martyrdom there, for the governor had sent out troops of soldiers to hunt down God's beloved ones. Not only that, but Christians were being brought back from exile to be persecuted anew.

Among these were two bishops, Agapius and Secundinus, who came into the house where we were staying at Muguae. Filled with the spirit of grace and love for the brethren, they broke the bread of God's word to us, and our souls were stirred to fuller life by their wise discourse. By the time these holy men were taken on their way a few days later, Marian and James were determined to persevere in following their glorious example.

And the summons soon came. For suddenly a gang of soldiers and a rabble of people descended on our house, as if it were some great Christian stronghold. I was dragged off to Cirta,* and my beloved friends after me—those came second who were destined to be first. Nor had they long to wait: their joy in adversity showed that they were Christians, and when taxed with it they confessed the Name. Thereupon they were imprisoned, and subjected to grievous tortures—as if faith of the soul could be overcome by mangling of the body. James had already beaten off the attacks of the Decian persecution nine years before, and he now declared not only that he was a Christian but a deacon as well.

But by so doing he involved Marian in torture, because he had said that he himself was only a reader, which in fact was what he was. He was hung up that his flesh might be torn, hung up, moreover, by his thumbs, with unequal weights fastened to his feet. But strength was given him, he exulted in his agony, and heathen wickedness found itself helpless against this temple of God and joint heir with Christ. So he was returned to prison, and there with James and the rest his triumph was happily celebrated with prayer. And Marian told us that while he lay in deep sleep after his torments he had a dream, and it was this.

"I saw a lofty white bench on which there sat, not the governor, but a judge, beautiful of countenance. There was, too, a high platform, with many steps up to it, to which confessors were brought one by one, and the judge ordered that each be slain by the sword. When my turn came, I heard a tremendous voice say, 'Make Marian come up.' And while I was climbing the steps I suddenly saw Cyprian† sitting on the judge's right, and he lifted me higher, saying

---

* Now Constantine in Algeria.

† St Cyprian of Carthage had been martyred eight months previously.

with a smile, 'Come and sit by me.' When the judge rose
we escorted him to his palace, through a country of green
fields surrounded by groves of great cypresses and pines,
and in the midst a hollow place with water. There Cyprian
picked up a bowl from the side of a brook, and filled and
drained it. Then he filled it again and gave it to me, and I
drank and said, 'Thanks be to God.' And at the sound of my
voice I awoke and got up."

This reminded James that he too had had a vision, while
travelling in a carriage on their journey. He had gone to
sleep, and saw a young man in shining garments, whose
feet did not tread the earth and whose face overtopped the
sky. And he threw two purple girdles into James's lap, one
for him and one for Marian, and said, "Follow me quickly". . . .
There were others similarly favoured. One of the prisoners
was a man of equestrian rank called Aemilian, who had lived
unmarried for fifty years, and even in prison fasted the whole
day before receiving the Lord's body and blood. He dreamed
that he was being rudely questioned about his faith by one
of the heathen, who asked amongst other things whether
the rewards of Heaven are exactly the same for all. "That
is a thing I cannot judge," replied Aemilian. "But look at the
stars: do they all shine equally? Yet there is one light in them
all." The man persisted: "If there is variousness of reward,
which of you rank the higher in this respect?"—"Two whose
names I cannot tell you: God knows them," Aemilian
answered. "The slower and more difficult the victory, the
more glorious the crown . . ."

When Marian and James were brought before the magis-
trates at Cirta for further examination, one of the Christians
standing by was noticed because of the peace and happiness
shining in his face. Being angrily questioned, he confessed the
Name, and was seized and added to the other prisoners.*
Marian and James were sent to the governor at the legionary
city of Lambesa, where they found themselves guests of the

* The narrator had apparently already been released.

local gaol, for that is the only hospitality that the wicked extend to the righteous. But they and the other imprisoned clergy were disappointed to find that their final contest was delayed, because the governor was proceeding against the laity with great cruelty. He imagined that, deprived of their clergy, lay people would more easily yield to fear and worldly considerations. Among these victims were two women, Tertulla and Antonia, for whom before his passion the bishop Agapius had prayed with such importunity that he heard a heavenly voice ask him, "Why do you keep on praying for what you have earned by a single prayer?"

At last the governor pronounced the sentence by which Marian, James and the rest would be delivered from the misery of this world and joined with their fathers in the glory of the next. They were led to a hollow in a river valley, where the high ground on either side served for seats, as in a theatre. The river running through the midst received the blood of the blessed: two kinds of baptism were seen there, by blood and by water. So many were the holy victims that they were drawn up in rows, and the executioner passed with swift fury from one to the next, striking off their heads; thus he lightened his burdensome task and carried it out tidily and with dispatch.

While he awaited the coming of the executioner, James said: "I am happy to be going to the banquet of Agapius and the other blessed martyrs. Last night, brethren, I saw him and those others who were with us in the prison at Cirta: they were rejoicing and holding a festive meal. Breathing love and charity, Marian and I hastened towards them as to a love-feast, and a boy ran out to meet us. He had a garland of roses round his neck, and he must have been one of the twins who suffered with their mother three days ago: he carried a bright green palm-branch in his right hand. 'Why are you in such a hurry?' he said. 'Rejoice and be glad, for you will dine with us tomorrow.'"

The martyrs' eyes were blindfolded as usual, but to their

inward sight all was light. Many of them—and their friends
and relatives, too—declared that they saw as it were young
horsemen in Heaven, all dazzling white; others said they heard
the whinnying of the horses and the beat of their hooves.
And Marian spoke with the voice of prophecy, foretelling the
retributions that would soon fall upon the slaughterers of
the righteous; by so doing he gave strength to the brethren to
choose present death rather than the wrath to come.

When all was over, Marian's mother, like another mother
of the Maccabees, embraced and kissed the body of her son,
happy that she had given birth to so noble a child. Well was
she named Mary, a mother blessed in her son and in her name.
Surely the mother of such a son, the bearer of such a name,
has never strayed.

The mercy of Almighty God and his Christ towards his
children is beyond telling. Not only does he strengthen with
his grace those who trust in his Name, but he gives them life
by redemption through his Blood. Who can measure his
goodness to us? He does everything with a father's love, so
that even the ransom that seems to be paid in our own blood
comes from God Almighty, whose is the glory for ever
and ever. Amen.

MARTYRS OF THE ALEXANDRIAN PLAGUE

AT ALEXANDRIA, A.D. 262

In the seventh book of his Ecclesiastical History, *Eusebius quotes
a letter from St Dionysius, bishop of Alexandria, recounting the heroic
conduct of Christians during the plague that had recently been raging
in his episcopal city. Dionysius regarded death consequent on such*

C

selfless charity, shown by the brethren towards persecutors as well as friends, as equivalent to martyrdom; he was not alone in his opinion, and the following entry is found in the Roman Martyrology on February 28: "In Alexandria, the memory of the holy priests, deacons and many others who, when Valerian was emperor, willingly met their death through caring for the sick during a deadly pestilence: whom the religious faith of godly people is wont to honour as martyrs." The following is what St Dionysius wrote.

To heathen men this might not seem a suitable time for a festival*—nor is it for them, or any other time either, whether sorrowful or what might seem to them joyful. At present, indeed, everyone is in tears and mourning, the sound of weeping is heard in the city every day, because of the multitude of dead and dying; it is as it was before, when "there arose a great cry in Egypt, for there was not a house wherein there lay not one dead" [Exodus 12: 30]. And that is not the whole story. First we were driven out; but we kept the feast even when we were alone and persecuted and killed. We made every place of affliction a place of rejoicing—field, desert, ship, inn, prison: but the happiest festival of all was that of the perfected martyrs, making merry in Heaven. And after that there was war and famine. These we endured in common with the heathen; but only we suffered the things they did to us, while we were not exempt from feeling the effects of what they did to and suffered from one another. But we ever rejoiced in the peace of Christ, which was given to us alone.

And then, when there had been a very short respite, there came this plague of sickness. To the heathen it is more terrifying and difficult to bear than any other calamity: one of their own writers has said that it is the only thing that extinguishes all hope. It is not like that with us: still, it is no less a test and a trial than the other things, for it has not spared us, though the heathen have felt it more severely. . . .

Most of the brethren were prodigal in their love and brotherly kindness. They supported one another, visited the

* Probably written just before the Easter of the year 263.

sick fearlessly and looked after them without stint, serving them in Christ. They were happy to die with them, bearing their neighbours' burdens and taking their disease and pain on themselves, even to the death which they caught from them. They put reality into what we look on as a courteous formula, accepting death as "humble servants" of one another.

The best among our brethren died in this way, including several priests and deacons and those men and women who were most looked up to. Thus to bring oneself to the grave evinced such religious dutifulness and strength of faith that it seemed, indeed, not to fall short of martyrdom itself.

With their own bare hands they closed the eyes and mouths of the saints; they carried their bodies away and laid them out; they embraced and kissed them, washed them and put on their grave-clothes. And it was not very long before they were tended in the same way themselves, for the survivors were continually following those who had already been taken. But the heathen behaved very differently. . . .

ST ALBAN

AT VERULAMIUM, *C.* A.D. 287 OR 304 (?)

Unlike the martyrdoms that have just been related (except St Lawrence), there is no certainly authentic account of the passion of St Alban. But he is of special interest to people of English speech as being traditionally the protomartyr of the Church in the Island of Britain, and his story as it has come down to us is a good example— if a relatively mild one—of a martyr-narrative which has been embellished by imaginative hagiographers. The earliest existing accounts of St Alban are those of Gildas, who was writing about the year

540, and the Venerable Bede, who finished his Ecclesiastical History *in 731. All subsequent accounts derive substantially from these two writers, especially from Bede, who in turn must have relied on a narrative or narratives no longer extant.*

Both Gildas, by implication, and Bede, explicitly, assign the martyrdom to Verulamium, whose site adjoins the present city called Saint Albans, and it is the opinion of most scholars that this tradition is reliable. Bede says further, and Gildas "conjectures" to the same effect, that Alban suffered in the persecution of Diocletian, though the contemporary Eusebius says that that persecution did not reach Britain; but he could have suffered in some sporadic outbreak, either then or earlier: the year 287 has been suggested as a likely date. There is no need to underline how strikingly different the following narrative is from those that are indubitably genuine. We have moved from the realm of factual record and living people into an atmosphere of formalized characters, pious fancy and didacticism.

GILDAS.—God, willing "all men to be saved" [1 Tim. 2:4] and calling sinners no less than those who think themselves righteous, accordingly magnified his mercy to us. Lest Britain should be wholly wrapped in thick darkness, he of his own free gift kindled for us bright lamps of holy martyrs, in the aforesaid time of persecution [of the tyrant Diocletian], as we conjecture. . . . Being moved by charity, Alban of Verulamium gave shelter to a confessor who was being pursued by his persecutors and was on the point of being captured, and thus Alban imitated Christ, who laid down his life for his sheep. For he hid the man in his own house and then exchanged clothes with him, gladly exposing himself to the risk of being pursued in the said brother's clothes. In this way Alban was well-pleasing to God; and during the time between his holy confession and cruel death, in the presence of godless men who bore the Roman standards in hateful delusion, he was wonderfully adorned with miraculous signs. His fervent prayer opened an unknown path across the bed of the noble river Thames,* like the dry untrodden way of the Israelites when the Ark of the Covenant stood

* Verulamium is not, of course, on the Thames, but on a little stream now called the Ver, a back-formation from the name of the city.

long on the ground in the midst of the Jordan; a thousand
men with him, he walked through dry-footed, the rushing
waters hanging on either side like steep cliffs. By the sight
of such wonders Alban changed his executioner from a wolf
into a lamb; he made him join with himself in thirsting more
deeply for the victorious palm of martyrdom and enabled
him to grasp it more boldly.

BEDE.—In those days [of the persecution of Diocletian and
Maximian] there suffered the holy Alban, of whom the priest
Fortunatus says (in his *Praise of Virgins*, wherein he mentions
all the blessed martyrs who came to the Lord from every part
of the world),

In fruitful Britain's land was noble Alban born.

When all kinds of cruelty were being used against Christians by order of those unbelieving emperors, Alban, being yet
a heathen, gave shelter to a priest who was fleeing from his
persecutors. When he saw how this man spent all his time in
prayer and worship, Alban was suddenly touched by God's
grace and he began to follow such an example of faith and
piety. Little by little the priest taught him the way of salvation, and Alban, casting off the darkness of idolatry, became
whole-heartedly a Christian.

In due course the wicked ruler heard that the holy confessor
of Christ, whose time of martyrdom was not yet come, was
concealed in Alban's house. Soldiers were sent to make a
thorough search, and they were met by the holy Alban,
dressed in his guest's long cloak. He surrendered himself in
place of his teacher, and was taken off bound to appear before
the judge.

It so happened that at the moment he arrived the judge
was standing before an altar, offering sacrifice to demons.
When he saw Alban he was furious that this man had en-
dangered himself by giving himself up in place of his guest,
and he ordered him to be dragged before the idols at the
altar. "You have chosen to hide a sacrilegious rebel," he said,
"instead of giving him up to pay the proper penalty for his

blasphemy. So you shall suffer all the punishment due to him if you dare to forsake our religion and its worship."

The holy Alban, who had declared himself a Christian to the enemies of the faith, was not intimidated by this threat; strong in his spiritual armour, he openly refused to obey the judge's order. He was asked what was his family and nationality. "What have my origins got to do with you?" he replied. "If you want to know the truth about my religion, I would have you know that I am a Christian and subject to the law of Christ."

"I insist on knowing your name. Tell it me at once."

"My parents named me Alban. I worship the true and living God, the creator of all things."

The judge was very angry, and he exclaimed, "If you want to enjoy everlasting life, sacrifice to the great gods at once."

"You offer sacrifice to devils, who are powerless to help their worshippers or to answer their prayers and petitions. Indeed, whoever sacrifices to such idols will receive the endless pains of Hell for his reward."

The judge, more angry than ever, ordered God's holy confessor to be scourged, hoping thus to break down the constancy of his heart, since threats achieved nothing. But Alban bore cruel torments patiently, indeed joyfully, for Christ's sake; and when the judge saw that torture did not shake his resolution or make him renounce the Christian religion, he ordered him to be put to death.

On his way to execution, Alban came to a river which flowed rapidly between the wall of the town and the place where he had to die. A great crowd of men and women, of all ages and conditions, were assembled there, doubtless come together by God's will to attend his blessed confessor and martyr. So many people had come out that the judge was left unattended in the city, and it looked as if the martyr would be unable to make his way across the river that evening because of the crowd. But he was thirsting for a speedy martyrdom and, approaching the water, he raised his eyes in appeal to Heaven. At once the river was stayed in its course, leaving a dry way for him to go over.

Among those who saw this was the executioner, who was so moved in spirit at the sight that he hastened forward to meet Alban: throwing away his sword, he fell at his feet, asking that he might die with him, if it was not possible for him to die in his place. While this man was being changed from a persecutor into a comrade in the true faith, and while the other executioners were hesitating to take up the sword from where it had been thrown, the noble confessor went on up the hill for about five hundred paces, the people with him. The sides of this hill were not steep or rough, but rose gently from the plain, and many kinds of flowers grew there: a beautiful place, worthy to be hallowed by the shedding of a blessed martyr's blood. When he reached the top, the holy Alban prayed that God would give him water, and at once a living spring broke out at his feet: it was a testimony to all men that the waters were at the martyr's service, for he for whom the river had dried up would not be left in want of water on the hill-top, unless he willed it so. The river, its sacred service fulfilled, returned obediently to its natural course.

At this spot, then, the valiant martyr's head was stricken off, and here he received the crown of life which God has promised to those who love him. But he who dealt the wicked stroke was not allowed to take pleasure in his deed, for his eyes dropped out and fell to the ground together with the martyr's head.

· At the same time there was beheaded the soldier who had been moved by God to refuse to execute the holy confessor. He had not been cleansed in the water of baptism, but he was certainly cleansed by the outpouring of his own blood, and so made fit to enter the kingdom of Heaven. The judge was struck with wonder at these unwonted miracles and he put a stop to the persecution forthwith; and he now began to honour the death of the saints where once he had thought

to use death to turn them away from Christ. The blessed
Alban suffered on the twenty-second day of June, near the
city of Verulamium. . . .

ST MARCELLUS
THE CENTURION

AT TANGIER, A.D. 298

*Among the early martyrs of whom genuine accounts have survived
there are three whose execution was concerned with military service,
namely, Marinus, Maximilian and Marcellus. Of these, the second and
third were not called on to deny their faith but were put to death
on disciplinary grounds: Maximilian for refusing to be enrolled in
the army, Marcellus for repudiation of his military allegiance. Because
of their religious reasons for their actions, they were venerated as
martyrs, and their names figure today in the Roman Martyrology
(Maximilian is therein called Mamilian, and the place of his passion
mistakenly given as Rome instead of in north Africa).*

*Another martyr at Tangier, St Cassian, is stated to have been the
shorthand-writer who took down the record of the trial of Marcellus
by Agricolanus, and to have been put to death for having openly
in court accused that officer of giving an unjust judgement in the case.
But Father H. Delehaye, Bollandist, has thrown serious doubt on this
story.*

In the city of Tingis [now Tangier], during the administration of the president Fortunatus, a festival was being
held on the occasion of the emperor's [Maximian] anniversary.
One of the centurions, a certain Marcellus, rejected such
festivities as heathen, and he cast aside his soldier's belt in
front of the legionary standards which stood there, declaring

in a loud voice: "I serve the eternal king, Jesus Christ. Henceforth I will not serve your emperors, and I disdain to worship your gods, deaf and dumb idols made of wood and stone."

The troops were astounded to hear such things, and they seized Marcellus and reported the occurrence to the president Fortunatus, who ordered him to be held in confinement. When the celebrations were over, Fortunatus had the centurion brought before him in council, and he asked him what he meant by ungirding himself contrary to military discipline, and throwing away his belt and centurion's insignia.

"On the twelfth of the kalends of August," answered Marcellus, "when you were celebrating the emperor's festival, before the standards of your legion I declared clearly and openly that I was a Christian and that I could not continue under this allegiance, that I could serve only Jesus Christ, the Son of God the Father Almighty." Thereupon Fortunatus said, "I cannot overlook your reckless behaviour, and accordingly I shall report this matter to the emperors and the *caesar*. You will be sent to my lord Aurelius Agricolanus, deputy of the praetorian prefect."

Marcellus was brought into court at Tingis on the third of the kalends of November (October 30), when an officer reported that "The president Fortunatus has referred Marcellus, a centurion, to your authority. There is a letter from him here, and at your command I will read it." Agricolanus ordered it to be read: "From Fortunatus, to you, my lord," and the rest. Then Agricolanus asked Marcellus, "Did you say these things that are set out in the president's official report?"

MARCELLUS: "I did."

AGRICOLANUS: "Were you serving as a regular centurion?"

MARCELLUS: "I was."

AGRICOLANUS: "What madness possessed you to throw away the badges of your allegiance and to speak as you did?"

MARCELLUS: "There is no madness in those who fear God."

AGRICOLANUS: "Did you say each of the things that are contained in the president's report?"

C*

MARCELLUS: "I did."

AGRICOLANUS: "Did you cast away your arms?"

MARCELLUS: "I did. For it was not right for a Christian, who serves the Lord Christ, to serve in the armies of the world."

AGRICOLANUS: "Discipline requires that what Marcellus has done should be punished." And he pronounced sentence: "Marcellus, who held the rank of regular centurion, has admitted that he degraded himself by openly repudiating his allegiance, and furthermore said other insane things, as related in the official report: it is therefore our pleasure that he be put to death by the sword."

When he was led away to execution, Marcellus said to his judge, "May God bless you, Agricolanus." In such seemly fashion did the glorious martyr Marcellus pass out of this world.

ST PROCOPIUS,
ST PAMPHILUS and Others

AT CAESAREA IN PALESTINE, A.D. 303 AND 309

St Procopius was the first of the Palestinian martyrs under the Emperor Diocletian and then under Galerius, particulars of whom are furnished by their contemporary, Eusebius. Procopius is interesting not only because of the moving little account of his passion that Eusebius gives; but also because this simple story gave birth to a family of preposterous legends that forms a museum-specimen of the process for students of hagiography. Eusebius, a native of Palestine and resident in Caesarea Maritima (he became bishop there about 313), was a close friend of St Pamphilus and for a time shared his imprisonment. Procopius suffered in the year 303 and Pamphilus on February 16 in 309, though he is named in the Roman Martyrology on June 1.

The first of the Palestinian martyrs was Procopius, a man filled with divine grace, who before his martyrdom had ordered his life so well that he dedicated himself to chastity and growth in every virtue from his childhood up. He so wore out his body that he looked almost like a corpse; but his spirit drew such vigour from God's word that his very body was strengthened thereby. Bread and water were his food, and these he ate only every two or three days: sometimes he fasted for a week on end, while meditation on the divine word so held his mind that he continued in it night and day without wearying. Procopius was all kindness and gentleness, and looked on himself as the least of men, but his utterances were a source of help and strength to everybody. He studied nothing but the word of God, and was but poorly informed in profane learning. He was born at Aelia (Jerusalem) and lived at Scythopolis (Bethsan), where he discharged three ecclesiastical offices: he was an ordained reader, he interpreted in the Syriac language, and by laying on of hands he cast out evil spirits.

With others, Procopius was sent from Scythopolis to Caesarea, and he had scarcely set foot there when he was taken before the governor. Straightway, before he was even imprisoned or manacled, the judge, Flavian, called on him to sacrifice to the gods. Procopius declared in a clear voice that there are not several gods, but One only, the maker and creator of all things. The judge was impressed by his words and cast about for something to say in reply; finding nothing, he tried to persuade him at least to sacrifice to the emperors. But God's martyr scorned the request. "Listen to this verse of Homer," he said, " 'It is not good to have several masters; let there be one master, one king.' "* It was as though he had uttered imprecations against the emperors: at once the judge ordered him to be led away to death. His head was cut off, and he passed happily to eternal life by the shortest way. It was the seventh day of the month of Desius, the day that the

* *Iliad*, ii, 204.

Latins call the nones of July, in the first year of the persecution
among us; and this was the first martyrdom in it that took
place at Caesarea. . . .

Now let us turn to Pamphilus, a man thrice dear to me,
and those who finished their course with him: there were
twelve of them, apostles in number as in grace. Pamphilus
was their leader, a priest of Caesarea, noted for his virtuous
life, for his charity to the poor and all who needed help, and
for his love of Holy Scripture.* He was first arrested and
gaoled, with two others, Valens, an aged deacon of Jerusalem,
and Paul, an earnest Christian from Jamnia (Yebnah).

Their imprisonment was brought to an end after two years
through the arrival in Caesarea of five Egyptian Christians.
These men had out of kindness accompanied some confessors
who had been sentenced to the quarries of Cilicia, and on their
way home were seized by the sentries at the gates of Caesarea.
Acknowledging that they were Christians, they were taken
before the governor, Firmilian, who had them tortured. When
asked his name, their leader replied that he was Elias: not
that that was his real name, but some Christians substituted
such Jewish names for heathen ones to show that they belonged to the true Israel of God. The names of his companions
have been transmitted as Jeremy, Isaias, Samuel and Daniel.
In the same way, when Firmilian asked where they came
from, Elias answered that Jerusalem was his country, meaning
"the city of the living God, the heavenly Jerusalem," as St.
Paul says. In an effort to extort more precise information
about this city, the young man was again tortured, but he
stood firm: he had, he declared, spoken the truth, the city
was the home of the godly alone, and it lay toward the
rising sun. But Firmilian was suspicious that the Christians
intended somewhere to found a city that would be a danger
to the Romans, and he continued to press his inquiries and

* Pamphilus founded the famous library of Caesarea. So devoted was
Eusebius to him that he called himself Eusebius Pamphili.

had Elias scourged. But at length he realized his efforts were vain, and he sentenced him to death, together with the others.

Firmilian then proceeded against Pamphilus and his two companions. When he was told that they had previously been tortured and had refused to deny their faith, he asked them if they would obey now; they gave the same answer and were condemned to death too. Thereupon a servant of Pamphilus, a young man who had been educated and trained by his master, called out from the crowd that they should not be denied burial. Firmilian at once called on him to sacrifice, and, when he would not, he was tortured by tearing his flesh till he was speechless and insensible. Firmilian then ordered him to be burnt to death at once. Porphyry, covered with dust and blood, threw his philosopher's cloak around himself and, after quietly and calmly telling his friends his last wishes, walked cheerfully to the stake. When the flames first touched him he called aloud for the help of Jesus, Son of God, and did not utter another sound after. Such was Porphyry's contest.

A Christian called Seleucus, formerly a soldier, brought word to Pamphilus that Porphyry was dead. This was noticed and, just as he had saluted one of the martyrs with a kiss, he was seized and carried off to immediate execution. This Seleucus was a Cappadocian, and as a soldier he had been distinguished for the qualities that the Romans admire, notably strength and comeliness of body; he left the army and led a life of religious asceticism and charity, looking after widows and orphans, the sick and the destitute, as if he were their father and guardian. He was the tenth of these martyrs, and after him came Theodulus. This venerable old man belonged to the governor's own household, and Firmilian had once honoured him for his age and faithful service; but now he was even more angry with him than with the others, and Theodulus was sent to his Saviour's death, by crucifixion.

The number of twelve who suffered on this day was made up by another Cappadocian, one Julian. He had just arrived from abroad, and upon approaching Caesarea heard what was going on. He hurried to the place of execution, and, when he saw the martyrs' bodies lying on the ground, he went joyfully forward and kissed each one. Thereupon he too was led before Firmilian, and straightway was condemned to the stake. Full of the Holy Spirit, he in a loud voice gave thanks to God who judged him worthy of such honour, and so received the martyr's crown.

Such was the company accounted worthy of martyrdom with Pamphilus. The impious governor directed that their sacred and truly holy bodies be left exposed for four days and nights, that they might be food for the beasts of the field. But through God's providence not one came near them—whether beast of prey or bird or dog—and being taken up whole, they were properly buried in the usual way.

ST AGAPE, ST CHIONE and ST IRENE

AT SALONIKA, A.D. 304

Among the victims of the persecution of Diocletian at Thessalonica (now Salonika) in Macedonia were three sisters, authentic particulars of whose confession have come down to us. Their names were Agape, Chione and Eirene, and, with three other women, Cassia, Philippa and Eutychia, and a man, Agatho, they were brought before the governor of Macedonia, Dulcitius, charged with refusing to eat food that had been offered in sacrifice to the gods.

Dulcitius first asked Agatho why he had acted thus, and Agatho replied it was because he was a Christian, adding that he was still of the same mind. To the same question, Agape, Chione, Irene and Cassia returned similar answers. The governor then questioned Philippa, who replied, "I say the same."

DULCITIUS: "What do you mean by 'the same'?"

PHILIPPA: "That I would rather die than eat of your sacrifices."

EUTYCHIA: "So would I."

DULCITIUS: "Have you got a husband?" (Eutychia was far advanced with child.)

EUTYCHIA: "He is dead."

DULCITIUS: "When did he die?"

EUTYCHIA: "Nearly seven months ago."

DULCITIUS: "How do you come to be in the condition you are in?"

EUTYCHIA: "By the husband whom God gave me."

DULCITIUS: "I strongly advise you to stop this nonsense, Eutychia, and to behave like other people. Will you obey the imperial decree?"

EUTYCHIA: "No, I will not. I am a Christian, a servant of the almighty God."

In consideration of her pregnancy, the governor ordered Eutychia back to prison. He then turned again to Agape and asked if she would obey the emperors.

AGAPE: "I cannot sacrifice to Satan. I am not under his sway, and my mind is made up."

DULCITIUS: "And you, Chione, what is your decision?"

CHIONE: "No one can change our minds."

DULCITIUS: "Have you any of those impious Christian writings, books or parchments?"

CHIONE: "No, none. The present emperors have taken them all away."

DULCITIUS: "Who put these ideas into your head?"

CHIONE: "Almighty God."

DULCITIUS: "Somebody must have persuaded you to this folly; who was it?"

CHIONE: "Almighty God, and his only-begotten Son, our Lord Jesus Christ."

The governor then gave his judgement: the prisoners had refused to forsake their religion at the bidding of the emperors, so Agape and Chione must be burned alive. As the others were very young, they would be kept in custody.

But after Agape and Chione had thus been put to death, Irene was examined again. Dulcitius had found out that she at any rate had kept sacred writings in her possession. When confronted with them she recognized them, but denied that they were hers. The governor told her it was still not too late to save herself if she would eat sacrificial food and offer to the gods. She refused.

DULCITIUS: "Who induced you to hide these writings for so long?"

IRENE: "Almighty God, who commands us to love him unto death. That is why we would rather be burnt alive or anything else than give them up."

DULCITIUS: "Who knew that you had them in the house?"

IRENE: "Nobody, except Almighty God, who knows everything. God is my witness that no one knew: we feared our own people as much as anybody, so we did not tell them."

DULCITIUS: "Where did you hide yourselves last year when the emperor's decree was first published?"

IRENE: "Where it pleased God—in the open air, in the mountains."

DULCITIUS: "Who sheltered you?"

IRENE: "We were in the open air, wandering about."

DULCITIUS: "Who fed you?"

IRENE: "God, who feeds everybody."

DULCITIUS: "Did your father know about this?"

IRENE: "No, he knew nothing at all about it—I swear it."

DULCITIUS: "Which of your neighbours was in the secret?"

IRENE: "Ask them, and see if anyone knew where we were."

DULCITIUS: "After you came back from the mountains, did you read these books when anyone else was about?"

IRENE: "They were hidden in the house, but we did not dare to take them out. We were very unhappy that we could no longer read them at all hours as we used to do."

The governor decided that Irene was to be subjected, not to physical, but to moral torture. She should be stripped of her clothing and exposed to outrage in a brothel; police would be on guard, and were not to let her leave the place for a moment. But she came through the ordeal without being once molested. Dulcitius then gave her another chance to conform, but again she rejected it, and he signed the death-warrant. She too appears to have been burnt at the stake.

The books, the sacred Scriptures, St Irene's love for which brought her to death, were destroyed: they also were publicly burnt.

ST PHILIP and ST HERMES

AT ADRIANOPLE, A.D. 304

Until Byzantium rose to power and became Constantinople, the principal city of Thrace was Heraclea, which during Diocletian's persecution had a revered and aged bishop named Philip. Just before the feast of the Epiphany in the year 304 his church was closed by the police, to which action Philip replied by pointing out that God dwells in men's hearts rather than in buildings, and by assembling the brethren for worship outside in the open air. Shortly afterwards, the authorities laid hands on the bishop and brought him before the governor, Bassus.

Bassus called on Philip to hand over the vessels used in his church's worship and also the sacred books, to which Philip replied that, if he must give up the vessels, he would, "for God is not honoured by precious metals but by awe and a right heart"; but for the Scriptures, no: "it is not fitting that you should ask for them or that I should surrender them." So the old man was tortured, till his deacon, Hermes, protested and told the governor that were all the Christian writings destroyed everywhere, Christ's word would still live on in the Church, and yet more writings would be written. Hermes was scourged, and then taken to the church, where books and vessels were found. An officer began to pocket valuables for himself, and when Hermes again protested, struck him violently in the face. This came to the ears of Bassus, who was vexed with his officer and ordered that the deacon's bruises be dressed.

While the church was being dismantled and the sacred writings publicly burned, Philip, Hermes and others were held in the market-place. The governor came to them and ordered Philip to sacrifice to a god. "I am a Christian," was the reply, "how can I worship a piece of stone?"

BASSUS: "To the emperors then—it must be done."

PHILIP: "We are taught to obey those in authority and to honour the emperors, but not to worship them."

BASSUS: "Then sacrifice to our goddess Fortune, who stands there in beauty looking down on us."

PHILIP: "She may please those who worship her, but no carver's skill can lead me away from God."

BASSUS: "Look at this beautiful great image of Hercules— just touch it."

Hercules was the name-deity of Heraclea. The bishop repudiated it, saying that graven images were useful to stone-carvers but helpless to aid their worshippers. So Bassus turned to Hermes, and was duly rebuffed by him; he said he followed his teacher, Philip, in everything.

BASSUS: "If Philip can be persuaded to sacrifice, will you follow him in that?"

HERMES: "No, I will not—but you will not succeed in persuading him. We share the same source of strength."

BASSUS: "If you persist in this folly you shall be burned alive."

HERMES: "Your fire does not last long. There are other flames, that burn the wicked everlastingly."

And so it went on. At length the confessors were led away, singing a psalm of praise to God, but the mob pressed in on them, repeatedly pushing the aged Philip to the ground. After a few days he and Hermes were transferred under guard to a private house, but the relative lenience of Bassus (whose wife was a Christian) came to an end with his term of office. His successor, Justin, again interrogated Philip, and at the end had him dragged through the streets by his feet, back to prison. Justin tried to move Hermes by appealing to his love for his children, but all to no purpose. Together with a priest named Severus, the bishop and his deacon underwent a most rigorous confinement that lasted seven months, when they were all removed from Heraclea to Adrianople. Twice did Justin interview them here, and he had Philip unmercifully beaten. Special efforts were made to save Hermes, who was a town-councillor and had been a magistrate, and had good friends in Heraclea; but he denounced idolatry so vigorously that Justin snarled, "You talk as if you wanted to make me a Christian, too." They were sentenced to be put to death by fire.

The old bishop was so weak with ill-usage that he had to be carried to execution. Hermes was not much better, but managed to walk. "We need not trouble about our feet, we shall not need them much longer," he said, and told the bystanders that he knew the Lord was calling him, for he had had a dream in which a white dove came and fed him with sweet-tasting food. The martyrs were first buried in the ground up to their knees, their hands tied behind them to a stake. Hermes was so unsteady getting into the pit that he remarked with a laugh, "Even here the Devil cannot bear me." He then beckoned to a friend, and asked him to tell his son Philip to discharge all his debts and obligations; "Tell him, too," he added, "that he is young and must work for his living and be honest with everybody, remembering his father's example." The fire was then lit, and the martyrs praised and gave thanks to God so long as they were able: "Amen" was the last word heard from them.

It appeared from the state of their dead bodies that these martyrs died from suffocation by smoke more than from the fire itself. Their companion, the priest Severus, was martyred on the following day.

ST JONAN and ST BERIKJESU

IN PERSIA, A.D. 327

One of the bitterest persecutions in the whole history of the Church is that which took place in Persia under Shapur II, the Sassanian king who ruled for the greater part of the fourth century. Christians shared the religion of the hated Romans—it was another case of "Christians are traitors"—and numberless clergy, lay men and women chose torture and death rather than abjure their faith and accept the Persian religion, Mazdaism. Among these martyrs were two of whom an early account, purporting to be by an eye-witness, has survived: these were Jonan and Berikjesu, who in the Roman Martyrology are called Jonas and Barachisius.

In the year 327, at a place called Hubaham in Persia, nine martyrs were put to death, and their passion was at once followed by the arrest of Jonan and Berikjesu. These two men, seemingly deacons or priests, were brothers, from the town of Bethiasa, and they had excited attention by their encouragement of the confessors imprisoned at Hubaham. Brought before the judge, they were invited to obey the king of kings, Shapur, and to worship the sun in accordance with his religion. To which the prisoners replied that it was more in accord with true wisdom to obey the real and eternal King of kings than a human sovereign who would one day die.

Thereupon Berikjesu was put aside in confinement, and Jonan was given the choice of offering incense in honour of fire or being beaten with thorn-covered boughs. He replied that he put all his trust in Jesus Christ; he would not break his promises to God and dishonour the church in which he ministered, for that would be to lose his own soul and betray those committed to his care. He was therefore stripped, stretched out with a stake under his belly, and beaten till his skin was in strips. When this had no effect, he was tied in an icy pond, and left there for the night.

When Berikjesu was brought up again he was told that his brother had disavowed his faith. Berikjesu said that he did not believe it, and went on to expound the power and majesty of God the Creator. He was so eloquent that his persecutors said, "It is dangerous to let this man defend his religion in public," and they put off his interrogation till darkness had fallen. He was then cruelly tortured, but all to no purpose.

Jonan was taken out of the pond the next morning, and asked if he had not had a very distressing night. "No," he answered, "from the day of my birth I have never spent a happier one, for the memory of Christ's sufferings sustained me." He too was told that his brother had abjured, to which he retorted, "I know it. He abjured Satan and his evil spirits long ago." Jonan was warned lest he perish miserably, forsaken by God and man, but he was not to be intimidated. "Life is like seed-corn," he said. "If you scatter it abroad, trusting in Christ, you will reap a rich harvest when he comes again in glory." So, too, when he was told he was intoxicated by what he read in his sacred books. "Yes," he said. "The love of Christ's cross is like wine: it makes you forget all the good things of this world, and you long only for the sight of the true King in his everlasting kingdom."

So they cut off his fingers and toes, one by one, saying as they cast them aside, "There! We have sown your hands and feet, and you can look forward to reaping them with increase at harvest-time!" To which sarcasm Jonan only replied, "God made my body, and he will renew it." Then, after more torments, he was crushed to death in a wooden press, and his dismembered body was thrown into a dry well.

When Berikjesu was urged to save himself, he answered as his brother had done: "I did not make my body, nor am I able to lose it. If you destroy it, God will restore it; but your wickedness will recoil on your own heads." He was tortured again, and at length killed by having burning pitch and sulphur poured down his throat.

A Christian bought the martyrs' bodies for a sum of money and three silk robes, after taking an oath that he would not divulge the transaction.

ST SABAS THE GOTH

IN DACIA, A.D. 372

From the third century there were Gothic settlements on both sides of the Danube, in the Roman provinces of Dacia and Lower Moesia, and Christianity appears to have been introduced among them by prisoners brought back from raids into Asia Minor. In the year 370 one of the Gothic rulers began to persecute his Christian subjects, and among the martyrs was this St Sabas. He is known from a letter written, on behalf of the local Christians to the church in Cappadocia and elsewhere, very shortly after the martyrdom. This appears to have taken place, on 12 April 372, at the place now called Targoviste, north-west of Bucarest in Rumania.

Sabas was the ordained reader of a priest named Sansala, and was so intransigent in face of persecution that for a time he had to leave his town, for not even all the Christians approved his attitude. Soon after his return persecution flared up again. Some of the leading townsmen came forward to swear that there were no Christians left, whereupon Sabas interposed: "No one is to swear for me," he said, "for I am a Christian." The magistrate looked at him, and asked the bystanders if he were a person of any standing or substance. "No," was the reply, "he has got nothing but the clothes he stands up in." So the magistrate dismissed him with contempt: "Let him go. Such a fellow can do us neither good nor harm."

Later on, when the persecution was again renewed, Sabas was prevented, by what seemed a heavenly interposition, from going to another place to help the priest there in the celebration of Easter; and three days after the feast the town where he lived was occupied by soldiers, under the command of a certain Atharid.

These broke into the priest's house and carried Sansala off, together with Sabas, who was pulled out of bed and dragged naked over the rough ground. Next day Sabas pointed out to his captors that, in spite of their brutality, there was not a bruise or a scratch on his body; whereupon they stretched out his limbs, tying them to the axles of two chariots, and left him thus for the night. A woman released him surreptitiously, but Sabas refused to escape, and when the soldiers found him again they slung him by his hands to the beam of a house.

When a meal-time came round, Sansala and Sabas were given food that had been offered to idols. They refused to eat it, and Sabas asked who had sent it. "My lord Atharid," he was told. "There is only one Lord, God in Heaven," said Sabas. "This devil's meat is as heathen and impure as Atharid himself." A soldier struck him violently with a spear, but Sabas did not turn a hair: "Did you think you had killed me?" he asked, "I felt that blow no more than if your spear were a skein of wool."

When he heard what had passed, Atharid gave orders for Sabas to be put to death, and he was accordingly marched to the river-bank to be drowned. Grieved that his master was seemingly not to have the martyr's crown, Sabas asked, "What wrong has the priest Sansala done, that he should not die with me?" He was told to mind his own business. One of the executioners suggested to his fellows that Sabas should be released: "The man is innocent and Atharid would never know." But Sabas objected. "You are wasting time," he said. "Get on with your duty. I can see what you cannot—on the other side of this river there are people waiting to receive my soul and carry it to glory."

The soldiers tied a pole to his neck, while Sabas raised his voice in God's praise: "Blessed art thou, Lord, and may thy Son's name be blessed for evermore. Amen." Then he was pushed into the water, and held under by means of the pole. "And this death by wood and water was an exact symbol of man's salvation."

When Sabas was dead, the soldiers drew his body out of the river and left it lying there. So the faithful were able to recover it, and soon after, at the instance of St Basil, it was conveyed to Caesarea in Cappadocia, where Basil was Bishop.

"And so, on the anniversary of the day on which this martyr was crowned, you offer up the Sacrifice and recall all these things to the brethren; and they, rejoicing with the whole Church catholic and apostolic, join in glorifying the Lord who chooses those who are to serve him."

MARTYRS UNDER
THE VANDALS

IN NORTH AFRICA, A.D. 484

From the year 437 until 484 the Vandal kings in north Africa, Gaiseric and his son Huneric, who professed Christianity in its Arian form, persecuted orthodox Christians with great determination and cruelty. Possidius writes of St Augustine seeing, in the early years of the Vandal invasion, towns ruined, people murdered and driven to flight, churches without clergy, maidens dedicated to God wandering about homeless or suffering in intolerable servitude, the sacraments disregarded or asked for in vain, refugees pursued into their very hiding-places or dying of want, and the leaders of the churches stretching out their hands for help where there was none (Life of Augustine, ch. xxviii). And to all this was soon to be added the demand for apostasy to Arianism, in response to which there were many martyrs, both direct and indirect.

For information about this persecution, and especially its very violent phase during the last days of King Huneric, we are indebted to a history of it written by a contemporary named Victor, who was of Vita in the African province of Byzacena. The following passages are taken from this work. The martyrs concerned, SS. Dionysia, Majoricus, Servus and Victorian are all mentioned in the Roman Martyrology.

Even before the bishops were sent off into exile brutality was at work all over the African provinces: no place was safe and no person, of whatever sex or age—unless one gave in to the persecutors. The scourge, the cord, fire, all were used one after the other upon the faithful. And where women were concerned, especially those of high rank, even their natural rights were violated: for they were stripped to the skin and tormented in public view. There was the case of my fellow countrywoman Dionysia.* Of all matrons she was the most

* Victor of Vita seems to have been of African origin.

beautiful and bravest, and therefore a natural object of barbarian ferocity. When she learned that her tormentors intended to strip and beat her in public, she implored them, "Torture me as much as you like, but do not shame me by exposing my body naked." But this only made them worse, and they dragged her up to a high place where everybody could see. As the blows rained down on her, she exclaimed, "You servants of Satan, you think to put me to shame: but my shame is my glory!" And indeed her courage put heart into the onlookers, and was an effective example to the whole country.

When Dionysia saw her young son flinch at the prospect of scourging, she gave him a look that inspired him with all his mother's strength. And, as the blows began to fall, she spoke words of encouragement to him: "Son, remember that we have been baptized in the name of the Holy Trinity. We belong to our mother the Catholic Church. We must not lose our wedding-garment of salvation, lest the Bridegroom cast us into outer darkness. That is the only pain that really hurts: we have to keep our eyes on everlasting happiness." Thus strengthened, Majoricus (for that was the youth's name) stood firm to the end, and received his palm with his last breath. . . . Dionysia buried his body in her own house, so that she could feel close to him every time she called upon the Holy Trinity at his grave. . . .

What words can tell the sufferings endured for Christ by the noble Servus, who came from Thuburbo? He had already been mistreated under Gaiseric, for refusing to disclose a secret; and since he had been so faithful to a man, it was not to be expected that he would betray the God-man. He was put to death by being hoisted into the air with pulleys, and then pulled up and down so that he fell each time with all his weight on the hard ground. . . . Words fail me, too, to do justice to the proconsul at Carthage, Victorian of Hadrumetum. He was the richest man in Africa, and a loyal servant of the king in secular affairs. But when Huneric sent him a private message that promotion was awaiting him if he would do a certain simple thing, Victorian replied: "Tell your master that he can do his worst with me, but to satisfy his request would be to repudiate my baptism into the Catholic Church. This I will not do." Victorian was put to death with atrocious cruelty.

ST MARTIN I

AT KHERSON, *c.* A.D. 656

The death of Pope St Martin I in captivity, which led to his veneration as a martyr, was brought about by his opposition to a religious aspect of the politics of the emperors at Constantinople. In order to conciliate his monophysite subjects, the Emperor Heraclius (d. 641) had given his support to what in fact was the associated heresy of Monothelism.* In the year he was elected pope, 649, Martin I presided over a council at the Lateran in which the upholders of Monothelism were again condemned, as well as two relevant imperial decrees, called the Ekthesis and the Typos respectively. The Typos was the work of the then emperor, Constans II, who was exceedingly angry at the action of the council and ordered the pope to be brought to Constantinople. Martin's subsequent sufferings and death caused him to be acclaimed as a martyr (the last martyred pope so far) in both East and West; in the Western church his feast is kept on November 12, and by Byzantine Catholics and Orthodox on April 13.

The imperial emissary who had to bring Pope Martin to Constantinople, Theodore Kalliopas, arrived in Rome in mid-

* *Monophysism:* the affirmation that there is only one nature in Jesus Christ, his manhood being absorbed in his divinity, and his body not of one substance with ours. *Monothelism:* the affirmation of one single will and one operation, or energy, in Christ.

June 653. When he heard of his coming, Martin, who was ill, had his bed put up before the altar in the Lateran basilica, and there Kalliopas found him and took him into custody. He was removed secretly from Rome and put aboard ship at Porto. The voyage lasted fifteen months, and there is discussion as to how much of this time was passed on the island of Naxos *en route*; but in any case Martin was very cruelly treated and suffered continually from sea-sickness, gout and dysentery. When he at last arrived in Constantinople he was left lying on deck a whole day, "a spectacle to the world and to angels," as he said, and was then taken on a stretcher to the Prandearia prison, where he was kept in close confinement for over three months. He wrote from there that:

For forty-seven days I have been given no water, whether hot or cold, in which to wash, and I am wasting away and frozen through with dysentery, which has never left me, on sea or land. At this time of bitter need I have nothing whatever to strengthen my broken and unhappy body, for the food that is given me is disgusting. But God sees all things, and I trust in him, hoping that when he shall have taken me out of this world he will enlighten my persecutors, that thus they may be led to repentance and better ways.

On 19 December 654, Pope Martin, too ill to walk, was brought before the senate, with the imperial treasurer presiding. He was charged with various political offences, and with such things as a want of proper respect for the Mother of God: his real offence, as he did not fail to point out, was his rejection of the emperor's theological Typos. Evidence adduced in support of the charges was so flimsy and untruthful that Martin said to his accusers, "If these are all the witnesses you have, let them say what they have got to say: but do not make them perjure themselves by saying it on oath." Seeing how things were, he asked that he should be sentenced to death without further delay. The treasurer went to report to the Emperor Constans. Martin was then carried in a chair to an open terrace where, before a large crowd, Constans watching from a window, he was stripped of his *pallium*— and perhaps publicly scourged—and handed over to the prefect to be marched half-naked through the streets to the prison of Diomedes. The crowd was called on to curse the prisoner, but hardly a score of voices replied; the rest bowed their heads in shame.

Martin was so weak that he stumbled and fell over the prison steps and hurt his legs. He remained in prison another three months, paralysed with cold, in spite of the kindness of two women, one of whom brought him a bed and bedding. Then he was reprieved, at the instance, it is said, of the patriarch of Constantinople, Paul II, who was on his deathbed and repenting of his part in these things. Instead of execution, the pope was to go into exile at Kherson, upon the Crimean peninsula. On his last morning in prison Martin offered the holy Mysteries, and afterwards embraced those who had been specially kind to him. Many of the bystanders were in tears, and "Do not weep," he said to them. "My sufferings are so much gain to me." But they replied, "We weep less for your hardships than for our own, for we are losing you."

Pope Martin arrived at Kherson, west of Yalta, on 15 May 655. The place was in the grip of famine: "Bread is talked about, but we never see it," he wrote to a friend at Constantinople, asking him to send food. As well as the miseries of hunger, he found the barbarousness and heathenry of the local inhabitants very trying. But most of all, surprisingly and pathetically, Martin suffered from neglect by his friends, particularly his own clergy in Rome. On this he wrote sadly in a letter:

I am surprised at the indifference of those who used to know me but have now so completely forgotten me that they apparently do not know that I am still alive. I am yet more surprised that the clergy of the church of St Peter show so little concern for one of themselves: the church may be without money, but it has corn, oil or other supplies out of which a little could be spared us. What is frightening these men that they neglect God's command to help those in distress? We are all made of the same clay, and we have to appear before Christ's judgement-seat. Am I looked on as an enemy, of the Church at large or of them in particular? Ah well, I pray God through St Peter's intercession to keep them strong and steadfast in the true faith, especially their new shepherd, Eugenius. As for this wretched body of mine, God will look after it: he is near at hand, so why should I be anxious? I hope that in his mercy he will not prolong my course.

His course was not prolonged, for Pope Martin I died soon after, in the place of his captivity, perhaps on 13 April 656. His relics now repose in the church of St Martin *ai Monti* at Rome.

ST HEWALD THE DARK and ST HEWALD THE FAIR

IN WESTPHALIA, C. A.D. 695

There are two English missionary martyrs, doubtless natives of Northumbria, who seem to be quite forgotten in their own land, though they are named in the Roman Martyrology on October 3, their feast is observed in several German dioceses, and their relics are still in St Cunibert's church at Cologne. They were both called Hewald (the name is sometimes spelt Ewald), and they figure in the Calendar of St Willibrord (c. 704), as well as in a few medieval English calendars. Little enough is known about them, and that little comes from Bede: his relevant passages are given below. St Willibrord, with eleven companions, went from Nothumbria into Friesland in 690.

Following the example [of Willibrord and his fellows], two other priests from among the English people went to the province of the Old Saxons; they had previously lived for a long time in Ireland as exiles for the sake of the everlasting kingdom, and now hoped to gain some of the heathen for Christ by their preaching. As they were one in zeal, so they were one in name, being distinguished as Hewald the Dark and Hewald the Fair, from the colour of their hair. Both were very good and religious men, but Hewald the Dark was the more learned in sacred Scripture. When they arrived in the province they were given lodging in the house of a certain reeve; him they asked to take them to his lord, for they had news that they must give him for his welfare. . . . The reeve looked after them for some days, promising to send them to his lord as they had asked.

The Hewalds gave themselves to psalmody and prayer, and every day they offered the sacrifice of the saving Victim to God (they had the sacred vessels with them, and a consecrated stone for altar). When the barbarous people of the place saw this, they realized that the strangers were of a different religion from themselves, and they began to be suspicious of them; they were afraid that, if the Hewalds met their lord and talked with him, the lord might be turned from his gods and receive this new religion of the Christian faith, and then the whole province would gradually have to change its old customs for new ones.

And so the heathen suddenly laid hands on them and slew them: Hewald the Fair was killed outright with a sword, but Hewald the Dark was put to slow torture. After they had been hacked about, the bodies were thrown into the river Rhine. When the lord heard of this, he was very angry that strangers who wanted to see him had not been allowed to: he sent and put all those villagers to the sword and burned down their village.

These priests and servants of Christ suffered on the third day of October, and heavenly portents greeted their martyrdom.

After their bodies had been thrown into the river as I have said, they were carried for nearly forty miles, against the stream, to the place where their companions were. Every night a great ray of light, reaching to the heavens, shone above the spot at which the bodies had arrived, and this was seen by the heathen who had slaughtered them. Furthermore, one of the martyrs appeared in a vision by night to one of their companions, Tilman (a distinguished man of good family, who had been a fighting-man before he was a monk), telling him that their bodies would be found at the place where the heavenly light should be seen. And so it came about: the bodies were found, and buried with the honour due to martyrs, and the day of their passion or of the finding of their bodies is kept in those parts with the respect that is befitting.

When the news of these happenings reached Pippin, the illustrious duke of the Franks, he ordered the bodies to be brought to him, and he had them buried with much honour in the church of the city of Cologne on the Rhine. It is said that a spring burst from the ground at the place where they were martyred, and that it gives a plentiful supply of water to this day.*

* The traditional place of the Hewalds' martyrdom is on a tributary of the Rhine at Aplerbeke, near Dortmund. They are esteemed the patron saints of Westphalia.

ST BONIFACE OF CREDITON

It has been said of St Boniface, the apostle of Germany and regenerator of the church of the Franks, that he "had a deeper influence on the history of Europe than any Englishman who has ever lived" (Christopher Dawson, in The Making of Europe, *p. 166); Father James Brodrick writes yet more strongly "A very strong case indeed could be made out for regarding St Boniface as the greatest Englishman that ever was born, even though he might not have been able to write* Hamlet *or to win the battle of Trafalgar" (A Procession of Saints, p. 71). He was born about the year 680, traditionally at Crediton in Devonshire, being called Winfrid at baptism; he became a monk at Nursling, near Southampton; and, after a preliminary visit to Friesland, he finally left England for Germany in 718, never to return. A few years after his death, a Life of Boniface was written by Willibald, an English missionary in Germany. A passage in this Life suggests that the primary motive for the killing of Boniface by the heathen, near modern Dokkum, right in the north of the Netherlands, was plunder, rather than hatred of the Christian faith; but from the earliest times St Boniface was venerated as a martyr, and as "one of the best and greatest teachers of the true faith," a patron of England equally with Pope St Gregory I and St Augustine, as Archbishop Cuthbert of Canterbury called him, who was one of his correspondents.*

When the Lord willed to deliver his servant from the trials of this world and to set him free from the vicissitudes of this mortal life, it was decided, under God's providence, that he should travel in the company of his disciples to Frisia, from which he had departed in body though not in spirit. And this was done so that in dying there he might receive the divine recompense in the place where he had begun his preaching.

To Bishop Lull he foretold in an astonishing prophecy the approaching day of his death and made known to him the manner in which he would meet his end. Then he drew

D

up plans for the construction of further churches and for the evangelization of the people. . . . When he had ended his instructions he added the following words, or words to this effect: "Carefully provide everything which we shall need on the journey, not forgetting to place in the chest, where my books are kept, a linen sheet in which my aged body may be wrapped."

At these sad words Bishop Lull could not restrain his tears and gave vent to his profound sorrow; but Boniface, having expressed his last wishes, went about his business unconcerned. After the lapse of a few days, he still persevered in his decision to set out on the journey, and so, taking with him a few companions, he went on board a ship and sailed down the Rhine. Eventually he reached the marshy country of Frisia, crossed safely over the stretch of water, which in their tongue is called Aelmere [Zuider Zee], and made a survey of the lands round about, which up till then had borne no fruit. . . .

When . . . the faith had been planted strongly in Frisia and the glorious end of the saint's life drew near, he took with him a picked number of his personal followers and pitched camp on the banks of the river Bordne [Boorne] which flows through the territories called Ostor and Westeraeche and divides them. Here he fixed a day on which he would confirm by the laying-on of hands all the neophytes and those who had recently been baptized; and because the people were scattered far and wide over the countryside, they all returned to their homes, so that, in accordance with the instructions laid down by the holy bishop, they could meet together again on the day appointed for their confirmation.

But events turned out otherwise than expected. When the appointed day arrived and the morning light was breaking through the clouds after sunrise, enemies came instead of friends, new executioners in place of new worshippers of the faith. A vast number of foes armed with spears and shields rushed into the camp brandishing their weapons. In the twinkling of an eye the attendants sprang from the camp to meet them and snatched up arms here and there to defend the holy band of martyrs (for that is what they were to be) against the insensate fury of the mob. But the man of God, hearing the shouts and the onrush of the rabble, straightway called the clergy to his side, and, collecting together the relics of the saints, which he always carried with him, came out of his tent. At once he reproved the attendants and forbade them to continue the conflict, saying: "Sons, cease fighting. Lay down your arms, for we are told in Scripture not to render evil for good but to overcome evil by good. The hour to which we have long looked forward is near and the day of our release is at hand. Take comfort in the Lord and endure with gladness the suffering he has mercifully ordained. Put your trust in him and he will grant deliverance to your souls." And addressing himself like a loving father to the priests, deacons and other clerics, all trained to the service of God, who stood about him, he gave them courage, saying: "Brethren, be of stout heart, fear not them who kill the body, for they cannot slay the soul, which continues to live for ever. Rejoice in the Lord; anchor your hope in God, for without delay he will render to you the reward of eternal bliss and grant you an abode with the angels in his Heaven above. Be not slaves to the transitory pleasures of this world. Be not seduced by the vain flattery of the heathen, but endure with steadfast mind the sudden onslaught of death, that you may be able to reign evermore with Christ."

Whilst with these words he was encouraging his disciples to accept the crown of martyrdom, the frenzied mob of heathens rushed suddenly upon them with swords and every kind of warlike weapon, staining their bodies with their precious blood.

When they had sated their lust for blood on the mortal remains of the just, the heathenish mob seized with exultation upon the spoils of their victory (in reality the cause of their damnation) and, after laying waste the camp, carried off and shared the booty. . . . Disappointed in their hope of gold and silver, they littered the fields with the books they found, throwing some of them into reedy marshes, hiding away others in widely different places. But by the grace of God and through the prayers of the archbishop and martyr Saint Boniface the manuscripts were discovered a long time afterwards, unharmed and intact, and they were returned by those who found them to the monastery, in which they are used with great advantage to the salvation of souls even at the present day. . . .

The bodies of the holy bishop and the other martyrs were brought by boat across the water called Aelmere, an uneventful voyage of some days, to the city of Utrecht. . . . There the bodies were deposited and interred until some religious and trustworthy men of God arrived from Mainz. From there they had been sent in a ship by Bishop Lull, the successor of our holy bishop and martyr, to bring the body of the saint to the monastery built by him during his lifetime on the banks of the river Fulda. . . .

From that moment the spot in which the sacred body was interred became the scene of many divine blessings through the intercession of the saint; many of those who came there, troubled by various sicknesses and diseases, were healed in soul and body. . . . God deigned to honour and enrich his servant, who possessed this great gift, and glorified him in the eyes of present and future ages. . . . Thus, in the manner described above, on the fifth day of June [754 or 755], crowned with the palm of martyrdom, he departed to the Lord, to whom be honour and glory for ever and ever. Amen.

ST STEPHEN THE YOUNGER

AT CONSTANTINOPLE, A.D. 765

During the eighth-ninth century the Church in the East was convulsed by a movement against the lawfulness of the veneration of holy images; it was accompanied by widespread destruction of such images, so that it is known in history as Iconoclasm, Image-breaking. The movement was a complex one: there was a religious reaction, partly "puritan," partly justified, against what was esteemed an excessive cult of images; and this was supported and used by certain of the emperors for the furtherance of their political aims. The leadership of opposition to iconoclasm came from the monasteries, and St John Damascene's writings in defence of Catholic teaching and practice in the matter are classical. But not a few of the monks met excess with excess, which had the effect of aggravating the violence of Iconoclasts against their opponents. Many of the upholders of the veneration of sacred images were put to death, and some of them are accounted martyrs in defence of a matter of Catholic orthodoxy. One of the most outstanding among these is St Stephen the Younger. He is called "the Younger" and "the New Martyr" presumably to distinguish him from St Stephen the Protomartyr; his feast is kept in the Byzantine churches on November 28.

Stephen was a hermit-monk on Mount St Auxentius, near Chalcedon on the Asiatic shore of the Bosporus, where he made a name for himself as an upholder of the veneration of holy images. Accordingly, when he was about forty-five years old, in 761, he had a visit from an emissary of the Emperor Constantine V, whose mission was to try to get Stephen's support for the decisions of a council of Iconoclast bishops that had been held seven years before. So far from threatening, the emperor sent a present of figs "and other food suitable for an ascetic." Stephen refused the imperial request, somewhat rudely, and the emperor, we are told, tried to compromise Stephen's reputation by accusing him of sinful relations with a nun named Ann. When Ann firmly denied the charge, she was atrociously beaten and shut up in another convent, where she died of neglect.

This scheme having failed, Stephen was trapped into giving the monastic habit to a young man, which had been forbidden, and thereupon he was forcibly removed to a monastery at Chrysopolis (Skutari). Here he remained for over a fortnight, fasting the whole time, in spite of the excellent meals served him, and stoutly resisting the blandishments and threats of the court bishops sent to win him over. He was then exiled to the island of Proconnesus in the sea of Marmara, where he was kept for three years; he had a relative freedom, and used it to good purpose.

In January 765, Stephen was brought before Constantine V at Constantinople and questioned. The monk produced a coin bearing the imperial effigy, and asked whether it was wrong to tread on it disrespectfully. All agreed that it was and that he who did so should be punished. "Very well," retorted Stephen. "Then how much more does he deserve punishment who stamps upon an image of Christ and his mother, and destroys it by fire!" And he threw the coin to the floor and trampled on it. The infuriated bystanders wanted to throw him from the balcony; but Constantine intervened and ordered that he be confined in the common prison, pending trial.

In the gaol Stephen found nearly 350 other monks, many of whom had been barbarously mutilated for their firmness: they had been flogged, too, their heads shaven and their beards burnt off.* During the ten months he was there, Stephen organized some sort of monastic life among these prisoners, and his enemies said that crowds of people flocked there "to be taught to worship idols."

On November 28, Constantine made a speech to the people, gathered outside the palace on the occasion of celebrations in honour of the empress. He referred to the trouble over images, and exclaimed, "These detestable monks are most discouraging: they ought to be altogether forgotten." A servile

* Tokens of degradation in the East.

courtier asked him where in the city trace or memory of them could still be found. Stephen was one answer to the question, and it was suggested that he should be killed. Constantine, however, replied that to be put to death was just what Stephen hoped for; moreover, he said, it would be disagreeable to the empress to have her festival spoiled by bloodshed.

In the afternoon of the same day, Constantine sent two officials again to ask Stephen to sign the decisions of the Iconoclast council, promising that if he did so all his offences would be forgiven. Stephen refused peremptorily. The emperor was furious, and is said to have complained that "this monk is really emperor: I don't count," thus anticipating another king in another land four hundred years later in provoking what followed.

A number of officers ran to the prison and fetched Stephen out, knocking him about till he was killed by a blow from a piece of wood. The mob that had gathered dragged his body through the streets, while children pelted it with stones, and left it lying exposed in the burial-pit of criminals.

ST FLORA, ST MARY, ST EULOGIUS and ST LEOCRITIA

AT CORDOVA, A.D. 851 AND 859

In the year 711 the Moslems from North Africa invaded Spain, and they remained the principal power in the Iberian peninsula till the dissolution of the Moorish khalifate of Cordova in 1031. The chief period of active persecution of Christians under this regime began in 850, and it is known mainly from the writings of St Eulogius of Cordova, who eventually was one of the victims. He was a priest of ancient family, considerable learning, and noble character, and came to be elected archbishop of Toledo, but he did not live to be consecrated to that see. Christianity in Spain was not in a wholly healthy condition at the time, so that when the persecution began St Eulogius greeted it as "a just judgement from God"; and indeed it was owing to the action of an apparently treacherous bishop that Eulogius himself was one of the first to be arrested in Cordova.

During his first imprisonment Eulogius wrote an Exhortation to Martyrdom, addressed to two young women, Flora and Mary. The first of these had been denounced by her own brother, a Moslem, and brutally beaten by the magistrate's order. Eulogius writes of her: "I, wicked sinner that I am, knew her from the beginning of her sufferings; these hands of mine have touched the scars made by the whip on that lovely and noble head, from which the hair was torn out." Handed over to the tender mercies of her brother, Flora ran away from home and joined forces with another girl, Mary, the sister of a martyred deacon: together they defied the authorities, and were shut up in a cell.* Loose women were

* Shortly afterwards, a church council at Cordova forbade Christians deliberately to do anything to provoke persecution.

sent to try and corrupt them, and Eulogius wrote from his prison: "They threaten to sell you into a shameful slavery, but do not be afraid: no harm can come to your souls whatever infamy they inflict on your bodies. Cowardly Christians will tell you that churches are empty and without the Sacrifice because of your obstinacy, and that if you will only yield for a time all will be well. But you may be certain that for you a contrite and humble heart is the sacrifice that pleases God most: you cannot now draw back and renounce the faith you have confessed."

Every effort was made to induce the girls to apostatize, and after the last time Flora, "smiling cheerfully, with her honey-sweet voice," told Eulogius how she had again outfaced the magistrate and her brother. "And I," writes Eulogius, "encouraged her as best I could, bringing to mind the crown she had earned. Bowing low before her, I asked her prayers; and then, new heart put into me by all she had said, I left her angelic presence and went back to my dungeon." In the afternoon of 24 November 851, Flora and Mary were beheaded, making the sign of the cross and bowing their heads to the sword.

Five days after this execution Eulogius was put at liberty, and he set himself by tongue, pen and example to strengthen the Spanish Christians, especially when persecution was intensified in 853. Not long after, he was appealed to for help by a young woman who had made herself liable to execution by forsaking Islam and being baptized. Her name was Leocritia (Lucrezia). Eulogius found shelter for her with several Christian families, but one evening his house was raided when Leocritia was there to see his sister. They were both arrested.

When they appeared before the magistrate, Eulogius was asked why Leocritia had been found under his roof. "I am a priest of Jesus Christ," he answered, "and it is my duty to instruct people when they seek the light of the Christian faith. I could not turn this girl away. So far as I was able, I enlightened her about our religion and showed her the way

*D**

to the heavenly kingdom. I would gladly have done as much
for you, had you asked me." The magistrate threatened to
beat him to death, to which Eulogius replied that to be put to
death for rejecting a false religion was to ensure one's life for
eternity.

He was then taken to be examined by the royal council.
A friend of his among the councillors took him aside, and said:
"Foolish and ignorant people throw their lives away, we
know: but a man of your good sense and standing ought not
to do such a thing. Listen to me: just say the one word that is
required here, and afterwards you can go back to your own
religion. We promise that you will not be interfered with
again." Eulogius smiled. "Thank you, my friend," he said.
"If you understood our religion and the happiness that awaits
those who are faithful to it, you would not talk to me like
this. Rather would you follow my example." Then he turned
to the council and began in liberty of spirit to expound the
good news of the kingdom of Heaven. But they did not want
to hear, and cut him short by sentencing him to death.

As Eulogius was led from the court, a bystander struck him
in the face. "Now the other side, lest this be jealous of the
honour," said Eulogius, and turned the other cheek. He was
struck again, and he turned his face again. Then the guards
dragged him away, and took him to the place of execution.
He made the sign of the cross and raised his hands to Heaven
in prayer; then he bowed his head, and the headsman slew
him with one blow.

It was three o'clock in the afternoon of Saturday, 11 March
859. Four days later Leocritia followed her teacher, by the
same death. Promises and cajolery had been powerless to turn
her from the way, the truth and the life. Her body was thrown
into the Guadalquivir; but it was recovered, and now rests
beside that of Eulogius in the cathedral of Oviedo.

ST THOMAS
OF CANTERBURY

AT CANTERBURY, A.D. 1170

Thomas Becket was the most famous martyr of the middle ages: the murder of an archbishop in his cathedral church riveted the shocked attention of Christians everywhere, veneration of his memory spread like wildfire, and his shrine became one of the half-dozen most frequented pilgrimage-places of medieval Christendom. Becket was not, of course, a victim of heathen fury or fear, nor did he suffer in some persecution of right-believing Christians by heterodox opponents: he died, in a sense accidentally, as the culmination of a long-drawn-out dispute between church and state, in which all the right was not necessarily on one side. But most of the mass of people whose enthusiasm carried the murdered archbishop to a swift canonization knew and cared little enough about "criminous clerks" and royal prerogatives; few of them perhaps realized that he had given his life in resisting—with whatever violence, exaggeration and lack of finesse at times—what in those days were governmental encroachments that were esteemed to threaten the Church of which they too were members. What they did see was the sacrilegious killing of a father in God, and they heard the mounting reports of wonders wrought at his tomb. And their instinct was right. Pope Alexander III was not ill-disposed towards King Henry II (Becket, indeed, had thought the pope was too forbearing in his opposition to the king's demands); but it was Alexander who, little more than two years after the murder, canonized Thomas of Canterbury as a martyr, "smitten by the swords of a party of wicked men for his defence of justice and the Church's freedom," as the Roman Martyrology puts it.*

After six years of bitter struggle between the contending adversaries the end came suddenly and unexpectedly, for in the summer of 1170 king and archbishop had met in Normandy and patched up a reconciliation. The exiled Becket returned to England, where he was received with delight by the lower clergy and the common people—and by them only. But before leaving France he had suspended from their

* When urged to follow a certain course because it was that of the revered Becket, St Hugh of Lincoln observed, "He was not a saint because of that: his title to holiness was the martyr's crown."

*offices the archbishop of York and those bishops who had assisted him
in infringing the primatial rights of Canterbury by crowning the king's
son at Westminster. York, with the bishops of London and Salisbury,
hurried overseas to complain to the king, who was at the castle of
Bur, near Bayeux. Someone said that there would be no peace and
quietness in England so long as Becket lived, and Henry fell into a
paroxysm of uncontrollable rage: it was then that he uttered the reckless and fateful words that proved to be Becket's death-warrant. The
king can hardly be held deliberately responsible for what followed:
later on, he took an oath that he had neither ordered nor desired
Thomas's death, but he admitted that his rash words could have
occasioned it. Certainly they were understood as a rebuke to his
courtiers for allowing "this upstart priest" to continue to trouble him.
Four knights at once set off for England: they were Reginald Fitz-
Urse, William de Tracy, Hugh de Morville and Richard le Breton.*

After dinner in the mid-afternoon of Tuesday, 29 December 1170, Thomas Becket, then in his fifty-third year, was
sitting in the bedroom of his house adjoining the monastery
of Christ Church at Canterbury, talking with friends and
members of his household. Word was brought that four of
the king's knights were below, wishing to speak with the
archbishop. They were brought up, and, after a little uneasy
sparring, they voiced the royal complaints about Thomas's
behaviour. He rejected them, appealed to his agreement with
Henry five months before, and in turn complained of insults
offered to himself as archbishop. Hugh de Morville asked why
he took the punishment of these upon himself, to which
Thomas replied heatedly: "When the Church's rights are
violated, I await no man's permission to vindicate them. I
will give the king the things that are his, but to God the things
that are God's. It is my business, and only I shall see to it!"
This defiance stung the knights to fury. "You threaten!" exclaimed FitzUrse. "Are you going to excommunicate us?"
"You threaten me," retorted Thomas, "but to no purpose.
All the swords in England will not frighten me from my
obedience to God and my lord the pope. I gave way once—
but not again. There is fealty between you and me, and I am
astonished that you should threaten the archbishop in his own
house."

FitzUrse called on the bystanders who had crowded in not to let the archbishop escape; but they did not stir, and "I am not going to escape," said Thomas. He implored the knights to come back as they left the room, uttering confused threats, but they pressed on into the garden, shouting "To arms!" Their soldiers ran in at the main gateway, while outside in the streets the people gathered in the dusk of midwinter, a dusk made gloomier by a gathering storm.

Becket returned into his room and sat down on the bed, while his friend John of Salisbury gently rebuked him for his headstrongness. "I am ready to die," replied Thomas. But John continued to expostulate: "We are sinners, and no one of us is yet fit to die. I know nobody who wants to die without cause except you." But now there was a noise of shouting and breaking of doors, and Thomas was persuaded, very unwillingly, to go to the church, by way of a private door into the cloisters; his metropolitan's cross was borne before him. As he proceeded at a leisurely pace, his attendants hustled and hurried, even tried to carry him; he shook them off, time and again. Thus they passed along the north and east walks of the cloister, till they came to the door into the north transept of the church.

The cathedral of Canterbury is a very different and much bigger building now than what it was in 1170; but there is still a north-west transept on the Norman foundations, with a doorway into the south-east corner of the cloisters. Outside the predecessor of this door Thomas stopped, met by frightened monks who had interrupted the singing of Vespers when the alarm reached them. "Come in! Come in!" they implored. "Get back to choir," answered the archbishop. "I will not come in all the time you are standing there." They drew back a little from the door, and as he stepped in Thomas saw the crowd in the transept. "What are all these people frightened of?" he asked. And voices came back, "Armed men! In the cloisters!" Thomas turned and saw them in the dim light, coming up the southern walk: the four knights with drawn swords, other knights, and an armed rabble; FitzUrse had picked up a carpenter's axe outside, and was shouting, "This way, king's men!"

The door was slammed to and barred, and in the confusion some monks were shut outside; these banged on the door. Thomas himself reopened it, crying to the others above the din, "Get away, you cowards! I order you by obedience not to shut this door—a church is not a castle!" Terror was now out of hand; the crowd in the transept broke and fled, leaving only three men with the archbishop: his old master, Robert, prior of Merton, William FitzStephen, his chaplain, and an English cleric, Edward Grim. These hurried him to a flight of steps leading to the choir, and at that moment the pursuers burst in. There was a babble of voices: "Stop!"— "Where has that traitor Thomas gone?"—and from FitzUrse as he stumbled in the darkness, "Where is the archbishop?" Becket's voice replied from the steps: "Here I am, Reginald. No traitor, but archbishop and priest of God. What do you want?" And he came down from the steps and stood between a central pillar and the altar of St Benedict.

They shouted at him to absolve the bishops whom he had excommunicated four days before, on Christmas-day. "I cannot do other than I have done," answered Thomas, and turning to FitzUrse, "Reginald, you have received many benefits from me. Why do you come into my church with arms in your hands?" FitzUrse's only reply was to threaten with his axe, exclaiming, "You shall die! I'll tear your heart out!" "I am ready to die for God and the Church," said Thomas, "but God's curse be on you if you harm my people." Then they fell upon him and tried to drag him out of the church, but he resisted with all his strength, bracing himself against the pillar and shaking off his assailants.

The knights drew back, and then FitzUrse, who had cast aside his axe, advanced on the archbishop with uplifted sword. "You pander!" exclaimed Becket. "You are my man; you have done me fealty—how dare you touch me!" "I owe you no fealty contrary to my fealty to the king," retorted FitzUrse: "Strike! Strike!" and he knocked the cap from Becket's head. He covered his face with his hands, calling aloud on God and St Denis and St Alphege. Tracy aimed a more dangerous blow, which Grim partly warded off with his own arm, sustaining a wound; but Thomas's head and shoulder were cut, and somebody struck again, with the flat of his sword. Blood was running down the archbishop's face; he wiped it away, crying, "Into thy hands, Lord, I commend my spirit!" The next blow, again from Tracy, brought him to his knees, his hands still clasped as when one prays. Murmuring "I am willing to die for the name of Jesus and in defence of the Church," he fell forward on his face, so gently that his long cloak was not disarranged.

Then Richard le Breton struck Thomas's head with such ferocity that the scalp was severed and the sword left broken on the pavement. Hugh of Horsea, well called Mauclerc, a subdeacon who had joined the knights, put his foot on Thomas's neck and scattered the brains from the skull with his sword-point: "Let us go," he said, " the traitor is dead and will rise no more." While, it is said, a great storm of rain and thunder broke overhead, the murderers rushed away, shouting "The king's men!", to ransack the archbishop's house, where they found two hairshirts among his clothes, which they cast contemptuously aside.

It was all over in a few minutes. The nave of the cathedral was now full of excited townsfolk; but the transept was still and empty save for the body of Thomas Becket, lying close by the corner wall. For some time no one dared touch or even go near it; but before morning he was being called martyr and saint, and cloths were dipped in his blood for relics.

ST BERARD, ST DANIEL
and Their Companions

It cannot be denied that medieval missionary methods were often somewhat crude, and liable to provoke violent retaliation. To get a sympathetic hearing for one's message it is necessary to try to make friends with one's auditors: this cannot be done by denouncing their religion and calling their prophet a scoundrel (even today it is still possible to meet people who do not seem to realize this). The approach of such as St Francis de Sales and St Peter Canisius to those inculpably in error was as yet hardly known. But a Franciscan tertiary in the second half of the thirteenth century was already devoting himself to promoting a better and more informed approach to the Moslems This man, Bd Raymund Lull, was before his time and received but little encouragement; but he laid down his life for his friends, dying in 1316 from the effects of being stoned while preaching in Algeria. However, defect of method does not necessarily invalidate self-sacrifice, and not a few missionaries of the later middle ages are recognized and honoured as true martyrs.

At the same time that St Francis of Assisi was seeking to preach the Gospel among the Moslem Saracens in Egypt, five of his brethren had set out from Italy in the year 1219 to do the same among the Moslems of the West. Their names were Berard, Otto, Peter, Accursio and Aiuto, the proto-martyrs of the order of Friars Minor. When they attempted to preach to the Moors in Seville they were at once ill-treated and thrown into prison, but were soon released on condition that they should leave the country. They were enabled to reach Morocco, where at Marrakesh they were taken under the protection of the exiled brother of King Alonzo II of Portugal.

This Don Pedro warned the friars against preaching in

the streets; but that was what they had come to do, and they set to work with more zeal than discretion, though apparently only one of them, Brother Berard, knew any Arabic. At first they were set down as lunatics, and vain efforts were made to persuade them to return to Spain. For a time they acted as chaplains to the sultan's Christian mercenaries, and then Don Pedro tried to keep them in safety in his own house; but they slipped away and began preaching again in public.

Haled before the magistrate, the friars denounced the iniquities of Mohammed and glorified Christ, whereupon each one was mercilessly scourged, and eventually they were put to death. The story goes that the sultan, Joseph al-Mostansir, himself tried to induce them to accept Islam. He promised beautiful wives, riches and honourable positions; but the friars only replied, "We do not want your women or your money: for love of Jesus Christ we despise all the good things of this world." At that, the sultan in a fury seized a sword and smashed open the head of each one, and then decapitated them as they lay. When he heard of the martyrdom, St Francis of Assisi exclaimed, "Now indeed I can say I have five brothers"; and it prompted St Antony of Padua, then at Coïmbra in his native Portugal, to seek admittance among the Friars Minor.

Only seven years later, seven other Franciscans perished in Morocco in similar circumstances. They were Brothers Daniel, Agnello, Samuel, Domno, Leo, Nicholas and Hugolino, all Italians. Having travelled by way of Spain, the leader of the band, Daniel, and three others arrived first in Morocco, at a place near Ceuta. Here they spent a little time ministering to the merchants from Pisa, Genoa and elsewhere who had agencies there. When the others arrived, they all prepared at once to begin their mission. Three days later they made their confessions, washed one another's feet, and spent the night in prayer and watching. Then, early the next morning, they appeared in the streets of Ceuta, carrying a cross and with penitential ashes on their heads.

Their unusual appearance at once attracted attention, but curiosity was soon turned to anger when they called on the crowd to forsake the evil deceits of Mohammed and follow Jesus Christ. They were hurried off to prison, where Daniel wrote to the friends with whom they had stayed, telling them what had happened: "Blessed be God, the Father of mercies," he concluded, "for he comforts us in all our tribulations." When it was disovered that the strangers were missionaries and not simply cranks, attempts were made to get them to renounce the Christian faith, accompanied by the usual threats and bribes. These they rejected with scorn, and they were sentenced to death. Each of the friars in turn knelt before their leader for his blessing and to ask leave to give his life for Christ. Then, amid the execrations of the Moors whom they had come to serve, Daniel and his brethren were beheaded.

BD ANTONY OF RIVOLI

IN TUNIS, A.D. 1460

In 1767 Pope Clement XIII confirmed the long-standing cultus of a martyr whose story is a rather remarkable one. Antony Neyrot was born at Rivoli in Piedmont about the year 1423, and joined the Order of Preachers at San Marco in Florence at the time when St Antonino was prior there. Antony seems to have been a good religious, but rather fond of ease and lacking in stability, a quality that was not supplied by his travels in the Levant and elsewhere. When he had reached the age of thirty-five he was living in Sicily, and in 1458 he was given permission to go to Rome. On the way his ship was captured by Barbary pirates, and Antony was taken to Tunis and

thrown into prison. His efforts to get released were so unmeasured
that the Genoese consul at first refused to help him. But after a time
he was set free, only to fall into a worse captivity—he renounced
Christianity, accepted Islam, and took a Moslem wife. (One writer*
says he was stung into doing this by the calumnies of a fellow priest.)

Antony remained in this state for about six months, during
which he employed himself in translating the Koran from
Arabic into Latin, with the help of a man who knew both
languages as well as Italian. Then he came to his right mind,
and "threw himself on the mercy of Christ, whose loving-
kindness is so great that no man can imagine it." He opened
his heart to a Franciscan friar who was then in Tunis, was
reconciled with the Church, and spent another six months in
penance, keeping his repudiation of Islam secret meanwhile;
but whatever had been given him by Moslems during the time
he was a renegade he gave away to the needy. He was awaiting the return of the Tunisian ruler, who had left the city
for a time. The day after this prince came back (it was doubtless the Berber Abu Omar Othman), Antony resumed his
Dominican habit and tonsure, and movingly took leave of his
Christian friends. "Goodbye, brothers," he said, "I beseech
you all in the name of Jesus Christ to pray that I may be
courageous and strong in what I have to do." He then went
and presented himself before the sultan. It was the Palm Sunday of 1460.

Before the assembled notables, Antony formally announced
his rejection of the religion of Islam, its prophet and its book,
and declared that they could do him no greater service than
to enable him to expiate his own unfaithfulness to Jesus Christ
with his life. The sultan argued, promised and threatened, to
no purpose, and afterwards sent him to a religious court,
which had no better success. So he was treated with indignity,
beaten, and shut up in jail, where he spent his time comforting
and encouraging his fellow prisoners. Three days later, before

* One of the English martyrs, Bd Edward Waterson, was invited to
do the same when a young man; see Butler's *Lives of the Saints*, vol. i,
p. 49 (1956 edn).

a large crowd, he was sentenced to death by stoning, to which he replied "Deo gratias!"

Antony was bound and led round the streets of the city, being scourged the while and asked every so often if he would return to the faith of Mohammed. When they reached the European quarter there was a brief pause; Antony took off his scapular and handed it to a bystander, asking him of his kindness to give it to one John of Novara, a brother Dominican who was then in the city. At the place of execution the guards formed a threatening ring round the martyr as he knelt and prayed. Then the word was given, and with a howl the crowd flung stones and bits of metal, till Antony and the whole place was covered with them; he died without another word or movement.

That day, we are told, the house of every Christian in Tunis was kept bolted and barred; any one of them seen out of doors was liable to lose his life and they were very frightened. But some of them were mindful of the martyrs of old, and were happy that one more had been added to the company of Heaven.

ST JOHN OF ROCHESTER

IN LONDON, A.D. 1535

John Fisher was born at Beverley in Yorkshire in 1469, son of a mercer. He was ordained priest, appointed master of Michaelhouse at Cambridge and, after being elected vice-chancellor and chancellor of the university, where he left his mark, was nominated to the bishopric of Rochester by King Henry VII in 1504. Bishop Fisher was an

*energetic and enlightened reformer, a "paragon of bishops in learn-
ing and holiness," as the imperial ambassador in England described
him. He actively upheld the validity of Katherine of Aragon's marriage
with Henry VIII, and consistently opposed the king's claim to be
head of the Church in England. When a bill was enacted providing
for the succession to the throne of the offspring of Henry VIII and
Anne Boleyn, Fisher was not opposed to this succession in itself;
but, like St Thomas More and unlike the other bishops, he refused
the pertinent oath, on the ground that it constituted a recognition
of the king's ecclesiastical supremacy. "Not that I condemn any other
men's conscience," he wrote. "Their conscience may save them, and
mine must save me." On 26 April 1534 he was imprisoned in the
Tower of London, on May 21 of the next year Pope Paul III made
him a cardinal, and on June 17 following he was arraigned in Westminster Hall before thirteen commissioners and a jury of freeholders.
He was in an extreme state of debility, being older than his years
(sixty-six) through ill-health, imprisonment and austerity of life. The
following narrative is from a Life of Fisher written probably soon
after 1567.*

Being thus presented before these commissioners, he was
commanded, by the name of "John Fisher, late of Rochester,
clerk, otherwise called John Fisher, bishop of Rochester," to
hold up his hand, which he did with a most cheerful countenance and rare constancy. Then was his indictment read,
which was very long and full of words, but the effect of it
was thus: That he maliciously, traitorously and falsely had
said these words: "The King, our sovereign lord, is not
supreme head in earth of the Church of England." And being
read to the end, it was asked him whether he was guilty of
this treason or no, whereunto he pleaded not guilty.

[The sole witness was Richard Rich, solicitor general,
whom the king had sent secretly to talk with the bishop in the
Tower. Fisher replied to Rich in court that, supposing he had
said the words Rich alleged, they were not spoken treason-
ably: Rich had told him that the king wished to know his
mind on the supremacy "for better satisfaction of his own
conscience"; with an assurance from the king that he would
not be put in peril for anything he might say, and that Rich
would communicate what was said to none but the king.]
This good father, perceiving the small account made of his

words and the favourable credit given to his accuser, might then easily smell which way the matter would go. Wherefore, directing his speeches to the lords his judges, he said, "Yet I pray you, my lords, consider that by all equity, justice, worldly honesty and courteous dealings, I cannot as the case standeth be directly charged therewith as with treason, though I had spoken the words in deed, the same being not spoken maliciously but in the way of advice and counsel, when it was requested of me by the king himself; and that favour the very words of the statute do give me, being made only against such as shall *maliciously* gainsay the king's supremacy, and none other."

To that it was answered by some of the judges that the word "maliciously" in the statute is but a superfluous and void word; for if a man speak against the king's supremacy by any manner of means, that speaking is to be understood and taken in law as malicious. "My lord," said he, "if the law be so understood, then it is a hard exposition and, as I take it, contrary to the meaning of them that made the law. But then let me demand this question: Whether a single testimony of one man may be admitted as sufficient to prove me guilty of treason for speaking these words, or no? And whether my answer negatively may not be accepted against his affirmative, to my avail and benefit, or no?" To that the judges and lawyers answered that, being the king's case, it rested much in conscience and discretion of the jury, "and as they upon the evidence given before them shall find it, you are either to be acquitted or else by judgement to be condemned." The jury, having heard all this simple evidence, departed according to order into a secret place, there to agree upon the verdict; but before they went from the place the case was so aggravated to them by my lord Chancellor [Sir Thomas Audley], making it so heinous and dangerous a treason, that they easily perceived what verdict they must return, or else heap such danger upon their own heads as was for none of their cases to bear.

[Meanwhile, some of the commissioners complained of

Fisher's singularity and obstinacy in standing out against Parliament and the bishops of the realm. He replied that he had the rest of the bishops of Christendom with him and thus] having on his part all the Catholic bishops of the world, from Christ's ascension till now, joined with the whole consent of Christ's universal Church, "I must needs," said he, "account mine own part far the surer. And as for obstinacy, which is likewise objected against me, I have no way to clear myself thereof but by my own solemn word and promise to the contrary, if you please to believe it; or else, if that will not serve, I am here ready to confirm the same by mine oath." . . . The twelve men, being shortly returned from their consultation, verdict was given that he was guilty of treason. . . . [When asked if he had anything further to say, Fisher replied,] "Truly, my lords, if that which I have before spoken be not sufficient, I have no more to say, but only to desire Almighty God to forgive them that have thus condemned me, for I think they know not what they have done." Then my lord Chancellor, framing himself to a solemnity in countenance, pronounced sentence of death upon him in manner and form following:

You shall be led to the place from whence you came, and from thence shall be drawn through the city to the place of execution at Tyburn, where your body shall be hanged by the neck; and being half alive, you shall be cut down and thrown to the ground, your bowels to be taken out of your body and burnt before you, being alive; your head to be smitten off, and your body to be divided into four quarters; and after, your head and quarters to be set up where the king shall appoint. And God have mercy on your soul.

[Before he left the precincts of Westminster, Fisher addressed the commissioners and formally denied the possibility of King Henry or any other sovereign being head of the Church in England or anywhere else. He was then taken back to the Tower. Four days later the king issued a writ for his execution, not according to the sentence but by beheading on

Tower Hill. Early the next morning the lieutenant of the Tower] came to him in his chamber in the Bell tower, finding him yet asleep in his bed, waked him, shewing him that he was come to him on a message from the king; and after some circumstances used with persuasion, that he should remember himself to be an old man and that for age he could not by course of nature live long, he told him at the last that he was come to signify unto him that the king's pleasure was he should suffer death that forenoon. "Well," quoth this blessed father, "if this be your errand, you bring me no great news, for I have long time looked for this message; and I most humbly thank the king's Majesty that it pleaseth him to rid me from all this worldly business, and I thank you also for your tidings. But I pray you, master lieutenant, when is my hour that I must go hence?" "Your hour," said the lieutenant, "must be nine of the clock." "And what hour is it now?" said he. "It is now about five," said the lieutenant. "Well, then," said he, "let me by your patience sleep an hour or two, for I have slept very little this night, and yet, to tell you the truth, not for any fear of death, I thank God, but by reason of my great infirmity and weakness." "The king's further pleasure is," said the lieutenant, "that you should use as little speech as may be, especially of any thing touching his Majesty, whereby the people should have any cause to think of him or his proceedings otherwise than well." "For that," said he, "you shall see me order myself as, by God's grace, neither the king nor any man else shall have occasion to mistake of my words." With which answer the lieutenant departed from him, and so the prisoner, falling again to rest, slept soundly two hours and more. And after he was waked he called to his man to help him up.

[Fisher ordered his hairshirt to be hidden away, and dressed himself in clean clothes with more than usual care. His man] demanded of him what this sudden change meant, seeing that his lordship knew well enough he must put off all again within two hours and lose it. "What of that?" said he. "Dost thou not mark that this is our marriage day, and that it behoveth us

therefore to use more cleanliness for solemnity of that marriage?" About nine of the clock the lieutenant came again to
his prison and, finding him almost ready, said that he was now
come for him. "I will wait upon you straight," said he, "as fast
as this thin body of mine will give me leave." Then he said
to his man, "Reach me my furred tippet and put it about my
neck." "Oh, my lord," quoth the lieutenant, "what need you
be so careful for your health for this little, being as your lordship knoweth not much above an hour?" "I think no otherwise," said this blessed father. "But yet in the meantime I will
keep myself as well as I can till the very time of my execution.
For I tell you truth, though I have (I thank our Lord) a very
good desire and willing mind to die at this present, and so
trust of his infinite mercy and goodness he will continue it, yet
will I not willingly hinder my health in the meantime one
minute of an hour, but still prolong the same as long as I can
by such reasonable ways and means as Almighty God hath
provided for me."

And with that, taking a little book in his hand, which was
a New Testament lying by him, he made a cross on his forehead and went out of his prison door with the lieutenant.
[Fisher was too weak to walk properly, so he was carried in a
chair. At the gate there was some delay,] during which space
he rose out of his chair, and standing on his feet leaned his
shoulder to the wall and, lifting his eyes up toward Heaven,
he opened his little book in his hand and said: "O Lord, this
is the last time that ever I shall open this book; let some com-
fortable place now chance unto me, whereby I, thy poor
servant, may glorify thee, in this my last hour." And with that,
looking into the book, the first thing that came to his sight
were these words: "Haec est autem vita aeterna. . . ." [Now
this is eternal life: That they may know thee, the only true
God, and Jesus Christ whom thou hast sent. I have glorified
thee on the earth; I have finished the work which thou gavest
me to do. And now glorify thou me, Father, with thyself, with
the glory which I had, before the world was, with thee" (John

17: 3-5).] And with that he shut the book together and said, "Here is even learning enough for me even to my life's end." . . . And when he was come to the foot of the scaffold, they that carried him offered to help him up the stairs; but then said he, "Nay, masters, seeing I am come so far, let me alone, and ye shall see me shift for myself well enough"; and so he went up the stairs without any help, so lively that it was marvel to them that knew before of his debility and weakness. But as he was mounting up the stairs, the south-east sun shined very bright in his face, whereupon he said to himself these words, lifting up his hands: "Accedite ad eum et illuminamini et facies vestrae non confundentur." ["Draw nigh to Him and receive his light, and you shall not be discountenanced."] By that time he was up the scaffold (it was about ten of the clock), where the executioner, being ready to do his office, kneeled down to him, as the fashion is, and asked him forgiveness. "I forgive thee," said he, "with all my heart, and I trust thou shalt see me overcome this storm lustily."

[When stripped of his gown and tippet, Fisher was seen to be so thin that he seemed "a very image of death."] He spake to the people in effect as followeth: "Christian people, I am come hither to die for the faith of Christ's holy Catholic Church, and I thank God hitherto my stomach hath served me very well thereunto, so that yet I have not feared death. Wherefore I do desire you all to help and assist me with your prayers that, at the very point and instant of death's stroke, I may in that very moment stand steadfast without fainting in any one point of the Catholic faith, free from any fear. And I beseech Almighty God of his infinite goodness to save the king and this realm, and that it may please him to hold his holy hand over it and send the king good counsel." These or like words he spake with such a cheerful countenance, such a stout and constant courage, and such a reverent gravity that he appeared to all men not only void of fear but also glad of death. Besides this, he uttered his words so distinctly and with so loud and clear a voice that the people were astonied thereat, and noted it for a miraculous thing to hear so plain and audible a voice come from so weak and sickly an old body. . . .

He kneeled down on both knees and said certain prayers, among which, as some reported, one was the hymn "Te Deum laudamus" to the end, and the psalm "In te, Domine, speravi." Then came the executioner and bound a handkerchief about his eyes, and so this holy father, lifting up his hands and heart to Heaven, said a few prayers, which were not long but fervent and devout. Which being ended, he laid his holy head down over the midst of the block, where the executioner, being ready with a sharp and heavy axe, cut asunder his slender neck at one blow, which bled so abundantly that many wondered to see so much blood issue out of so lean and slender a body. And so, head and body being severed, his innocent soul mounted to the blissful joys of Heaven. . . .

Two of the watchers took [the headless body] and carried it to a churchyard there hard by, called All Hallows Barking, where on the north side of the church hard by the wall they digged a grave with their halberds, and therein without any reverence tumbled the body of this holy prelate and blessed martyr, all naked and flat upon his belly, without either sheet or other accustomed thing belonging to a Christian man's burial, and so covered it quickly with earth, following herein the king's commandment, who willed it should be buried contemptuously. And this was done on the day of St Alban, the protomartyr and first martyr of England, being Tuesday the 22nd of June in the year of our Redemption 1535. . . . The next day after his burial, the head, being somewhat parboiled in hot water, was pricked upon a pole and set on high upon London Bridge, amongst the rest of the holy Carthusians' heads that suffered death lately before him. . . . [So great was the press of people coming to see it, attracted by devotion and the reported miraculously good state of the martyr's head, that after fourteen days] the executioner commanded to throw down the head in the night time into the river of Thames; and in place thereof was set the head of the most blessed and con-

stant martyr Sir Thomas More, his companion and fellow in
all his troubles, who suffered his passion the sixth day of July
next following.

BD CUTHBERT MAYNE

AT LAUNCESTON, A.D. 1577

*As with some martyrs at other times and in other places, the ques-
tion is sometimes raised whether some of the martyrs under Queen
Elizabeth I and subsequently were not put to death for political rather
than for religious transgressions. The Rising of the North took place
in November 1569, and in the following February Pope St Pius V
issued the bull "Regnans in excelsis," purporting to depose Elizabeth
and to absolve her subjects from their allegiance. This is not the place
to discuss that grave error of judgement, and its far-reaching effects
of aggravating the oppression and difficulties of Catholics in England.
But from then on till the end of her reign persecution, further
aggravated in due course by the Spanish Armada, was at its height,
and produced those statutes of 1581 and 1585 which made it high
treason to reconcile anyone or to be reconciled with the Catholic
Church, and for a "Jesuit or seminary priest" to be within the queen's
dominions (to maintain the Pope's authority had already been made
treason). It is true that there were individual English Catholics both
at home and abroad who were willing and anxious to use force and
political intrigue on behalf of their cause; some even among the
martyrs held the opinion that, were a Catholic prince to invade a
country to bring it back to Rome, Catholics ought to support him.
But they died for the faith nevertheless. The "treason" for which so
many were put to death was a legal construction. There is no need to
question that many of those who looked on them as political traitors
did so in complete good faith: but the religious motive, "hatred of
the faith," was always there as well.* Time and again a convicted*

* Alexander Mackay, the pioneer Protestant missionary in Uganda,
who with his colleague R. P. Ashe was very active in the efforts to
save the Christians there in 1886 (cf. below, pp. 197 ff.), remarked
with much truth that there is a political element in every religious
persecution.

"traitor" was offered his life if he would abjure his faith; and on the other hand, how many of the martyrs, standing on the scaffold, protested their innocence of treasonable intent and their loyalty to their sovereign, and publicly prayed for her or him and for the realm. Accordingly, the Holy See had no hesitation in recognizing, in 1886, that a first group of English and Welsh martyrs had been equivalently beatified by Pope Gregory XIII in 1583, and in formally beatifying 136 more in 1929.

The martyrs under Henry VIII are represented herein by St John of Rochester. But among the later and more numerous ones are names no less famous than those of Fisher and More, of the Carthusian and Benedictine monks, of Richard Reynolds and the Countess of Salisbury—such names as Edmund Campion, Robert Southwell, Anne Line, James Duckett. Of these later martyrs, only a very small selection can figure here, made up of some well-known, others not so well-known. And of those who suffered under Elizabeth I we may well begin with Bd Cuthbert Mayne, the protomartyr of the seminaries, that is, of the missionary priests trained and ordained in the English colleges established abroad.

Cuthbert Mayne was born at Youlston, near Barnstaple, in 1544, brought up a Protestant, and ordained in the Church of England. At St John's College, Oxford, he first came under the influence of Dr Gregory Martin and Edmund Campion, and some years later he was reconciled with the Catholic Church and went to the newly-founded college at Douay. Here in 1576 he was ordained priest, and sent back to England to minister. His headquarters was at Golden, Francis Tregian's house near Truro, and only a year later he was found there when the house was searched by the high sheriff of Cornwall, Richard Grenville. (When asked "What art thou?" Mayne made the famous retort, "I am a man.") At the following Michaelmas assizes at Launceston he was indicted on six counts: that he had traitorously obtained from Rome and published a "printed instrument containing a pretended matter of absolution"; had taught and upheld the ecclesiastical authority of the bishop of Rome; had brought into the realm and delivered to Mr. Tregian "a certain vain sign and superstitious thing called an agnus Dei*"; and had celebrated Mass at Golden. With Mayne there were indicted certain laymen for aiding and abetting in some of the counts. The evidence was of the feeblest. A specimen of it is referred to in the following particulars, which are from a manuscript concerning Tregian and Mayne, written in 1593 and now at St Mary's College, Oscott.*

After all this "substantial and inevitable evidence" against them had been by the [queen's] attorney in their proper colours soundly set forth, adding his accustomed speeches, that they were all papists and traitors, refusing to obey her

Majesty's proceedings in not coming to the church, and therefore not worthy of any favour, or fit to receive the benefit of law, he concluded in generality that what he had alleged was matter good and sufficient enough to prove them all guilty concerning the several indictments whereof they were accused, and so willed the jury to go together and bring in their verdict. The jury had not been long together but they came into the judgement-hall again, and yet sat down in the lower end thereof, staggering as though they had not been thoroughly resolved concerning their verdict. The which when the sheriff perceived, with speed he arose out of his seat and went unto them; and there, in the sight both of the judges and all the people, contrary to the course and order of law, contrary to all use and custom, and contrary to the oath of their forsworn keeper, he talked to them, and that very vehemently a long time—to what effect God knoweth.

But he was no [sooner] departed and returned to his seat again, but they cried, as the manner is, "A verdict!" And then being called forth, they found Cuthbert Mayne and all the rest guilty of all and every one of the surmised offences, whereof they had been most unjustly accused. This sentence thus given, they were all (saving Cuthbert Mayne, who was conveyed into a vile place to be close prisoner, kept from conference with the rest) returned again into the common gaol, where their beds were a bare floor and their pillows hard stones. . . .

The next day, therefore, they were all brought forth again to receive judgement, coupled like dogs, two together with chains of iron (saving Cuthbert Mayne who, also with iron fast fettered both hand and foot, went all alone as their captain before them) in which sort they marched on as well as they could, to the great admiration of the people, from the common gaol into the place of judgement. Where when they came, first Cuthbert Mayne, as the manner is, was demanded what he could say why he ought not to receive judgement upon those several indictments whereof he was found guilty.

Whereunto he answered that he never committed or intended to commit any treason towards her Majesty or his dear country; and, as touching the copy of the jubilee [indulgence] found in his custody which they enforced to be a matter of great offence, as he had already said, the thing to his knowledge and to his account was no other than a void paper which he brought from Douay and not from Rome, where he never was; besides, the date of the same is expired, and so out of all use long before his coming into England, and therefore, if he would, yet by no means he could have committed any such act contrary to the law, as was alleged. Further, admitting the date thereof had not been expired but in full force, yet could he not thereby have committed any treason by any means whatsoever: for any act that was thereby to be done was only but to give absolution of sin unto penitent sinners, and therefore, if the thing had been in full force as it was altogether out of use, yet he had committed no treason, unless they would make it treason to forgive sins.

Thus speaking, the judge who was chief in commission [Manwood] said: "We have not to do with your papistical use in absolving sins—you may keep it to yourselves; and although the date of this bull was expired and out of force, as you have alleged, so was it always out of force with us, for we never did nor do account any such thing to be of force or worth a straw; and yet the same is by law of this realm treason, and therefore thou hast deserved to die." Hereunto he answered, what he had deserved God did best know; but if it were as [the judge] said, he was very sorry this land had any such law.

Whereupon the other judge [Jeffreys], who was second in commission, communed with his fellow somewhat softly a long time, as it seemed in defence of that which Cuthbert Mayne had alleged, for much contrariety and disagreement appeared in their talk. In the end therefore he who was chief in commission, in some choler to be contraried, was heard to say thus: "Well, it maketh no matter; for all that, I will give judgement." [He then sentenced Mayne to death, in similar terms to those noted under St John of Rochester, above.] Which sentence thus pronounced, Cuthbert Mayne, with a most mild and gladsome countenance, lifting up his eyes and hands unto Heaven, only said, "God be thanked." [The other prisoners were sentenced to forfeiture of goods and life imprisonment for aiding and comforting.]

The condemnation of Cuthbert Mayne not being liked nor allowed, as hath been declared, by Mr Jeffreys . . . , it was thought necessary by some in authority, as we have heard, that all the judges of the realm should meet and consider of the matter. But being carried into divers minds, they departed leaving the same undetermined, although the most ancient, most learned and most in number maintained with Mr Jeffrey's opinion, not allowing of the condemnation. Notwithstanding, the state of the time considered, it was by the Council thought good and expedient that one should die for the sins of the people. Whereupon there was a warrant sent unto the sheriff of Cornwall, subscribed with seven or eight of the Council's hands, for the execution of Cuthbert Mayne.

The day assigned for the same purpose was dedicated unto St Andrew; but on the eve before, all the justices of that county, with many preachers of the pretended reformed religion, being gathered together at Launceston aforesaid, Cuthbert Mayne was brought before them, his legs being not only laden with mighty irons, but his hands also fast fettered together (in which miserable case he also remained many days before): when he maintained disputation with them concerning the controversy in religion at this day in question, from eight of the clock in the morning until it was almost dark night, continually standing, no doubt in great pain in that pitiful plight, on his feet.

Those preachers besides the offer of his life and liberty if he would have conformed himself to their religion and renounced the authority of the bishop of Rome, used many other persuasions to draw him from his opinion and received religion. But their labour was all lost, for they could not, with all their bitter railing and reproachful speeches, which they poured forth in great plenty, so much as once move him to the least impatience in the world.

Wherefore, according to the judgement he had received, the next day he was uneasily laid on a hurdle, and so spitefully drawn, receiving some knocks on his face and his fingers with a girdle, unto the market-place of the said town, where of purpose there was a very high gibbet erected, and all things else, both fire and knives, set to the show and ready prepared. At which place of execution when he came, he was first forced, for the more despite, to mount the ladder backward, and after permitted to use very few words. Notwithstanding, he briefly opened the cause of his condemnation, the which how justly he deserved he referred to the judgement of Almighty God; and withal solemnly protested, and took it on his death, that his master [Mr Tregian] was never privy or any way acquainted with his having of those things whereupon he was condemned, which was the jubilee and the *agnus Dei*.

Then, beginning to use some words in way of exhortation, one of the justices [Treffry], interrupting his talk, commanded the hangman to put the rope about his neck, "And then," quoth he, "let him preach afterward." Which done, another [Mohun of Boconnoc] commanded the ladder to be overturned, so that he had not the leisure to recite the verse "In manus tuas, Domine" to the end. With speed he was cut down, and with the fall had almost ended his life, which before remained very perfect in him: for the gibbet being very high and he being yet in the swing when the rope was cut, he fell in such sort that his head first encountered the scaffold which was there prepared of purpose to divide the quarters, so that the one side of his face was very sorely bruised and one of his eyes far driven out of his head.

After he was cut down the hangman first spoiled him of his clothes . . . and then in butcherly manner opening his belly, he rent up his bowels and after tore out his heart, the which

E

as a plausible spectacle he held up aloft in his hand, showing it unto the people. Lastly his head was cut off and his body divided into four quarters, which afterwards were dispersed and set up on the castle of Launceston, one quarter sent unto a town called Bodmin, the most populous town in Cornwall, another unto a town called Barnstaple in Devonshire, whereabouts he was born, the third unto a town called Tregony, not above a mile distant from Mr Tregian's house, the fourth unto Wadebridge, the most common travelled way in that county. And thus was the most innocent maintainer of unity murdered and dismembered with great cruelty.*

BD RICHARD GWYN

AT WREXHAM, A.D. 1584

Wales contributed over fifty to the martyrs of the British Isles during the sixteenth and seventeenth centuries; fifteen of them are numbered among the beati, including that notable man John Roberts of Trawsfynydd, one of the founders at Douay of what is now St Gregory's Abbey at Downside. The first Welshman to suffer in his own land was a schoolmaster, Richard Gwyn. He was born at Llanidloes in the county of Montgomery about 1537. On coming down from St John's College at Cambridge he taught school at various places in Flintshire and Denbighshire, married a wife and begot six children, and eventually became unambiguously a Catholic. In July 1580 he was finally arrested near Wrexham as a recusant schoolmaster.

* A considerable relic of Bd Cuthbert Mayne's skull is preserved at the convent of Carmelite nuns at Lanherne, not far from Newquay. This community, the oldest of English Carmelites, was founded at Antwerp in 1619.

Richard Gwyn was held in prison for over four years, though brought up at assize after assize. He was a troublesome prisoner. When carried in chains to Wrexham parish church he interrupted the sermon by rattling his fetters; on another occasion, when he and two other recusants were brought into court to hear the arguments of a minister, they preached back at him—in Welsh, English and Latin: the stocks and confinement in irons could not break his spirit. He was accordingly fined a preposterous sum for "brawling in church," and again for not attending his parish church while actually in jail; towards the payment of these fines he said he had something, namely, sixpence. Some of the time he passed writing topical verse in his own tongue, and there too his energy was evident, in the spirited and sometimes bitter tone of his words. In 1583 Gwyn, with four others, including Father John Bennet the elder, the first Welsh member of the Society of Jesus, were taken before the Council of the Marches. They were by its orders all fiercely tortured to extort the names of other Catholics, but only one gave in, and that temporarily.

In October 1584 Richard Gwyn, with two other laymen, John Hughes and Robert Morris, appeared at the Wrexham assizes for the eighth time. He was indicted for high treason, in that he had tried to reconcile a certain Lewis Gronow with the Church of Rome and had maintained the pope's ecclesiastical supremacy. Gronow later admitted that his evidence was false, and the two other witnesses were bribed. The jury, collected on the spot because the original jurymen had failed to appear, asked the judge, Sir George Bromley, what their verdicts should be, and accordingly convicted the first two and acquitted Morris. Gwyn and Hughes were therefore sentenced to be hanged, drawn and quartered.* After the sentence was read Gwyn said coolly, "What is all this about? Is it any more than one death?"

* The sentence on Hughes was commuted to imprisonment for life. He probably died in jail. Because he protested against being treated differently from the others, Morris was fined a huge sum for not attending church.

Mrs Gwyn and Mrs Hughes, both with babies in arms, were lectured by the court and warned against emulating their husbands. Katherine Gwyn rounded on the sheriff, Simon Thelwall. "If it is blood that you want," she exclaimed, "you may take my life as well as my husband's. Fetch the witnesses and give them a little bribe, and then they will give evidence against me too!" She spent some days in jail for her pains.

A few days later Gwyn was offered his freedom if he would acknowledge the royal ecclesiastical supremacy. On 15 October 1584 he was led out to die. As he left the prison he blessed the sorrowing bystanders, saying, "Do not weep for me: I am only paying my rent before rent-day." It was pouring with rain, and he said to the crowd, "God is merciful to us—even the elements are weeping for our sins." The vicar of Wrexham pressed him to the last, urging the queen's ecclesiastical supremacy. Gwyn replied that she was lawful queen of England, he was her subject and he prayed for her: "I offered the Council to leave the realm if it would please them, to go to any place my sovereign might choose to send me, anywhere where my conscience would not be an offence to others: but it was no good." He forgave those who had brought him to death, and asked the people to pray for him, calling on them to be witnesses that he died for the Catholic faith: "I have been a jesting fellow," he added, "and if I have offended any that way, or by my songs, I beseech them for God's sake to forgive me." They in turn clamoured that he should not be disembowelled before he was dead.

But it was not allowed. The whole horrible business was gone through, and beneath the headsman's knife Gwyn cried out in Welsh, "Holy God, what is this?" "An execution for the queen's majesty," observed an official. "Jesus, have mercy on me," said Gwyn, still in Welsh, and a few seconds later his head was struck off.

BD MARGARET CLITHEROW

Margaret Middleton was the daughter of a wax-chandler, a man of substance and repute and a freeman of the city of York, and about the age of sixteen she married John Clitherow, of similar position and a grazier and butcher by trade. A few years after marriage she became a Catholic; her husband did not follow her example, but he put no difficulties in her way and paid the fines her recusancy incurred. Periods of imprisonment (one of two years) did not discourage her great activity in sheltering priests and providing places where Catholics could meet in secret for Mass. But there was nothing of the fanatic about Margaret Clitherow: "Everyone loved her," we are told, and turned to her for comfort in distress; she combined a lively temperament with deep religion, care for her children with efficient help in her husband's business. On 10 March 1586, when Margaret was something over thirty years old, the Clitherows' house in The Shambles at York was searched and several boys were found at their lessons. One of them was bullied with threats of beating into disclosing a secret room, wherein were found incriminating books, Mass vestments, and the like. Margaret was straightway haled off to gaol in York castle. What follows is taken from a contemporary account.

Four days she remained [in York castle] before she came to her trial, during which time she never spoke with her husband but once, and that in the presence of the jailer, after which time she could never be admitted to see him, or speak with him, notwithstanding all the suit she and her friends could make, unless she would do something against her conscience and contrary to the rules of a good Roman Catholic. During her imprisonment in the castle she gave herself more strictly to abstinence and prayer, and it being reported to her that the boy had accused her of harbouring divers priests, but two especially, by name Mr Francis Ingleby and Mr John Mush, and that according to law newly enforced she was to suffer death for the same, she was much pleased with the news; and smiling, thanked the messenger, wishing she had some good thing to give him, but wanting better means, having a fig in her hand, she gave him that for a reward.

The fourth day, the 14th of March, she was brought from the castle to the common hall (the place of justice), where the two judges, Clench and Rhodes, with the vice-president, council and other justices, were sitting on the bench. There she was indicted of felony, for that she had harboured and maintained Jesuits and seminary priests contrary to the law then in force, and by that law made traitors to the Queen, her crown and dignity. The indictment being read, Judge Clench stood up and demanded of her whether she would plead not guilty or confess the indictment. She, offering to answer, was commanded to take off her hat; whereunto obeying, with a mild, sweet boldness she answered she knew of no offence committed by her for which she should acknowledge herself guilty. The judge told her she had offended the law in harbouring Jesuits and priests, enemies to her Majesty. "I have neither harboured, nor do I know, any such persons," quoth she, "and God defend me from harbouring or maintaining those that are otherwise than the queen's friends."

The judge demanded how she would be tried. "Having not offended," quoth she, "I need no trial." Answer was made that she had offended the statutes made against the maintenance of priests and therefore she must have her trial, urging her to say how she would be tried. "If you say," quoth she, "that I have offended and that I must be tried, then I will be tried by none but God and your own conscience". . . .

Thereupon the judges commanded the two chalices, divers pictures and some vestments, with other ornaments of the altar in use in the Catholic Church, to be brought to them. These sacred ornaments were by way of derision put on two fellows' backs, who with plenty antic faces made themselves apes to please the judges and the multitude, and holding up some wafer breads said to the martyr, "Behold thy God in whom thou believest." They asked her how she liked the vestments. "I like them well," quoth she, "if they were on the backs of those that know how to use them unto God's honour."

The judge Clench asked her in whom she believed. "I believe," quoth she, "in God the Father, in God the Son and in God the Holy Ghost, in three Persons and one God, and that by the passion, death and mercy of Jesus Christ I must be saved." The judge told her she said well, and he, having paused a while, demanded of her again if she were contented to be tried by God and the country, the which she refused. Hereupon the judge bid her consider well what she did: "For," quoth he, "if you refuse to be tried by your country, you make yourself guilty of your own death, for we cannot try you but by order of law, and you need not fear this kind of trial, for I do think the country cannot find you guilty upon the bare evidence of a child." Yet this trial she still refused, and her reason was (as hath been reported) that she saw they intended to have her blood, whereof she would not have the child guilty, being brought to accuse her, for fear of whipping, as is before declared.

"Well!" quoth the judge. "Since you refuse this trial we must proceed by order of law against you, which will condemn you to a most cruel and sharp death." "God's will be done," quoth she, "and I do humbly thank him that he thinketh me worthy to suffer any kind of death for so good a cause." Which she spake with so much joy and sweetness that some said she was mad, others that she was possessed with a smiling spirit. . . . For that time the judge rose without giving sentence, and she was sent prisoner to a house on the bridge guarded by many halberdiers. . . .

The next morning about eight of the clock she was carried back into the common hall and, being brought into the bar, the judge began to tell her of the clemency that was used towards her the day before in not pronouncing sentence on her, as they might have done, hoping that now upon better consideration she would put herself on the country, otherwise she must undergo the rigour of the law, "and I see," quoth he, "no reason why you should not consent unto it, for the witness that is against you is very slender, and the country will consider your case.' "Indeed," said the martyr, "I do think your witnesses are slender, for you have no witnesses against me but children who with an apple and a rod you may cause to say what you please."

"It is plain," replied the judges, "that you have had priests in your house by those things which were found." "I know no cause," said the martyr, "why I should refuse good Catholic priests, since they come for my good and for the good of others." Judge Rhodes and some others replied that they were traitors and seducers of the queen's subjects. "God forbid," said the martyr. "If you knew them you would not speak so of them." They replied she would detest them herself if she knew their treasons and wickedness as they did. "I know them," quoth she, "for virtuous men sent by God to save our souls," which speech she uttered very boldly, and yet with modesty.

[Another vain attempt was made to induce Margaret to plead. Then a Protestant minister, a puritan very adverse to the Catholic Church, intervened and asked leave to speak.] "My lord,' quoth he, "be well advised what you do. You sit here to do justice. This woman's case is upon life and death, and you ought not by the laws of God and man to judge her to die unless you had two or three witnesses against her, and here is the witness but of one poor boy." "The law doth warrant the doing of it," quoth the judge. The minister demanded what law. The judge replied, "The Queen's law." "That may well be,' quoth the minister, "but I am assured you cannot do it by God's law." And he said no more. . . .

It would seem that these speeches of the minister did somewhat move the conscience of the judge, for presently he bent himself to the martyr and said, "Good woman, I do pray you to put yourself on the country; here is nothing but the evidence of a boy against you, and though the country should

find you guilty, yet we have power to be merciful unto you."
But his speech did nothing move her, whereupon the other
judge demanded of him why he did spin forth the day upon
that naughty woman, and urged him to dispatch. "If then,"
quoth the judge to the martyr, "you will not put yourself on
the country, hear your judgement.

"You shall return unto the place from whence you came, and
there in the lower part of the prison be stripped naked, laid
down on your back to the ground, and so much weight laid
on you as you are able to bear, and this you shall continue
for three days without any other food than a little barley
bread and puddle water; and the third day you shall have a
sharp stone put under your back, and your hands and feet
shall be tied to posts that, more weight being laid upon you,
you may be pressed to death."*

The martyr, not dismayed with the sentence, told the judge
that if this judgement was according to his conscience she
prayed God to send him a better judgement in the latter day,
and so gave humble thanks to God for that which was done to
her. The judge replied that he had proceeded according to
law, and that the judgement must be executed upon her accordingly, unless she would put herself to be tried by the
country. He put her in mind of her husband and children,
wishing her in regard for them not to cast herself away. "I do
honour my husband and love my children," replied the
martyr, "according as duty and nature bindeth me, but I am
so far from seeking to help them by yielding unto your desires
as that I wish both husband and children might suffer death
with me in this good cause."

[Clench made a last effort to get Margaret to plead, and
then handed her over to the sheriff; she was bound and taken
to the house of detention on York bridge. She] smilingly rejoiced that she was bound for Christ's sake, which did not a

* *Peine forte et dure*, the penalty for standing mute and refusing to
plead to a charge of felony. Since 1828 refusal to plead is taken as a
plea of not guilty.

little enrage them against her. The council sent to mark her countenance on her return to prison, which, witnessing an inward joy, divers diversely censured, malice making some to say she was possessed with a merry devil, others of a more indifferent disposition attributed it to the comfort of the Holy Ghost, but all were astonished that beheld her. . . . In her passage from the common hall into the prison she bestowed her alms on both sides of the street, as well as her pinioned arms would give her leave. When her husband had notice of her condemnation he was like a man distracted, crying out that they would murder the best wife within the kingdom, and the best Catholic, wishing they would take all he possessed so that her life might be saved.

[The question was raised whether Margaret were not pregnant. She was uncertain about it, and a jury of matrons was appointed who found, "so far as they could perceive or gather from her," that she was so. Clench accordingly wanted to reprieve her, but a faction of the York council and ministers was bent on her death.] Hurleston (the mouth of this elect congregation) urged mainly for her death, and to strike the nail on the head he took it on his conscience that she was not so. Clench, thinking it was a fair occasion to take the thorn out of his own heel and to put it into another's, referred the whole matter to the council, with caution that they should stay the execution until the five and twentieth of March, and then to do as they thought good, if they heard not from him to the contrary, and so departed the town.

Thus was this innocent lamb delivered up into the butcher's hands. Some of the council and divers ministers at several times repaired unto her, and pressed her to go to their church for the saving of her life, wherein she constantly resisted them. They also demanded of her many questions concerning religious priests resorting unto her house, and of some particularly by name, but she, aiming at their ill intentions, by her discreet answers frustrated their hopes. Wherefore, hopeless to draw her into their desires or to get anything from her to the

prejudice of others, they resorted no more unto her, but, resolved she should die according to the judgement given against
her, and the better to colour her death under the show of justice, they raised of her many false and slanderous reports. . . .

The night before her death she spake unto the man's wife
that had custody of her to have some woman watch with her
that night: "Not that I fear death," quoth she, "for that is comfort; but the flesh is frail." The woman told her that the jailer
had locked the door and was gone to bed, and therefore none
could be had; but the woman herself, being ready to go to bed,
put on her clothes again, and sat by her until towards midnight, the martyr spending her time in prayer. About midnight the woman went to rest, and within some hour after the
martyr rose up from her prayers, put off her apparel, and put
on a linen habit, which she made on purpose for her martyrdom. In this habit, without any other garment, she betook
herself again unto her prayers on her knees, until three of the
clock, at which time she came down unto the fireside and laid
herself flat down upon the stones a quarter of an hour, and so
went to bed, where she lay until six in the morning.

Then preparing for death, she entreated this Yoward's wife,
that had custody of her, to see her die, wishing she might be
accompanied with some Catholics in that time of her agony,
to put her in mind of God. Yoward's wife refused to be present at so cruel a death, but preferred to procure some friends
to lay on store of weight to put her quickly out of pain, the
which the martyr absolutely refused.

About eight of the clock the sheriff came, who found her
ready. Expecting this rich banquet prepared for her, with
the linen habit on her arm, and some inkle [tape] which she
had provided to tie her feet and hands, she went barefoot and
her gown loose about her, but her headgear was decently put
on. And so she went cheerfully to her marriage, as she called
it.

The place of execution was the Tolbooth, some twenty
feet distant from the prison, and she must of necessity come

into the street to go unto this place. The street was full of
people, insomuch as she could hardly pass, yet as she went she
dealt alms. The sheriff hastened her to come away, to whom
she answered merrily, "Good Mr Sheriff, let me deal my poor
alms before I go I have but a short time in this world." There
was admitted into the room where she suffered no more but
the two sheriffs, one gentleman, one minister, four women,
three or four men, four serjeants and those the serjeants had
hired to do the execution.

The martyr coming into the room kneeled down and prayed
unto herself. The officers and standers by bid her pray with
them, and they would pray with her, which she refused, saying she would not so much as say Amen to their prayers, nor
willingly should they do to hers. Then they willed her to
pray for the queen. Whereupon the martyr in hearing of them
all began as followeth: "I do pray for the Catholic Church,
for the Pope's Holiness and cardinals, for all such as have care
of souls, and for all Christian princes in the world." At which
words the officers interrupted her, and commanded her not to
put the Queen's Majesty amongst that company. Yet the martyr proceeded: "And for Elizabeth, queen of England, and
I humbly beseech God to turn her to the Catholic faith, that
after this mortal life she may enjoy the joys of Heaven, unto
whose soul I do wish as much joy as unto mine own."

One of the sheriffs, called Gibson, moved with compassion
towards her, withdrew himself to the door and stood weeping; the other named Fawcett, commanded her to put off her
apparel, saying she must die naked according to the judgement
given against her. She fell on her knees and the rest of the
women with her, requesting him for the honour of woman-
kind that she might not be seen naked, but be suffered to die
in her smock, which he would not grant. Then she requested
that the women might unclothe her, and that they would
turn their face from her during the time of her unclothing,
which was granted. And the women put upon her the long
linen habit which she had brought with her, and so was

quickly laid down upon the ground, a sharp stone being laid under her back; her face was covered with a handkerchief.

When the boards that were joined together in the fashion of a broad door were laid upon her to bear the weight, she raised up her hands towards her face and joined them together, which the sheriff seeing commanded two of the serjeants to part them, and to tie them to two posts set there for that purpose, which was done with the inkle she brought with her; and so her arms extended and her body made a perfect cross.

Then they called upon her again to ask the Queen's Majesty's forgiveness and to pray for her. They willed her to ask her husband's forgiveness: "If ever I have offended him," replied the martyr, "I do ask him for forgiveness from the bottom of my heart." After this they laid the weights upon her, which when she felt she cried out, "Jesu, Jesu, Jesu, have mercy on me!" which were the last words that were heard to come from her. She was dying about one quarter of an hour. They laid on her about seven or eight hundredweight, which did not only break her ribs but caused them to break through the skin.

And this was the end of this virtuous and glorious martyr, the protomartyr of her sex in the kingdom of England since heresy infected it in these latter times. The day of her death was the 25th of March [1586], on which day she was desirous to offer up her soul, which is very remarkable, being a day that she did highly honour in regard of the general opinion that the world was made on that day, and that our Saviour was then incarnate in the womb of the Blessed Virgin Mary.*

* Bd Margaret Clitherow's right hand is preserved at the Bar Convent at York, a community founded near Fountains only a half a century after the martyrdom.

BD EDMUND GENINGS and BD SWITHIN WELLS

A proclamation of Queen Elizabeth I on 18 October 1591 at once brought about a stricter enforcement of the laws against Catholics, and within eight weeks more martyrs had suffered. On November 8 the priest-hunter Topcliffe raided a house in Gray's Inn Lane, the residence of a Hampshire gentleman, Swithin Wells, and his wife. Mass was being celebrated by Edmund Genings, a young priest of Lichfield, not long arrived from the college at Rheims. Some of the congregation managed to keep Topcliffe and his men out till Mass was over, and then Genings was arrested, together with another priest, Bd Polydore Plasden, two laymen, Bd John Mason and Bd Sidney Hodgson, Mrs Wells, and others. Mr Wells was absent, but was arrested soon after when he went to protest to Justice Yonge about what had been done. The following account is taken from Bishop Challoner's Memoirs of Missionary Priests *(1741-42).*

On the 4th of December, Mr Genings and all the rest were brought upon their trial, and a jury was impanelled to find them all guilty; and yet all they could prove against them was no more than that one of them had said Mass in Mr Wells's house and the rest had heard the said Mass. Many bitter words and scoffs were used by the judges and others upon the bench, particularly to Mr Genings, because he was very young and had angered them with disputes. And the more to make him a scoff to the people, they vested him, not now in his priestly garments (in which they had before carried him through the streets), but in a ridiculous fool's coat, which they found in Mr Wells's house. In conclusion, the next day the jury brought in their verdict, by which the priests were found guilty of high treason for returning into the realm contrary to the statute of 27 Elizabeth, and all the rest of felony for aiding and assisting the priests; and it was appointed that they should all die at Tyburn, except Mr Genings and Mr Wells, who were to be executed before Mr Wells's own door in Gray's Inn Fields. The judges, after pronouncing sentence, began to persuade them to conform to the Protestant religion, assuring them that by so doing they should obtain mercy, but otherwise they must certainly expect to die. But they all bravely answered that they would live and die in the true Roman Catholic faith, which they and all antiquity had ever professed, and that they would by no means go to the Protestant churches, or once think that the Queen could be head of the Church in spirituals.

At their return to Newgate, the priests were cast into the dungeon; and whilst they were there, Justice Yonge, Mr Topcliffe and others twice or thrice came to the prison, and calling for Mr Genings, promised him both life and liberty if he would go to their church and renounce his religion, giving him also hopes of a living and promotion in that case. But they found him still constant and resolute, with which they being highly offended, put him into a dark hole within the prison, where he could not so much as see his own hands nor get up or down without hazard of breaking his neck. Here he remained in prayer and contemplation, without any food or sustenance, till the hour of his death.

On the 10th of December, at eight in the morning, Mr Plasden and the rest were carried to Tyburn and there executed. Mrs Wells, to her great grief, was reprieved, and died in prison. Mr Genings and Mr Wells were brought, according to sentence, to Gray's Inn Fields, over against Mr Wells's door, to suffer there; where, after a few speeches of some ministers that were there present, Mr Genings was taken off the sled and, like St Andrew, joyfully saluted the gibbet prepared for him. "Being put upon the ladder, many questions were asked him by some standers by, whereto he still answered directly. At length Mr Topcliffe cried out with a loud voice, 'Genings, Genings, confess thy fault, thy popish treason, and the queen by submission no doubt will grant thee pardon.' To which he mildly answered, 'I know not, Mr Topcliffe, in what I have offended my dear anointed princess; for if I had offended her, or any other, in any thing, I would willingly ask her and all the world forgiveness. If she be offended with me without a cause, for professing my faith and religion, because I am a priest, or because I will not turn minister against my conscience, I shall be, I trust, excused and innocent before God. I must obey God, saith St Peter, rather than men, and I must not in this case acknowledge a fault where there is none. If to return into England priest, or to say Mass, be popish treason, I here confess I am a traitor; but I think not so, and therefore I acknowledge myself guilty of these things, not with repentance and sorrow of heart, but with an open protestation of inward joy that I have done so good deeds; which, if they were to do again, I would, by the permission and assistance of God, accomplish the same, although with the hazard of a thousand lives.' "*

Mr Topcliffe, being very angry at this speech, scarce giving him liberty to say a *Pater noster*, bid the hangman turn the ladder, which being done, he presently caused the rope to be cut. The holy priest, being little or nothing stunned, stood on his feet, casting his eyes towards Heaven till the hangman tripped up his heels to make him fall on the block on which he was to be quartered. After he was dismembered, the violence of the pain caused him to utter these words with a loud voice, "Oh, it smarts!" Which Mr Wells hearing, replied, "Alas! sweet soul, thy pain is great indeed, but almost past; pray for me now, most holy saint, that mine may come." After he was ripped up and his bowels cast into the fire, "if credit may be given," says his brother, "to hundreds of people standing by, and to the hangman himself, the blessed martyr (his heart being in the executioner's hand) uttered these words, 'Sancte Gregori, ora pro me!' Which the hangman hearing,

* This quotation is from a life of Bd Edmund written by his brother John, and published at Saint Omers in 1614.

swore a most wicked oath: 'Z . . . ds! See, his heart is in my hand, and yet Gregory is in his mouth. O egregious papist!' " . . .

Mr Wells received the sentence of death with undaunted courage, and religiously prepared himself for it. The morning he was to die, his wife (who had also received the like sentence for the guilt of harbouring priests) was brought out of prison with him and Mr Genings, in order, as it was supposed, for execution; but she was remanded back to prison by the sheriff, there to wait the queen's pleasure. That which would have afforded great joy to another was grievously afflicting to this good lady, who lamented to see herself left behind and not suffered to bear her husband and her ghostly father company in so glorious a death. She lived ten years a close prisoner in Newgate, exercising herself there in fasting, watching and continual prayer, and died most holily in 1602.

Mr Wells was carried to be executed with Mr Genings in Gray's Inn Fields, over against his own door. In the way, seeing by chance an old friend of his, he could not forget his wonted mirth, but saluted him in these words: "Farewell, dear friend! Farewell all hawking, hunting and old pastimes. I am now going a better way." At the place of execution he was first witness of the bloody butchery of Mr Genings; but so far from being terrified by it, or desiring any respite or delay of execution, he rather expressed a desire to have his death hastened. "Despatch," said he, "Mr Topcliffe, despatch. Are you not ashamed to suffer an old man to stand here so long in his shirt in the cold? I pray God make you of a Saul a Paul, of a persecutor a Catholic professor." And in these and other like sweet speeches, says my author, full of Christian piety, charity and magnanimity, he happily consummated his course the 10th of December 1591.*

[Father Thomas Stanney, s.j., who had been Wells's confessor,] adds that when he was under the gallows, Topcliffe

* Bd Swithin Wells was esteemed guilty of felony but not of treason, and so was hanged without the accompanying barbarities.

said to him, "You see now, Mr Wells, what your priests have brought you to.' To whom he replied, "Mr Topcliffe, I am very glad, and give great thanks to God and look upon myself exceedingly happy, that I have been so far favoured as to have received so many and such saint-like priests under my roof."

BD ALEXANDER RAWLINS and BD HENRY WALPOLE

AT YORK, A.D. 1595

On 7 April 1595 two priests, Bd Alexander Rawlins and Bd Henry Walpole, were hanged drawn and quartered for their priesthood at York. Rawlins was born somewhere on the Worcester-Gloucestershire border, and was ordained priest from the English College at Rheims in 1590. He ministered in England for five years before he was apprehended, in Yorkshire. When Bd Edmund Campion was butchered at Tyburn in 1581, his blood splashed a young man present, who was thus sealed to follow his example. This was Henry Walpole, who was born in 1558 at Docking in Norfolk; after studying for the law at Gray's Inn he went, at the age of twenty-four, to Rheims and then Rome, where he entered the Society of Jesus. After ordination and various employments on the continent, he landed in England at Flamborough Head on 4 December 1593, and within twenty-four hours was arrested. He was kept for a year in the Tower of London, where he was subjected to torture no less than fourteen times. These two priests were not associated in life, but they died together.

When Mr Rawlins was arraigned at York he pleaded not guilty, but objected to being tried "by God and my country," *i.e.*, by a jury, on the ground that the jurymen were uneducated and therefore incapable of judging the matters at issue: he was unwilling, he said, that his blood should lie at their door—the judges should take it upon their own conscience. The three judges adjourned for some hours to consider this; but the trial went forward, and Rawlins was sentenced to the penalty for treason, as a priest ordained abroad and come into the realm.

Henry Walpole wrote to a fellow priest from prison: "I know not as yet what will become of me; but whatever shall happen, by the grace of God it shall be welcome." He spent some of the time of his incarceration writing verse; already before he went abroad his poem, then anonymous, on Father Edmund Campion's martyrdom had stirred the wrath of the authorities. At his trial he made a good defence, but resolutely refused to "make submission to the queen in matters of religion"; he told the jury that he was a priest and a Jesuit, come to convert his countrymen and to invite sinners to repentance: "If you find anything else in me, that is not agreeable to my profession, show me no favour. Act according to your consciences, and remember you must give an account to God." They showed him no favour.

A few days later, Alexander Rawlins was brought out of prison and he laid himself down on the hurdle, on the left side, for, he said, "I leave the more honourable place for my betters." But he had to wait there two full hours before Walpole was brought out. They were then ranged side by side on the hurdle, but with the head of one against the feet of the other, Walpole's head towards the horse's tail; this was so far as possible to prevent their talking with one another. At the place of execution, Rawlins was ordered up the ladder first; he kissed it and the gallows and the rope, but he was not allowed to speak to the people. He was quickly turned off, "having the sweet name of Jesus in his mouth, and so happily finished his course."

Father Walpole had to look on while his companion was being drawn and quartered, in the hope that the sight would break down his nerve. But upon being again offered his life if he would conform and acknowledge the queen's ecclesiastical supremacy, he would not. They told him that this was treason, but that they hoped he would die in peace and join with them in prayer. To which he answered that by God's grace he was at peace with all the world and prayed to God for all, particularly for those that were the cause of his death; as they were not of his religion, he ought not to join in prayer with them, but he prayed heartily for them, that God would enlighten them, bring them back to his Church, and dispose them for his mercy.

"Then, begging the prayers of all Catholics, he lifted up his hands and eyes to Heaven and recited aloud the Lord's Prayer; and after it began the Angelical Salutation, which the persecutors had not the patience to hear, and therefore turned him off the ladder and quickly cut the rope, and so dismembered, boweled and quartered him: a spectacle which drew tears from the eyes of a great part of the beholders, and served not a little to advance the glory of God and the propagation of His Church in those northern parts of the kingdom."

ED JOHN OGILVIE

AT GLASGOW, A.D. 1615

John Ogilvie, the Scottish martyr beatified by Pope Pius XI in 1929, was the eldest son of Walter Ogilvie, baron of Drum-na-Keith in Banffshire, and was brought up a Protestant. But at the age of seventeen, in 1556, he was received into the Catholic Church at

Louvain, and eventually was admitted to the Society of Jesus, at the place now called Brno in Czechoslovakia. He was ordained priest in 1610, and three years later was allowed to go back to Scotland, where the state of Catholics was at a very low ebb. He was at liberty for only nine months, being betrayed to Archbishop John Spottiswoode, King James VI's agent in Glasgow.

During five months Father Ogilvie was subjected to at least the same number of examinations, in Glasgow and Edinburgh, and he defended himself with pertinacity and skill. He was high-spirited, too, in spite of ill-health and suffering, and returned Spottiswoode and the rest as good as they gave. After one passage, Bishop Knox of the Isles said, "You have a sharp wit, Mr Ogilvie. I wish I had many of your sort with me; I would make good use of them."

OGILVIE: "I would rather follow the hangman to the gallows, for you are going straight to the devil."

KNOX: "How dare you talk to me like that?"

OGILVIE: "I beg your pardon, my lord. I have not learned to speak like a courtier: we Jesuits say what we think. I will not flatter. I respect your secular rank and I honour your grey hairs, knowing your age. But I give nothing for your episcopal dignity. You are a layman, and you have no more spiritual jurisdiction than your stick. If you do not want me to say what I think about you, say the word, and I will be silent. But if you want me to speak, I must say what I think and not what you want to hear."

KNOX: "I am sorry that bread and butter made you turn papist."

OGILVIE: "You judge me by your own standard, for you abjured two articles of your faith for two bishoprics.* I am my father's firstborn, and a gentleman by birth. . . ."

When a serving-man threatened to throw him on the fire, Father Ogilvie retorted that, "I am so cold that nothing would please me better. But think what a mess it would make, and it would be your job to clear it up." A laird raged at him,

---

* Andrew Knox was bishop of Raphoe in Ireland as well as of the Isles.

"Were I king you should be boiled in oil!" And Ogilvie passed it off with, "No doubt if God wanted to make a king of you, he would have given you better brains."

After the first examination he was threatened with "the boot" to extort information about his alleged infringements of the law and his associates therein; this does not seem to have been inflicted. But after the second, he was subjected to an abominable trial: for eight days and nine nights he was kept from all sleep by various cruel devices, so that after the next examination he wrote, "I scarcely knew what I said or did, or where I was, or indeed what city I was in." But throughout all the prolonged interrogatories he clung to his impressive plea, made at the second: "Let the king do as his mother and all the preceding kings of Scotland did: then he will have no more reason to fear Jesuits than the king of Spain has. What do we owe him more than our ancestors owed his ancestors? Why does he seek for more than the inheritance of rights they left him? They never had spiritual jurisdiction, nor did they claim it. They never had any faith other than the faith that is Catholic and Roman."

When Father Ogilvie was finally brought to trial in the townhouse at Glasgow, the indictment was based on his answers to five questions put to him on behalf of King James, which all bore on the relations between Church and king. It came to this: he was charged with curtailing the king's jurisdiction by asserting that of the bishop of Rome, and with failing to assert the royal prerogatives implied in the doctrine of the divine right of secular rulers. Ogilvie summed up his answer in three sentences: "In every duty that I owe the king's Majesty I will be most obedient. If any attack his temporal rights, I will shed my last drop of blood for him. But if the king unjustly claims things of spiritual jurisdiction, then in that case I cannot and must not obey." After much argument and bickering and speech-making, the prisoner was found guilty of treason and sentenced to death. Everyone knew it was a foregone conclusion—indeed, the gallows had

already been set up. A week before, Ogilvie had written in a
letter to the Jesuit provincial in Bohemia, Father Ferdinand
Alberi: "I commend myself to your Reverence's prayers.
This is written from prison in Glasgow, where I am loaded
with 200 lbs. of iron fetters and look forward to death unless
I accept the king's gifts with thanks, namely, a fat benefice
and abjuration of the faith. I was tortured once by enforced
sleeplessness for nine nights and eight days; now I await the
second torture and—afterwards death."

John Ogilvie was executed in Glasgow on 10 March 1615
(new style). Before he set out from the jail he forgave the
executioner, and embraced him in token of it. He had been
told not to address the crowd, so that when the minister
Robert Scot told the people that the execution was for treason
and not for religion, he protested against such unfairness: "I
have simply maintained the pope's spiritual jurisdiction in
these realms and over all Christians in the world," he declared,
"and his power to excommunicate heretical kings. . . . I am
ready to shed my last drop of blood against the king's enemies.
I die for the Catholic religion, and for that I am ready to
endure a thousand deaths." At one point Scot exclaimed, "I
have said and I repeat that you may live with honour." "Are
you willing to say that so as all these people can hear it?"
asked Ogilvie quickly. "By all means," answered Scot, and
spoke to the crowd: "I promise Mr Ogilvie his life, the
archbishop's daughter in marriage, and a very rich living,
provided he will come over to our side."

"Then there is no fear that I shall be held as guilty of
treason hereafter?"

"None at all."

"So I stand here as a criminal for the cause of religion
alone?"

"For that alone," shouted the people.

"Very well; that is all I wanted to hear. I am condemned
for religion alone, and for that I would happily give life

many times over. Take the one that I have, and do not delay—
for you shall never take my religion from me."

A friend of Ogilvie, one Abercromby, then engaged him
in conversation, till he was impatiently pitched off the scaffold
by the officers, who came to bind the prisoner's hands. Father
Ogilvie tossed his rosary towards the Catholics in the crowd,
where it struck a young Hungarian visitor, a Calvinist: from
that moment he had no peace of mind till he was reconciled
with the Church.* Then Ogilvie kissed the gallows and went
up the ladder, saying, "Maria, mater gratiae, ora pro me. Omnes
angeli, orate pro me. Omnes sancti sanctaeque, orate pro me,"
and then repeated the words in Scots. The hangman spoke
to him: "Say, John, 'Lord have mercy on me; Lord receive
my soul.'" Meekly the priest obeyed. The ladder was taken
away, and John Ogilvie was left hanging; the executioner
pulled at his feet to hasten his end.

Across the sea at Louvain, word of these things came to
the ears of the biblical exegete Cornelius a Lapide, and he
wrote in his commentary on Isaiah (50:7): "Such [martyrs]
were the soldiers whom the heavenly Captain used to lead
into battle. . . . Such, too, was Ogilvie; who at one time was
my catechumen at Louvain and lately of our Society. From
the account of his martyrdom it is clear that he astonished the
Calvinists: though he overcame torture and remained bold and
ready in debate, yet he did not open his mouth against his
tormentors."

* It is not commonly realized what inroads the Protestant Reforma-
tion made in Hungary. At the census of 1941, over a quarter of the
people were Protestants.

FOUR JAPANESE

AT YENDO, A.D. 1617

St Francis Xavier brought Christianity to Japan in 1549. Before the century was out, Japan had its first martyrs, and twenty-six of them were canonized in 1862. Of these, eighteen were Japanese, with six European missionaries, a Mexican Spaniard and another, said to have been Indo-Portuguese but perhaps really Indian. These were soon followed by other victims, of whom some particulars are given below of four Japanese laymen who have not so far been included among those beatified. The names given them at baptism were Thomas, Lewis, Vincent and Lawrence. We know of them from a report written by a Spanish Franciscan, Father James-of-St-Francis, who for a time shared their captivity.

Early in 1616 Father James, with two Japanese, Lewis and Thomas, was brought before the governor of Yendo, and asked why he had continued to preach Christianity after all ministers of that religion had been ordered to leave the country. The friar answered that he had come from Spain, a matter of five thousand leagues, with the sole purpose of preaching Christ, who so loved the Japanese that he wanted them all to learn the way to everlasting happiness. The governor asked, "And where do you propose to go when you leave here?" Father James named a neighbouring territory. The governor turned to Thomas and Lewis: "What places has this priest passed through?"

THOMAS: "He has come from Nagasaki, and has been to Firando, Myako and Mino."

GOVERNOR: "Where did he lodge?"

THOMAS: "In the houses of our people."

GOVERNOR: "Did none of them recognize him?"

THOMAS: "No, sir. As you see, he dresses like a Japanese and speaks our language very well."

GOVERNOR: "Are there many Christians here?"

THOMAS: "Yes, sir."

GOVERNOR: "Who are they?"

THOMAS: "We do not know. They are being pursued and are in hiding."

GOVERNOR: "Well, you will be quite safe if you give up Christianity."

THOMAS: "That is impossible, sir. It is our duty to suffer anything rather than do that. And we cannot cut ourselves off from our beloved priest here."

GOVERNOR: "Why do you love him so much?"

THOMAS: "Because at all costs he wants to teach us the way to everlasting life."

They were remanded to the supreme council, which sentenced them to be confined in a crowded jail, where they were so insufficiently fed (it was part of their sentence) that a Japanese called Vincent smuggled food in to enable them even to live. He was caught and accused before the governor, who asked, "Why did you do this? To get a little money, I suppose."

VINCENT: "You are mistaken, sir. The priests of St Francis have not got any money, they live in poverty. I am only a carpenter but, like other Christians, I put aside a little from my earnings for him."

GOVERNOR: "Why do you do that?"

VINCENT: "Because I am a Christian."

One of the guards said to him, "Keep your mouth shut if you value your life."

VINCENT: "What does it matter? I am a Christian, and I say so. And because I am a Christian, I love this priest and try to help him."

GOVERNOR: "Which other Christians do this?"

VINCENT: "All of them."

So Vincent joined the others in the prison, where he was very happy to be able to suffer with them. He was so abominably treated that he lost his sight—but he was still happy and cheerful. The conditions in the prison got more and more atrocious, and Father James was prevented by main force from carrying on his mission there. But at the end of six months he was released, at the instance of a representative of the king of Spain, and he was enabled to make his way to Mexico. In due course he was back in Japan, where his first thoughts were for his prison companions.

He found his four friends were all dead. Soon after he left, Thomas and Lewis, who had accompanied him on his journeys and shared his missionary work as catechists, had been executed, to be followed soon after by Vincent, the carpenter. The fourth was a disciple of the missionary and martyr Bd Luis Sotelo. His name was Lawrence, and his father, a man of high position, tried to get out of an embarrassing situation on his son's conversion by marrying him off to a girl of a heathen family. But Lawrence proceeded to convert his wife. Not only that, eventually they sold their property, gave the proceeds in charity, and Lawrence went to work in a leper-hospital. With other workers there, he was thrown into jail for his religion and lingered in squalid confinement for many months. He rejected all his father's efforts to get him to apostatize, and then was found to have leprosy himself. After grievous suffering, Lawrence died of this disease, still in prison, on 10 December 1617.

THE GREAT MARTYRDOM

IN JAPAN, A.D. 1622

The year 162. is distinguished in Japanese Christian history as the year of "the great martyrdom," and many of its victims were among those beatified by Pope Pius IX in 1869. In that year of blood and terror, no event is more striking to the imagination than the mass execution that took place on a hill outside Nagasaki on September 10: it is, indeed, one of the most startling, terrible and awe-inspiring events recorded in the long annals of martyrdom.

It is said that 60,000 people were assembled on that hill above the sea at Nagasaki, where, twenty-five years before, the first canonized martyrs of Japan had suffered. On this occasion, the new martyrs arrived in two separate parties. First, those who had been confined in the horrible prison at Omura (where, two days later, Bd Apollinaris Franco and seven others were to be burned to death). Leaders among them were two Jesuits, the Japanese Father Sebastian Kimura, a kinsman of one of St Francis Xavier's converts, and the astronomer Father Charles Spinola, an Italian.* There was a delay of an hour, during which confessions were made and preachers addressed the spectators. Then the party from Nagasaki itself arrived under its escort. The two groups met, and gravely saluted one another. There were men, women and children, Japanese and European.

Two ways of execution were assigned: slow fire for those esteemed the more heinous offenders, the sword for the rest. A huge pyre was ready, with stakes disposed around it at a sufficient distance for the victims not to be consumed at once; they were bound only lightly to the stakes, so that any who gave in could signify it by breaking away. Facing the stakes

* For Bd Charles Spinola's unintended visit to England in 1597, see Dr George Oliver's *Collections* (London, 1857), p.3.

outward knelt those to be beheaded, a headsman with a sword standing by each one. There was dead silence. Then the drums rolled, thirty swords flashed, and thirty heads fell to the ground. They were picked up at once and methodically arranged on a table. Then the fire was lit. No one of its victims lived on for less than an hour; many lingered in unspeakable agony till the evening, one at least, Father Hyacinth Orfanel, till after midnight. Two young Japanese men broke from their stakes and begged to be beheaded: they were picked up, thrown into the fire, and held there with poles.

Those who perished by fire numbered twenty-five: one Japanese and eight European priests (Franciscans, Dominicans, Jesuits), one Spanish and two Japanese laybrothers, one Korean and twelve Japanese lay people. One of them was a woman, Lucy de Freitas, the Japanese widow of a Portuguese, condemned for looking after Father Richard-of-St-Ann when he was ill. All the thirty beheaded were lay people and all Japanese, except a Spanish widow, Isabel Fernandez, whose four-year-old son, Iñigo, was executed with her. She was sentenced for sheltering Father Spinola. Of the rest, eleven were men, eleven women and six children, aged from three to twelve. Five couples were husband and wife.

Impressive as this relation is, it does not stand alone, for only three weeks before a somewhat similar thing on a smaller scale had taken place at the same spot. The leading victims were two Spanish priests, an Augustinian friar, Peter Zuñiga, and a Dominican, Luis Flores. They were on shipboard from Manila, when they were captured by a Dutch privateer off Japan and, with the master and crew of the ship, handed over to the Japanese authorities, who had decreed death for anybody concerned in bringing Christian priests to the country. They were all taken in chains to Nagasaki, where an apostate Japanese priest was used to try and make them renounce Christ; two appear to have wavered but eventually stood firm. Twelve of these martyrs were beheaded first, seven of them sailors and five other Japanese who had tried to rescue Father Flores. Then the two friars were burnt, together with Joachim Firaiama, the master of the ship, who was a Japanese. They kissed one another and walked cheerfully to the stakes, Joachim treading down the soil round his to make it stand firmer. As he was bound, he made his profession of faith in a loud voice, amid a deep silence from the crowd of onlookers.

Numerous are the other *beati* and *beatae* of this year in Japan. As representative of their spirit, here is the last of several letters that have survived from Father Paul Navarro, a Jesuit who suffered a few weeks after the events just narrated. It was written to another priest on the very day of his martyrdom.

My very dear Father, may all happiness be yours! Since this solemn day [he feast of All Saints] is to be the last of my life, I give boundless thanks to the eternal Goodness. I die full of happiness and confidence, trusting in the merits of Jesus Christ, my Master who died for me; I am longing with my whole soul to be with him. I ask your Reverence to forgive my faults and delinquencies; please do not fail to help me by your sacrifices and prayers, to which I commend myself. Written from Shimabara, on the 1st of November 1622.

PETER PAUL NAVARRO
who in a few hours
will be burned alive
for the sake of Jesus Christ.

Similar testimony comes from a very different source. The skipper of an English ship, Richard Cocks, witnessed a mass-execution at Miyako (Kyoto), and wrote: "Among them little children five or six years old burned in their mothers' arms, crying out, 'Jesus, receive our souls!' Many more are in prison who look hourly when they shall die, for very few turn pagan."[*]

[*] *Calendar of State Papers, Colonial East Indies, 1617-1621*, p. 537.

ST JOSAPHAT OF POLOTSK

AT VITEBSK IN BYELORUSSIA, A.D. 1623

In 1595, at Brest-Litovsk in Byelorussia, the Orthodox metropolitan of Kiev with five of his bishops (whose territories were then part of Poland-Lithuania), on behalf of themselves, their clergy and their flocks, returned to Catholic communion. Their action was far from meeting with unanimous approval: political, social and cultural factors were mixed with religious considerations, and the resulting struggle, lasting off and on for over a century, was at times carried on with detestable bitterness and violence on both sides. In the earlier period, there were Orthodox as well as Catholics who died for conscience' sake: for instance, on the one hand, Abbot Athanasius of Brest in 1648; on the other, St Andrew Bobola, of the Society of Jesus, who was ferociously tortured and murdered by Cossacks near Pinsk in 1657. But before these there was Josaphat of Polotsk.

Josaphat Kunsevich was a monk of the Holy Trinity monastery at Vilna, who was engaged with the famous J.B. Rutsky in promoting Slav-Byzantine monasticism. In 1617, at the age of about forty, he became archbishop of Polotsk. For some years he had considerable success in building up a sound and healthy life in his diocese, but an Orthodox reaction against communion with Rome set in (the leader of the opposition, Archbishop Melety Smotritsky, was himself eventually reconciled with the Holy See). A strong centre of this disaffection was the town of Vitebsk, and here Josaphat was done to death. It would certainly seem that, after being so careful to avoid provoking violence, his detention of the priest Elias, even though brief, was an error of judgement. But it was no more, and in 1867 Pope Pius IX canonized Josaphat Kunsevich as a martyr in the cause of Christian unity; in 1882, Leo XIII added the feast of this saint of the Eastern church to the general calendar of the Western Church, for November 14.

In October 1623 Josaphat determined to go to the disturbed town of Vitebsk to see what he could do there in person. The danger of this was obvious to all, but he could not be turned from his purpose and he would not take with him more than a few necessary persons, such as his archdeacon and a

small body of singers for the Liturgy. "I do not want to en-
danger anybody unnecessarily, though if anybody is to die it
will only be me. What is this great danger you want to put
me in fear of? Death? Why, I have just made arrangements
for my tomb to be made."

For a fortnight Josaphat was busy in Vitebsk, preaching,
hearing confessions visiting churches and calling on wavering
families. But there had arrived there at the same time the
leader of dissidents in Polotsk, Peter Vassilievich, and he was
busy too, stirring up the people against the archbishop, who
was mobbed and threatened in the streets. The situation grew
ugly, and on the feast of St Demetrius the Great Martyr,
Josaphat preached on John 16:2, "The hour cometh that
whosoever killeth you will think that he doth a service to
God," which occurs in the gospel of the day in the Byzantine
rite. "You people of Vitebsk," he said, "want to kill me. You
lie in wait for me, in the streets, on the bridges, everywhere.
Well, here I am, and I have come here of my own free will.
I am your shepherd, and I should be happy to give my life for
you. If it please God that I should die for unity under the
earthly headship of St Peter's successor, so be it. I am ready
to die for truth."

Josaphat's opponents were doing all they could to provoke
his attendants and his supporters in the town to violence, and
so to get a pretext for proceeding against the archbishop. He
saw this clearly enough, and imposed a strict forbearance on
his friends, so successfully that in desperation a plot was laid
to kill him directly. Throughout the day of November 11
(Julian calendar) a crowd surged round the archbishop's
house, led by a priest named Elias, who shouted insults at
all who went in or came out. Josaphat was visiting outside
Vitebsk, and when he returned in the evening a magistrate of
the town, Peter Lanovich, told him about the plot and urged
him to go away at once. The most the archbishop would do
was to write to the lord of Vitebsk, informing him of the plot
and naming the ringleaders; but he did authorize the seizure

and detention of Elias, should that priest repeat his behaviour. He then sat down to supper with his archdeacon, Dorotheus, his steward, Emmanuel Cantacuzen, Gregory Uszacky and other faithful friends. During the meal the archdeacon remonstrated with him for talking so much about death. "Do you not think, then," was the reply, "that death for Christ and his Church is a good subject of conversation, even at table?"

Josaphat did not go to bed that night. He spent it in prayer and in conversation with an old beggar, whom he had picked up off the street. Early the next morning he went to Utrenya (Lauds) in the neighbouring church, and during the office the priest Elias again began his disorderly behaviour outside the bishop's house. So the servants took him and locked him in the kitchen, as leave had been given them. At once the news spread, the bell of the town-hall rang the alarm, and a mob assembled, shouting against the archbishop. On Josaphat's return from church, he reprimanded and warned Elias, and then let him go free. But by eight o'clock the mob had been incited to greater fury than ever, and stones flying at the windows of the house were a signal for breaking into the courtyard. Here the crowd was confronted by the archdeacon, the steward and the aged Uszacky: they were knocked down and trampled on.

Josaphat appeared at the door of his room. "God be with you, my children," he exclaimed. "Why are you ill-treating my servants? What harm have they done you? If you have anything against me, here I am: but let them alone!"* There was a momentary hesitation, the crowd wavered. Then two men ran forward, shouting "Kill the papist!" One struck Josaphat with a stick, the other with an axe; the mob fell on him with yells and blows, and then, leaving him for dead, again attacked the others. But Josaphat was not dead; he raised one hand in appeal to Heaven, and uttered two words: "My God!" So he was dragged out of the courtyard and shot

---

* Compare the words of St Thomas of Canterbury in the like circumstances.

F

through the head. A dog that tried to defend him was cut to pieces, and thrown with his master's mangled body into the river Dvina.

With the rioters pillaging the archbishop's house and the Catholics cowering in fear and trembling, only the Jews of Vitebsk dared openly to mourn for Josaphat and rebuke his murderers; and at the risk of their own lives they rescued Archdeacon Dorotheus, Cantacuzen and Uszacky, still alive, from the hands of the mob. St Josaphat's body was recovered and was for long enshrined at Polotsk; later on it was at Biala Podlaska in Poland, and in 1916 it was translated for safety to the Ukrainian church of St Barbara in Vienna.

BD ALBAN ROE

IN LONDON, A.D. 1642

Bartholomew Roe was born in Suffolk in 1583 and was brought up in Protestantism; he was reconciled with the Catholic Church and eventually, in 1612, was professed a monk of St Benedict at the English monastery at Dieulouard in Lorraine,* under the name of Alban. Roe was a man of a very lively disposition: he had been dismissed from the English College at Douay, and in England he upset some of the bien pensants *of the time; but this did not hinder—probably it helped—his being a successful missionary during the time he was at liberty. After his final arrest, about 1627, he spent fourteen years in prison in London, with, however, a certain freedom to go out on parole. During this time he translated some ascetical writings into English; he suffered much from ill-health, especially the stone, for which he was operated on more than once, but his liveliness remained unimpaired.*

* Successor of the abbey of St Peter at Westminster, predecessor of St Lawrence's at Ampleforth.

Alban Roe was brought to trial for his priesthood at the Old Bailey on 19 January 1642. Like Bd Alexander Rawlins and Bd Mark Barkworth before him, he at first protested that responsibility for his blood should not be laid upon an ignorant jury. When the judge pointed out the penalty for refusing to plead (cf. Bd Margaret Clitherow, above), he answered, "My Saviour suffered more for me than that, and I am willing to suffer the worst of torments for his sake." However, after consulting other priests, he pleaded not guilty, was speedily condemned, and was sentenced to death in the usual form.

On the day of his execution, two days later, Alban Roe found means to celebrate Mass in Newgate jail, and was then drawn to Tyburn on a hurdle, together with a very infirm old priest, Bd Thomas Reynolds. "With his usual facetiousness," as Challoner puts it, he felt Reynolds' pulse, and asked him how he felt. "In very good heart," was the reply, "blessed be God for it; and glad I am to have a person of your undaunted courage for my companion in death." At the scaffold they gave one another absolution and, while Reynolds addressed the people, Roe ministered to one of the three felons who were to die with them (whom he had reconciled in prison the day before). Then he came forward and looked at the crowd. "Here's a jolly company!" he exclaimed, "I know you have come to see me die. My companion here has in great measure said what I would have said. However, I repeat the words I used at the bar. I say then, here again, that for a man to be put to death for being a priest, the most sacred and highest order in the world, is an unjust and tyrannical law. I say that the law of the 27th of Queen Elizabeth, which condemns a man to death only for being a priest, is a wicked, unjust and tyrannical law—a law not to be found even amongst the Turks or anywhere else in the whole universe, England excepted."

The sheriff interrupted him, saying he could not allow such criticism of the law. "Very well, sir," said Roe. "May I ask you a question? . . . If I will conform to your religion and go to church, will you secure me my life?" "Upon my word, I will," replied the sheriff. "My life for yours if you will but do that." Roe turned again to the people: "You see, then," he said "what the crime is for which I am to die, that my religion is my only treason." Then he asked for prayers, expressed his forgiveness of all who had harmed him and in turn asked theirs.

While the executioner was adjusting the ropes, Reynolds called out to him, "Pray, friend, let all be secure, and do your duty neatly—I have been a neat man all my life"; while Roe, catching sight of one of his former jailors, said to him with a smile, "Friend, I find you are a prophet. You have often told me that I should be hanged, yet my unworthiness was such that I could not believe it—but I see you are a prophet." The two priests said the psalm *Miserere* together in alternate verses aloud, and while they were saying it a second time, the executioner came to bind their eyes: "I have already disposed of my handkerchief," said Roe, "but I dare to look death in the face." They commended themselves to God, saluted the people cheerfully, and the cart was drawn away. While they were hanging, Father Roe was seen twice to separate and close his hands, as one praying at the altar.

They were allowed to hang till they were dead, before the remainder of their sentence was carried out.

THE NORTH AMERICAN
MARTYRS

AT OSSERNENON AND ELSEWHERE, A.D. 1642–1649

The first Christian recorded to have been slain out of hatred of the faith in North America was a Franciscan friar, John de Padilla, in 1544, but just whereabouts is not known. In 1549 a great missionary, Luis Cancer of Barbastro, and two other Dominicans, were murdered by Indians near Tampa, on the coast of Florida. Of these, and others, a process of beatification has never been undertaken, and the first martyrs of North America to be beatified were the six priests of the Society of Jesus who, with two lay helpers, were finally canonized by Pope Pius XI in 1930.* They were John de Brébeuf, Noel Chabanel, Antony Daniel, Charles Garnier, Isaac Jogues, Gabriel Lalemant, René Goupil and John Lalande, all Frenchmen. Brébeuf was the first in the field, in 1615, working among the Huron Indians, and being later joined by Daniel, Garnier, Chabanel and Lalemant; Jogues was the apostle of the Mohawks, and the first European and missionary to penetrate to the eastern entrance of Lake Superior, a thousand miles inland. The two lay helpers (donnés), Goupil and Lalande, worked on the mission with Father Jogues. On 2 August 1642 he, Goupil and another donné, named Couture, were captured by Iroquois and carried off to one after another of three villages, in each of which they were abominably tortured.† They were then kept at Ossernenon (now Auriesville in upper New York State) for some weeks, uncertain of what would happen to them. The following accounts are from The Jesuits in North America, by Francis Parkman, who made full use of the pertinent Jesuit "Relations" and other contemporary documents.

Jogues, however, lost no opportunity to baptize dying infants, while Goupil taught children to make the sign of the

---

* In South America, three Jesuits, Roque Gonzalez, Alonso Rodriguez and John de Castillo, martyred in Paraguay in 1628, were beatified in 1934.

† Jogues' hands were so mangled that it was unfitting for him subsequently to celebrate Mass, until Pope Urban VIII gave a special permission, saying, "It would be unjust that a martyr for Christ should not drink the blood of Christ."

cross. On one occasion, he made the sign on the forehead of a child, grandson of an Indian in whose lodge they lived. The superstition of the old savage was aroused. Some Dutchmen had told him that the sign of the cross came from the Devil, and would cause mischief. He thought that Goupil was bewitching the child; and, resolving to rid himself of so dangerous a guest, applied for aid to two young braves. Jogues and Goupil, clad in their squalid garb of tattered skins, were soon after [September 29] walking together in the forest that adjoined the town, consoling themselves with prayer, and mutually exhorting each other to suffer patiently for the sake of Christ and the Virgin, when, as they were returning, reciting their rosaries, they met the two young Indians, and read in their sullen visages an augury of ill.

The Indians joined them, and accompanied them to the entrance to the town, where one of them, suddenly drawing a hatchet from beneath his blanket, struck it into the head of Goupil, who fell, murmuring the name of Christ. Jogues dropped on his knees, and, bowing his head in prayer, awaited the blow, when the murderer ordered him to get up and go home. He obeyed, but not until he had given absolution to his still breathing friend, and presently saw the lifeless body dragged through the town amid hootings and rejoicings.

[After a year of servitude and suffering, Isaac Jogues was able to escape, with the help of the Dutch at Fort Orange. Three years later, in 1646, he was back in Ossernenon, as a missionary, with John Lalande; but he had become suspect of being a sorcerer, responsible for the misfortunes of the place, and the Bear clan determined to get rid of him.]

The warriors of one of these bands were making their way through the forests between the Mohawk and Lake George when they met Jogues and Lalande. They seized them, stripped them, and led them in triumph to their town. Here a savage crowd surrounded them, beating them with sticks and with their fists. One of them cut thin strips of flesh from the back and arms of Jogues, saying as he did so, "Let us see if this white flesh is the flesh of an oki."—"I am a man like yourselves," replied Jogues, "but I do not fear death or torture. I do not know why you want to kill me. I come here to confirm the peace and show you the way to Heaven, and you treat me like a dog."—"You shall die tomorrow," cried the rabble. "Take courage, we shall not burn you. We shall strike you both with a hatchet, and place your heads on the palisade, that your brothers may see you when we take them prisoners." The clans of the Wolf and the Tortoise still raised their voices in behalf of the captive Frenchmen; but the fury of the minority swept all before it.

In the evening—it was the 18th of October—Jogues, smarting with his wounds and bruises, was sitting in one of the lodges, when an Indian entered and asked him to a feast. To refuse would have been an offence. He arose and followed the savage, who led him to the lodge of the Bear chief. Jogues bent his head to enter, when another Indian, standing concealed within at the side of the doorway, struck at him with a hatchet. An Iroquois, called by the French Le Berger, who seems to have followed in order to defend him, bravely held out his arm to ward off the blow; but the hatchet cut through it, and sank into the missionary's brain. He fell at the feet of his murderer, who at once finished the work by hacking off his head. Lalande was left in suspense all night, and in the morning was killed in a similar manner. The bodies of the two Frenchmen were then thrown into the Mohawk, and their heads displayed on the points of the palisade which enclosed the town.

[A little over eighteen months later, on 4 July 1648, Father Antony Daniel was killed at the Huron village of Teanaustaye (near Hillsdale in Ontario). He had just celebrated Mass.]

. . . the forest around basked lazily in the early sun. . . . Here some squalid wolfish dog lay sleeping in the sun, a group of Huron girls chatted together in the shade, old squaws pounded corn in large wooden mortars, idle youths gambled with cherry-stones on a wooden platter, and naked infants crawled in the dust. Scarcely a warrior was to be seen. Some were absent in quest of game or of Iroquois scalps, and some had gone with the trading-party to the French settlements. . . . Suddenly an uproar of voices, shrill with terror, burst upon the languid silence of the town. "The Iroquois! The Iroquois!" A crowd of hostile warriors had issued from the forest, and were rushing across the clearing towards the opening in the palisade. [Father Daniel was surrounded by panic-stricken women and children and old men, imploring to be saved. He baptized as many as he could, sprinkling them with water from a dripping handkerchief.]

The fierce yell of the war-whoop now rose close at hand. The palisade was forced, and the enemy was in the town. The air quivered with the infernal din. "Fly!" screamed the priest, driving his flock before him, "I will stay here. We shall meet again in Heaven." Many of them escaped through an opening in the palisade opposite to that by which the Iroquois had entered; but Daniel would not follow, for there still might be souls to rescue from perdition. The hour had come for which he had long prepared himself. In a moment he saw the Iroquois, and came forth from the church to meet them. When they saw him in turn, radiant in the vestments of his office, confronting them with a look kindled with the inspiration of martyrdom, they stopped and stared in amazement; then recovering themselves, bent their bows, and showered him with a volley of arrows that tore through his robes and flesh. A gun-shot followed; the ball pierced his heart and he fell dead, gasping the name of Jesus. They rushed upon him with yells of triumph, stripped him naked, gashed and hacked his lifeless body, and, scooping his blood in their hands, bathed their faces in it to make them brave. The town was in a blaze; when the flames reached the church, they flung the priest into it, and both were consumed together.

[In the following spring, the Iroquois made an attack in the heart of the Huron country. Father John de Brébeuf and Father Gabriel Lalemant were captured, and carried to the village of Saint-Ignace. Four days later some Frenchmen found their mutilated bodies there, confirming what escaped Hurons had already reported.]

On the afternoon of the sixteenth [of March]—the day when the priests were captured—Brébeuf was led apart, and bound to a stake. He seemed more concerned for his captive converts than for himself, and addressed them in a loud voice, exhorting them to suffer patiently and promising Heaven as their reward. The Iroquois, incensed, scorched him from head to foot to silence him; whereupon, in the tone of a master, he threatened them with everlasting flames for persecuting the worshippers of God. As he continued to speak, with voice and countenance unchanged, they cut away his lower lip and thrust a red-hot iron down his throat. He still held his tall form erect and defiant, with no sign or sound of pain; and they tried another means to overcome him. They led out Lalemant, that Brébeuf might see him tortured. They had tied strips of bark, smeared with pitch, about his naked body. When he saw the condition of his superior, he could not hide his agitation, and called out to him with a broken voice, in the words of St Paul, "We are made a spectacle to the world, to angels, and to men." Then he threw himself at Brébeuf's feet; upon which the Iroquois seized him, made him fast to a stake, and set fire to the bark that enveloped him. As the flame rose, he threw his arms upward, with a shriek of supplication to Heaven. Next they hung around Brébeuf's neck a collar made of hatchets heated red hot; but the indomitable priest stood like a rock.

A Huron in the crowd, who had been a convert of the mission but was now an Iroquois by adoption, called out, with the malice of a renegade, to pour hot water on their heads, since they had poured so much cold water on those of others. The kettle was accordingly slung, and the water boiled and poured slowly on the heads of the two missionaries. "We baptize you," they cried, "that you may be happy in Heaven; for nobody can be saved without a good baptism." Brébeuf

F*

would not flinch, and in a rage they cut strips of flesh from his limbs, and devoured them before his eyes. Other renegade Hurons called out to him, "You told us that, the more one suffers on earth, the happier he is in Heaven. We wish to make you happy; we torment you because we love you; and you ought to thank us for it." After a succession of other revolting tortures, they scalped him; when, seeing him nearly dead, they laid open his breast, and came in a crowd to drink the blood of so valiant an enemy, thinking to imbibe with it some portion of his courage. A chief then tore out his heart, and devoured it. . . .

Lalemant, physically weak from childhood and slender almost to emaciation, was constitutionally unequal to a display of fortitude like that of his colleague. When Brébeuf died, he was led back to the house whence he had been taken, and tortured there all night until, in the morning, one of the Iroquois, growing tired of the protracted entertainment, killed him with a hatchet. "We saw no part of his body," says Ragueneau, 'from head to foot, which was not burned, even to his eyes, in the sockets of which these wretches had placed live coals." It was said that at times he seemed beside himself; then, rallying, with hands uplifted he offered his sufferings to Heaven as a sacrifice. His robust companion had lived less than four hours under the torture, while he survived it for nearly seventeen. . . .

[Before this year, 1649, was out, the other two martyrs had received their crowns. On December 7 the Iroquois raided the village of Saint-Jean, where Father Charles Garnier was alone with his flock.]

Garnier ran to his chapel, where a few of his converts had sought asylum. He gave them his benediction, exhorted them to hold fast to the faith, and bade them fly while there was yet time. For himself, he hastened back to the houses, running from one to another, and giving absolution or baptism to all whom he found. An Iroquois met him, shot him with three balls through the body and thigh, tore off his cassock, and rushed on in pursuit of the fugitives. Garnier lay for a moment on the ground, as if stunned; then, recovering his senses, he was seen to rise into a kneeling posture. At a little distance from him lay a Huron, mortally wounded, but still showing signs of life. With the Heaven that awaited him glowing before his fading vision, the priest dragged himself towards the dying Indian, to give him absolution; but his strength failed, and he fell again to the earth. He rose once more, and again crept forward, when a party of Iroquois rushed upon him, split his head with two blows of a hatchet, stripped him, and left his body on the ground. . . . Saint-Jean lay a waste of smoking ruins thickly strewn with blackened corpses of the slain.

[Garnier's companion, Father Noel Chabanel, had been away at this time, and he never returned. Suspicions were confirmed soon afterwards by a] renegade Huron, who confessed that he had killed Chabanel and thrown his body into the river, after robbing him of his clothes, his hat, the blanket or mantle which was strapped to his shoulders, and the bag in which he carried his books and papers. He declared that his motive was hatred of the faith, which had caused the ruin of the Hurons. The priest had prepared himself for a worse fate. Before leaving Sainte-Marie on the Wye to go to his post in the Tobacco Nation, he had written to his brother to regard him as a victim destined to the fires of the Iroquois. He added that, though he was naturally timid, he was now wholly indifferent to danger; and he expressed the belief that only a superhuman power could have wrought such a change in him.

BD PETER WRIGHT

IN LONDON, A.D. 1651

*Peter Wright was born at Slipton in Northamptonshire in 1603.
After a somewhat disordered youth, he entered the noviceship of
the Society of Jesu at Watten in Flanders in 1629, was in due course
professed and ordained priest, and became chaplain to Sir Henry
Gage's regiment of English soldiers in the army of Spain. When
Gage returned home to support King Charles I, Father Wright came
with him, and in 1645 became chaplain in the Marquess of Winchester's house. It was here that he was arrested on Candlemas day 1651,
and committed to Newgate as a suspected priest. During the pro-
tectorate of Oliver Cromwell, Catholics were severely repressed, but
only a few were put to death: Bd Peter Wright was one of them.
The account below follows the record made by an eye-witness of
the events.*

Upon his being brought to trial at the Old Bailey, the
principal witness against Father Peter Wright was the apostate
younger brother of Sir Henry Gage, in spite of the efforts of
another brother, an Anglican clergyman, to dissuade him
from testifying against the innocent. When asked by Rolle,
L.C.J., what he had to say in reply to the evidence, Father
Wright answered: "My lord, I give Almighty God thanks
from the bottom of my heart that he has been pleased I
should be here arraigned—to use the words of St Peter—not
as a murderer nor as a thief nor as a reviler, nor as guilty of
any other crime but my religion: that is the Catholic religion,
which was, is and ever will be illustrious over all the earth.
And I have nothing more to say."

The judge objected that he was not arraigned for his
religion, but for returning into the realm after he had been
ordained priest, and there seducing the people. To this Wright
replied that the persecutors of old might just as well have
objected against the apostles and early priests that they came

into foreign countries and preached the faith contrary to those countries' laws, calling it treason and seducing of the people. "But," said the judge, "they preached the Gospel, while you preach errors contrary to the Gospel." "That is the very point in question," retorted Father Wright; and he went on to declare that all sorts of errors and heresies were then tolerated in England, but only the Catholic religion was persecuted, which was a sign of its being God's truth. Nevertheless the jury returned a verdict of guilty, whereat Wright bowed low to them, saying, "May God Almighty's holy name be blessed, now and for evermore." The next day he was sentenced to be hanged, drawn and quartered.

Father Wright's last days were over Whitsuntide. Many Catholics came to the prison to talk with him and ask his blessing; he made a general confession of his life to a fellow prisoner, a secular priest, Mr Cheney, and slept the nights even more soundly than usual; he offered Mass for the last time on the morning of Whit Monday. The jailers arrived to fetch him soon after, and when he heard the noise of their knocking he cried, "I am coming, sweet Jesus, I am coming!" He embraced Cheney, saying, "Farewell, my room-mate and bedfellow. Before long we shall see one another again in Heaven." He hurried out to the hurdle, and as he lay down on it said to Cheney, "Upon this bed I lie alone, as you also henceforward will have your bed to yourself." Before he was dragged away through the thronged streets to Tyburn, Mr Cheney gave him a last absolution. Father Wright looked, says the eye-witness, "more like one sitting than lying down: his head was covered, his countenance smiling, a certain air of majesty, and a courage and cheerfulness in his comportment, which was both surprising and edifying, not only to the Catholics who crowded to ask his benediction but to the Protestants themselves, as many of them publicly declared." As the hurdle was pulled abreast of the Marquess of Winchester's house, Father Wright raised himself as best he could, to give a blessing to the family where they stood on a balcony, "which they all received with their heads bowed down."

There was a huge crowd, with many in coaches and on horseback, at the place of execution. Thirteen criminals were to die with Father Wright, and he tried to speak comfort to them; but he was interrupted by the importunities of a minister, who told him to save his life by renouncing the errors of popery. To which Wright answered that had he a thousand lives he would most willingly give them all up in defence of the Catholic faith. When the rope was fitted about his neck, Father Wright spoke briefly to the people, in some such words as these:

"Gentlemen, my time is now short, and I have not much to say. I am brought here charged with no crime but with that of being a priest. I willingly confess I am a priest. I confess I am a Catholic. I confess I am a religious man of the Society of Jesus—a Jesuit, as you call it. This is the cause for which I die; for this alone was I condemned, and for teaching the Catholic faith, which is spread through the whole world, taught through all ages from Christ's time, and will be taught for all ages to come. For this cause I most willingly sacrifice my life; and I look upon it as my greatest happiness that my most good God has chosen me, most unworthy, to this blessed lot, the lot of the saints. This is a grace which so unworthy a sinner could scarce have wished, much less hoped for. And now I beg of the goodness of my God with all the fervour I am able, and most humbly entreat him that he would drive the darkness of error from those of you that are Protestants, and enlighten your minds with the rays of truth. As for you Catholics, my fellow soldiers and comrades, I earnestly beseech you to join in prayer for me and with me till my last moment; and when I shall come to Heaven I will do as much for you. God bless you all. I forgive all men. From my heart I bid you all farewell, till we meet in a happy eternity."

Having recollected and commended himself, the cart was

drawn away, and he was allowed to hang till he was dead before the butchery was carried out. It was 19 May 1651, and Peter Wright was forty-eight years old.

BD JOHN WALL

Of the English and Welsh martyrs hitherto beatified, eighteen were victims of the persecution provoked by the bogus plot concocted by Titus Oates. Among them was John Wall, born near Preston in Lancashire in 1620, who became a Franciscan friar minor at Douay in 1651. He ministered in Worcestershire for twenty-two years, and was arrested during the Oates terror.

While in prison, Father Wall wrote an account of his apprehension and trial, in the course of which he says: "Imprisonment, in these times especially, when none can send to their friends, nor friends come to them, is the best means to teach us how to put our confidence in God alone in all things, and then he will make his promise good, 'that all things shall be added to us' (Luke xii), which chapter if every one would read and make good use of, a prison would be better than a palace; and a confinement for religion and a good conscience' sake more pleasant than all the liberties the world could afford. As for my own part, God give me his grace, and all faithful Christians their prayers; I am happy enough." He was tried at Worcester before Mr Justice Atkins, on the charge of being a priest unlawfully within the kingdom. Of the witnesses for the prosecution, three had to be subpoenaed, and the fourth had a grudge against the prisoner. He was found guilty and sentenced, whereupon he bowed to the bench and said, "Thanks be to God! God save the king; and I beseech God to bless your lordship and all this honourable bench." To which the judge replied, "You have spoken very well. I do not intend you shall die, at least not for the present, until I know the king's further pleasure."

"I was not, I thank God for it," wrote Father Wall, "troubled with any disturbing thoughts, either against the judge for his sentence, or the jury that gave such a verdict, or against any of the witnesses. . . . And I was, I thank God, so present with myself whilst the judge pronounced sentence, that without any concern for any thing in this world, I did actually at the same time offer myself and the world to God. . . . Several Protestant gentlemen and others who had heard my trial came to me, though strangers, and told me how sorry they were for me. To whom with thanks I replied that I was troubled they should grieve for me or my condition, who was joyful for it myself. For I told them I had professed this faith and religion all my lifetime, which I was as sure to be true as I was sure of the truth of God's word on which it was grounded; and therefore in it I deposed my soul, and eternal life and happiness. . . ."

Father Wall was taken up to London to be examined by Oates and his creatures. They announced that they found him innocent of any plot, and offered him life and liberty in return for apostasy: "But I told them I would not buy my life at so dear a rate as to wrong my conscience." He was returned to Worcester and there executed at Red Hill on 22 August 1679. Three days later, the following letter was written by a brother Franciscan, William Levison:

Of late I was desired, and willingly went to visit our friend Mr Webb [one of Wall's several aliases], prisoner at Worcester, whose execution drew near at hand. I came to him two days before it, and found him a cheerful sufferer of his present imprisonment, and ravished, as it were, with joy, with the future hopes of dying for so good a cause. I found, contrary to both his and my expectation, the favour of being with him alone; and the day before his execution I enjoyed that privilege for the space of four or five hours together; during which time I heard his confession and communicated him, to his great joy and satisfaction. I ventured likewise, through his desire, to be present at his execution, and placed myself boldly next to the under-sheriff, near the gallows, where I had the opportunity of giving him the last absolution, just as he was turned off the ladder.

During his imprisonment, he carried himself like a true servant and disciple of his crucified Master, thirsting after nothing more than the shedding of his blood for the love of his God: which he performed with a courage and cheerfulness becoming a valiant soldier of Christ, to the great edification of all Catholics and admiration of all Protestants, the rational and moderate part especially, who shewed a great sense of sorrow for his death, decrying the cruelty of putting men to death for priesthood and religion. He is the first that ever suffered at Worcester since the Catholic religion entered into this nation, which he seemed with joy to tell me before his execution.* He was quartered, and his head separated from his body, according to his sentence. His body was permitted to be buried, and was accompanied by the Catholics of the town to St Oswald's churchyard, where he lies interred. His head I got privately, and conveyed it to Mr Randolph [Father Leo, o.s.f.], who will be careful to keep it till opportunity serves to transport it to Doway. . . .

The martyr spoke but briefly from the scaffold because, as he said, he had given all he would say to a friend to be printed. A copy of this last speech exists in manuscript at Oscott College, and it was printed in a government broadsheet about the execution: the two versions differ in wording but are the same in substance. His last words were: "I will offer my life in satisfaction for my sins and for the Catholic cause; and I beg for those that be my enemies in this my death and desire to

* The writer's brother, also a Franciscan, the Venerable Francis Levison, died in prison there five months later.

have them forgiven, because I go to that world of happiness sooner than I should have gone. I humbly beg pardon from God and the world, and this I beg for the merits and mercy of Jesus Christ. I beseech God to bless his Majesty, and give him a long life and happy reign in this world and in the world to come. I beseech God to bless all my benefactors and all my friends, and those that may have been any way under my charge, and I beseech God to bless all the Catholics and this nation. I beseech God to bless all that suffer under this persecution and to turn our captivity into joy, that they that sow in tears may reap in joy."

BD OLIVER PLUNKET

IN LONDON, A.D. 1681

Among the Irish who defended their faith to death during the sixteenth and seventeenth centuries, three bishops were outstanding. The first of them was a Franciscan, Patrick O'Hely, who was appointed to the see of Mayo when in Rome in 1576. In 1578 or 1579 he landed in Kerry, and within a few days was arrested by the mayor of Limerick. The bishop refused to acknowledge Queen Elizabeth's ecclesiastical supremacy, stated that his business was to serve religion, and remained mute when tortured to elicit information about a Spanish invasion of Ireland. Accordingly, he was at once hanged at Kilmallock, under martial law, together with his chaplain, Father Conn O'Rourke. In somewhat similar circumstances the archbishop of Cashel, Dermot O'Hurley, was hanged in Dublin in 1584, again under martial law, as no jury would have convicted him. He was well over sixty years old, but had previously been tortured in most abominable fashion, by having his feet and legs roasted over a fire.

*But the only Irish martyr of those days who has so far been
beatified (apart from some, such as Bd John Roche, who were
domiciled in England) is Oliver Plunket, archbishop of Armagh, who
suffered in the panic attendant on Titus Oates's fictitious plot. He
was born of noble family at Loughcrew in county Meath in 1629
and was ordained priest in 1654 in Rome, where he was appointed
to a chair of theology in the College de Propaganda Fide. He arrived
in Ireland as archbishop of Armagh in 1670, at a time when there
were only two other bishops in the country, but with his troubled
and difficult episcopate of nine years we are not here concerned.
Among Titus Oates's "revelations" in 1678 was the existence of a
plot concocted by King Louis XIV, Pope Innocent XI and the
Jesuits to land a French force in Ireland. Consequently, Archbishop
Plunket was seized and brought to trial at Dundalk, on a concerted
charge of being concerned in the alleged conspiracy. The Crown
witnesses did not put in an appearance and the case broke down,
so, after three months in jail in Dublin, Plunket was brought over to
London and lodged in Newgate among the common-side felons (he
spent altogether eighteen months in prison).*

Oliver Plunket was finally arraigned in Westminster Hall
on 8 June 1681. The judges were Pemberton, L.C.J., and
Dolben and Jones, JJ., and there was an imposing array of
counsel for the Crown. In those days, the accused was not
represented by counsel, and Plunket—though well able to
conduct his own case—had only one witness that appeared:
he had not been allowed enough time to get his proper witnesses over from Ireland. The tedious indictment and lengthy
proceedings were summed up in a few sentences by the archbishop afterwards, in a letter to his kinsman Michael Plunket.

On the eighth of this month I was brought to trial, accused
of introducing the Catholic religion, of preparing 70,000
men for rebellion, collecting money for them, exploring the
fortresses and forts of Ireland, and of destining Carlingford
as the landing-place for the French. I applied for time to
bring my witnesses from Ireland, but in vain. I argued that
the pretended crime having been committed in Ireland, it
should be there discussed, or that at least a jury should be
brought thence, who would be better acquainted with the
circumstances and condition of those concerned; but everything was denied to me. Two Franciscan friars were the

principal accusers against me, the one named [John] Mac-
Moyer, and the other Hugh Duffy, and a certain priest of the
MacClanes. Four seculars [laymen] also appeared against me,
viz., two of the O'Neills, a certain Hanlon, and Florence Mac-
Moyer. As to these four I never saw them in my life*. . . .
When I alleged that no one was ever known, when accused before the tribunals in Ireland, to have been afterwards summoned
to answer to the same charges in England, the judge eluded
my argument. . . . Sentence of death has been passed against
me . . . and thus those who beheaded me in effigy have now
attained their intent of beheading the prototype. . . . My
conscience never reproached me with being guilty of any
conspiracy or rebellion, direct or indirect. Oh, would to God
that I were as free from every other stain and sin against the
divine precepts as I am from this. Therefore it is necessary
for all my friends to pray for me, as I confide they will.

When the verdict of guilty was brought in, Oliver Plunket
uttered those words that, from the earliest times to the latest,
have helped to make of martyrs' trials a sort of liturgy: "*Deo
gratias.* God be thanked." He was brought up for sentence a
week later, and in a dignified speech he again declared that
had time for his eight witnesses been allowed (they had by
then reached Coventry) his innocence of conspiracy would
have been demonstrated.† In the course of Pemberton's judg-
ment the religious animus operating in these cases was made
clear once again: "You have done as much as you could to
dishonour our God in this case; for the bottom of your treason
was your setting up your false religion, than which there is
not anything more displeasing to God, or more pernicious to
mankind, in the world. A religion that is ten times worse than

* The archbishop was charitably reticent about these gentry. The
two friars were suspended by the superiors of their order for gross
indiscipline; Florence MacMoyer was an embittered man of good
family who had turned informer; Edmund Murphy (not mentioned
by Plunket) was a priest under discipline for drunkenness; and so on.
  † In his *Lives of the Chief Justices* (1849-57), Lord Campbell called
the conduct of Plunket's trial a disgrace to Pemberton and to his
country.

all the heathenish superstitions; the most dishonourable and derogatory to God and his glory of all religions or pretended religions whatsoever, for it undertakes to dispense with God's laws and to pardon the breach of them." Sentence of death was passed in the usual form, and the archbishop said, "My lord, I hope I may have this favour, of leave for a servant. and some few friends that I have to come to me."

PEMBERTON: "I think you may have liberty for any servant to come to you. I know nothing to the contrary."

PLUNKET: "And some few friends that I have in town."

PEMBERTON: "But I would advise you to have some minister to come to you, some Protestant minister."

PLUNKET: "My lord, if you please, there are some in prison that never were indicted or accused of any crime, and they will do my business very well; for they will do it according to the rites of our own church, which is the ancient usage— they cannot do better, and I would not alter it now."

PEMBERTON: ". . . Mr Richardson [the keeper of Newgate], you may let his servant come to him, and any friend in your presence, to see there be no evil done nor any contrivances that may hereafter have an influence upon affairs. . . . [to Plunket] Well, sir, we wish better to you than you do to yourself."

PLUNKET: "God Almighty bless your lordship. And now, my lord, as I am a dead man to this world, I was never guilty of any of the treasons laid to my charge, as you will hear in time. . . ."

On the night before his execution the archbishop slept well, and arose betimes on July 1 (old style) to celebrate Mass. He had prepared his last speech on the previous day, and entrusted various personal matters and messages to his good friend the Benedictine monk Maurus Corker, to whom he wrote: "I do most earnestly recommend myself to your prayers and to the holy sacrifices of all the noble confessors who are in this prison, and to such priests as you are acquainted with. And I hope soon to be able to requite all your and their kindness." He had already written to Michael Plunket that: "The English Catholics were here most charitable to me; they spared neither money nor gold [work?] to relieve me, and in my trial did for me all that even my brother would do: they are rare Catholics and most constant sufferers." The archbishop was duly drawn on a hurdle from Newgate to Tyburn, where he addressed the people from the cart beneath the gallows. He gave a careful summary of what had passed at his trial, expounded his innocence of the charges brought, and declared that "a great peer [Lord Shaftesbury] sent me notice that he would save my life if I would accuse others; but I answered that. . . , to save my life, I would not falsely accuse any nor prejudice my own soul." Finally, he asked forgiveness of all whom he had offended in any way, as he forgave others. He expressed aloud his sorrow to God for his sins, called on the saints for their prayers, and said the psalm *Miserere*. As the cart was drawn away and his body swung, he was heard to commend his soul to God. He was dead before his body was cut down from the gallows.

In a long letter to the martyr's friend Mrs Sheldon, Dom Maurus Corker wrote: "If we may measure this happy martyr's love by the rule of our Saviour, 'This is the greatest love a man can show, that he should lay down his life for his friends,' we shall find him perfect in love. For in him was fulfilled that saying of the Canticles, 'love is strong as death.'"

The executioner (who was the notorious Jack Ketch) enabled the martyr's friends to recover his head, and today it rests above an altar in St Peter's church at Drogheda. The mutilated body was, in accordance with Oliver Plunket's own wish, buried near the grave of Bd Thomas Whitbread and four other recent Jesuit martyrs, in the chuchyard of St Giles-in-the-Fields; in 1684 it was removed to the English Benedictine monastery at Lamspring in Westphalia, and it is now enshrined in the abbey church at Downside.

ST JOHN DE BRITTO

IN INDIA, A.D. 1693

According to a tradition, old but of very uncertain value, the first Christian martyr in India was St Thomas the Apostle. Certainly there have been Christian communities in India continuously since the sixth century at least, possibly from the fourth, and they will have had their martyrs. In later times there have been martyrs among the European missionaries, beginning with those of Salsette in 1583, BB. Rudolf Aquaviva and his four companions, Jesuits. A century later, St John de Britto was also a Jesuit, a man of noble Portuguese birth, who came to Goa as a missionary in 1673. He was an upholder of the methods of Father Robert de' Nobili, of adapting oneself to Indian ways of life and observing the lawful customs of the country. He was a successful missionary in Madura in most difficult and trying conditions; but already in 1686 he was abominably tortured for refusing to give honour to the Hindu deity Siva, and narrowly escaped with his life.

Among Father de Britto's converts in the Marava country was the *poligar* of Siruvalli, and this potentate duly put away all his wives except one. Of these repudiated ladies, the youngest, we are told, was the most seriously upset. She was the niece of the raja Raghunatha, and she complained to her uncle, who was already opposed to the Christian missionary and to his niece's former husband. He then ordered that all missions in his territory be pillaged, their churches burnt and obstinate Christians fined; and Father de Britto was to be arrested.

He was seized on 8 January 1693 and, with three Christian Indian youths, taken to the raja at Ramuad. It was a long journey on foot and in fetters, and the missionary was in a very weak state. Time and again he fell, and was forced to his feet with blows, and at one place they were put in a cart and left all day exposed to the sun for the entertainment

of the villagers. On their arrival they were put in prison, while
Raghunatha, worked on by the leading Brahmans, tried in
vain to win over the *poligar* and carried out various "magical"
rites directed against his prisoner. When at length Father de
Britto was brought before him, the raja showed him the
Breviary that had been taken from him, and asked whether
it was from this book that he drew the power to make spells
harmless. Father de Britto answered that in a sense this was
so. "Very well," said Raghunatha. "We will see if it is a
protection against bullets too." He then ordered that the book
be tied round the priest's neck and that he should be taken
out and shot. Hereupon the Christian *poligar* jumped up in
protest, declaring he would die himself before allowing his
teacher to be killed. Raghunatha knew that the *poligar* had
a following and, seeing mutinous looks among the soldiers,
he recalled his order just as the sentence was about to be
carried out, and sent the priest elsewhere. Three days later
Father de Britto wrote to his superior and colleagues at
Madura:

You will have heard from the catechist what had happened
to me up to the time he left. The next day, January 28, I was
brought to trial and sentenced to be shot. I had already arrived
at the place of execution, and all was ready, when other
orders came. The raja of Marava, fearing trouble, had me
separated from the other confessors of Jesus Christ—those
dear children of mine—and handed over to his brother at
Oriur, who was told to put me to death without delay. After a
very hard journey I got here this last day of January, and was
at once interviewed. There was a long palaver, at the end of
which I was brought to this prison, where I await the death
that I must suffer for God.

It is the hope of having this happiness that has twice driven
me to India. Certainly it has been bought at no small price; but
the recompense I look for from Him to whom I offer myself
up is worth all the suffering and a very great deal more. The
only crime with which I am charged is that I teach the
religion of the true God and do not worship idols. It is indeed

glorious to suffer death for such a crime! That is what fills me with happiness and joy in our Lord. My guards are keeping a sharp eye on me, and I can write no more. Farewell, Fathers! I ask your blessing and commend myself to your holy sacrifices.

Your Reverences' very humble servant in Jesus Christ,

JOHN DE BRITTO

From prison at Oriur, 31 January 1693.

Four days later, February 4, John de Britto was led about midday into a wide open space, which was full of people. The executioners allowed him to kneel and pray for a quarter of an hour; then he rose to his feet, saying with a smile, "Now, friends, you can do what you like with me." First they tore off his yellow gown, and, seeing a small reliquary round his neck, cut it away roughly for fear of being bewitched. The same fear of magic made them use a heavy axe instead of the usual swords for execution. Then they tied a cord tightly from the martyr's beard round his middle, to keep his head down. At this moment two Christians ran from the crowd, asking to die with this man who was dying for them. They were flung aside, and the chief executioner, half-drunk as he was, smote off John de Britto's head. Hands and feet were hacked away, and trunk and head were hung on a high pole for all to see.

Later, the two Christians who had intervened were sent to the raja; he dismissed them—after having their noses and ears cut off.

BD GOMIDAS KEUMURGIAN

AT CONSTANTINOPLE, A.D. 1707

Gomidas (Cosmas) Keumurgian, who was beatified by Pope Pius XI in 1929, was perhaps the most noteworthy martyr in Constantinople since the era of Iconoclast persecution. At the beginning of the eighteenth century the Armenian Catholics there were subjected to a persecution in which, as in England a few generations before and in other places at other times, political considerations were a considerable factor, and the purity of Christian witness might easily be compromised. But, whatever the follies (if not worse) of the French ambassador to the Porte, and the acerbity of conflicts between Christians of differing communions, Bd Gomidas was clearly a martyr for the faith: he refused to purchase his life by passing to Islam, not once but several times.

A word should perhaps be said about the term "Frank" that occurs in the following narrative. The term was applied in the Levant to any foreigner from western Europe, especially a Frenchman, and to any Latin Catholic; it was rarely used of a Catholic of any other rite. This usage gave plentiful scope to equivocal use of the word. At this time the Turks did not, in civil affairs, recognize the existence of any Catholics except Latins, and Bd Gomidas was justified in repudiating—as he did—the application of the epithet to himself.

Gomidas Keumurgian was born at Constantinople about the year 1656, son of a priest of the dissident Armenian Church. In due course he was called to follow in his father's footsteps, and he studied for the priesthood under the Armenian scholar Minas of Aintab. In accordance with Eastern custom, he married before ordination to the diaconate, and became the father of two sons and five daughters. For some fourteen years he ministered in the Armenian church of St George at Constantinople, where he was noted for his studious habits, apostolic energy and preaching ability. When he was about forty, Father Gomidas, together with his family, came into communion with the Catholic Church; he continued his ministry in the Armenian rite, and devoted himself to the cause of Christian unity.

At this time the dissident Armenian authorities were very bitter against Catholics, and in 1701, by playing on Turkish fears of French political influence, their patriarch obtained from the sultan a decree for the suppression of Armenian Catholics. Persecution followed both in Constantinople and Asia Minor; the Catholic Armenian leaders went into hiding for a time, and Gomidas went on pilgrimage to Jerusalem. On his return home he still had to live in hiding for nearly a year; being a poet he occupied this time by writing a para- phrase of the Acts of the Apostles in verse.

Some years later persecution began afresh, and Gomidas was among those arrested. His friends soon obtained his release by the judicious use of money in the right quarter; but Gomidas believed he had received certain signs that he was destined for martyrdom, and this time he made no attempt to conceal himself. Six months later, in the evening of 23 October 1707,* he was again arrested. He was about to go to bed and, like St Fructuosus centuries before, he asked leave of his captors to dress himself properly. It was refused, but clothes were brought and Gomidas had to put them on hastily in the street, while his wife and children stood by weeping. "Don't cry," he said to them. "We must trust in God. Perhaps I shall be back tomorrow."

Father Gomidas was charged with betraying his national group within the Turkish state by adhering to "the religion of the Franks" and encouraging others to do the same, and the case was referred for examination to the jurist Mustafa Kemal. He was not at all happy about it, and he warned the witnesses to keep "your prophet Jesus and his mother Mary" before their eyes and speak nothing but the truth. But a dozen of them swore that Gomidas Keumurgian was "a

* October 23 by the Julian reckoning. The day of the martyrdom of Gomidas is given on his tomb as the feast of St Demetrius, a martyr very greatly revered in the East, but it was actually on the eve.

Frank," therefore an enemy to the sultan and a danger to public order, and there was a clamour for his death. Mustafa Kemal asked him why he had forsaken the religion of his people. Gomidas replied that his accusers had presented a wrong idea of his religion, so they evidently did not understand it; he was simply following the ancient fathers of the Armenian Church, and so he knew he was doing right; and, being a priest, it was not enough that he should be in the right way himself—he must lead others into it as well.

Mustafa Kemal said he did not want to listen to any sermons: Gomidas was accused of subversion in the interests of the Franks, and the penalty for that was death. "I ask nothing better," answered Gomidas, "for my conscience is clear of any such crime." If he were condemned, he went on, it would be for his religion, and such a condemnation would exceed the authority of those who did not share his religion and so were not competent to understand it; if, however, that sentence should be pronounced against him in defiance of justice, he appealed to the justice of God to vindicate his blood at the Last Judgement.

There was present in court the patriarch of the dissident Armenians John of Smyrna, who for years had been a bitter adversary of Gomidas and had instigated the present proceedings. Mustafa Kemal now turned angrily to this hierarch, saying, "His blood is on *your* head if you have lied." "So be it," replied John. "Let his blood be on our heads—and on the heads of all those Frankish priests who have perverted so many of our people." "Very well," said Mustafa, turning to Gomidas. 'You hear—they take the responsibility because, they say, you have corrupted true Christianity."

"Which seems to you the best among the faiths of the Christians?' asked Gomidas quietly.

"I am a Moslem. They are all equally detestable to me."

"Then what does it matter to you which one I choose?"

When he returned the prisoner to the judge, Ali Pasha, for sentence, Mustafa Kemal reported that the facts were proved; but he declared in court that a condemnation to death on the strength of them would be a crying injustice.

That night Father Gomidas received the sacraments, bade farewell to his family and friends, and gave his watch and ring to his wife, with a sum of money for the executioner. When he was taken before Ali Pasha in the Old Seraglio the next morning, a new charge had been added to the indictment, namely, that he had helped Moslems who had become Christians to escape abroad. This at once turned all Turkish opinion against him. Ali Pasha invited him to accept Islam. Gomidas refused peremptorily, and was sentenced to death by beheading. For what followed we are indebted to an Armenian monk, Father Elias, who accompanied Father Gomidas to the end. He afterwards related what happened to Father Matthew of Eudokia, the martyr's biographer.

Together with two other confessors, both laymen, and followed by a great crowd, Father Gomidas was marched off to the place of execution at Parmak Kapu in the Psamatia quarter. His hands were tied to his shoulders, and as he walked, strongly and serenely, he was heard saying Psalm 118, "Blessed are the perfect in the way, who walk in the law." Close by walked his wife and daughters. Twice on the way he was, by Ali Pasha's orders, offered his freedom if he would accept Islam: the executioner kissed his beard respectfully in the Eastern fashion, and urged him to think of his family and save his life, and his sister Irene implored him at any rate to pretend he had changed his mind. Gomidas replied only by repeating his profession of faith. He then recited the opening passage of St John's Gospel. After "the Word was made flesh . . ." he stopped and, turning to his two companions, he spoke words of encouragement to them. They had now reached the place of execution, at the crossroads of Parmak Kapu.

Gomidas was led forward and told to kneel down. He made the sign of the cross on the ground with his foot (for his hands were still tied) and did so, facing east. The crowd called to him to face south, in the direction of Mecca. "This is my south," he answered, and moved his head crossways. "In the name of the Father and of the Son and of the Holy Spirit, one only God. Glory be to Jesus Christ!" A last opportunity was given him to apostatize. "Don't waste time talking. Do what you have to do," said Gomidas, and began to rehearse aloud the eucharistic symbol of faith in its Armenian form. "We believe in one God, the Father Almighty. . . ." Before he reached the end, he was beheaded at one stroke.

After the body had been left exposed for three days in accordance with the provisions of the law, it was delivered to the martyr's relatives for burial. But no Catholic priest came forward to commit it to the grave; hearing this, the Greek Orthodox patriarch* sent a bishop and other clergy to celebrate a solemn funeral service and bury the body in the Armenian cemetery. Here the tomb may still be seen, with a long inscription to the memory of "the blessed Der Gomidas, minister of the altar, priest of the great family of Keumurgian, and citizen of Byzantium"; but later his body was translated to Lyons in France, where it disappeared at the Revolution.

* His name deserves to be recorded: it seems to have been Neophytos V.

BD PETER SANZ
and His Companions

AT FOOCHOW, A.D. 1747

*Since the early years of the seventeenth century persecution of
the Church in China in varying degrees of extension and intensity
has been grievously frequent. The earliest in date among the victims
who has been beatified was a Spanish Dominican missionary, Francis
de Capillas, who was executed in the province of Fukien in 1648.
In his last moments he summed up the lives of so many Christian
missionaries when he said, "The open air has been my dwellingplace,
the ground my only bed, my food has been what God sent me from
day to day. My only aim has been to work and to endure for the
glory of Jesus Christ and to bring people to eternal happiness through
belief in his name." There was a considerable outbreak of persecution
in the Fukien province in 1729 which, after a lull, got worse in 1746.
Among its victims was the local vicar apostolic, a Catalan pro-
phetically named Peter Martyr Sanz, who had been a missionary in
China for over thirty years, and four of his Spanish clergy suffered
soon after. They were all members of the Order of Preachers, and
were beatified in 1893.*

In June 1746 a man who had a grudge against Bishop Sanz
denounced the Christians of the town of Fugan to the authorities, and troops, under an officer called Fan, were sent there
to seize the missionaries. A number of arrests were made, including Father John Alcober, and torture soon brought about
the betrayal by a serving-man of Father Francis Serrano and
Father Francis Diaz. A day or two later, fearing that those
who sheltered him would be subjected to reprisals, Bishop
Sanz gave himself up; Father Joachim Royo followed his
example. Serrano and Diaz had already been barbarously mal-
treated for not saying where the bishop was (which, indeed,
they did not know). These five clergy and several Christian

girls, including one named Teresa, were then brought before a magistrate.

Teresa was questioned first, as to why she was not married: "Who advised you to remain maiden?" "Nobody," she answered. "I chose to do so for myself."—"But at any rate you put yourself at the disposal of Europeans for their pleasure." She rounded on her accuser: "That shows how little you know about them. Such a shameful idea is hateful to me too." To similar questions the other girls made similar answers, that nobody had tried to prevent them from marrying, that they had voluntarily followed Teresa's example. "Yes," interposed Teresa, "I advised them. If that is a crime, I am the only culprit. Let them go." Whereupon she was taken away to torture.* Father Alcober was then asked why he had come to China. "To preach the religion of Christ," he answered, and explained what that religion is. The officer Fan interrupted to make suggestions about the young women, which the priest said were too diabolical to deserve any reply. The bishop and Father Royo spoke in the same sense, but the other two clergy were not questioned. Then they were sent off, manacled hand and foot, to the governor of the province at Foochow.

Here the examination followed the same lines. They were also asked who sent them to China, and whether they bribed Chinese to become Christians. Bishop Sanz said that they were sent by the Christian chief bishop in Rome, and that nothing was further from their mind than to buy converts. "I simply show by explanation how true and good this religion is. I deceive nobody. I baptize only those who sincerely want me to do so. All China will come to this religion one day, when it is really understood. For those who live in accordance with it, there is everlasting happiness in Heaven after death; for those who knowingly reject it, there is an eternity of suffering. It does not matter how exalted the person was in

---

* It was one of the official charges against Christians in China at this time that many of their young women renounced marriage entirely.

this world—even you, my lord Governor, are liable to this sentence." For this bold reply the bishop was repeatedly struck in the face with a pliable leather instrument like the sole of a shoe. The missionaries were charged with unchastity and practising magic. It was alleged that they killed babies and used their bones to compound love-potions for their own use; this accusation was based on the finding in Father Alcober's care of certain medicines and a box of bones—treasured relics of a previous martyr. But a physician deposed that the bones were of an adult and at least a century old, much to the embarrassment of Fan, whom the judges now rebuked for bad faith and making frivolous charges. They said the prisoners should be discharged.

What we know of Fan is somewhat suggestive of a Chinese Titus Oates. He at once went to the governor and succeeded in convincing him that the Christians had been bribing people wholesale. Accordingly, named Christians were thrown into jail, traders who had done business for Sanz were arrested, military officers were disciplined and cashiered, and a new investigation ordered. But, although the five missionaries were cruelly beaten on face and feet, the fresh judges were no more successful than their predecessors in getting satisfactory evidence. So they changed their ground, and eventually found the bishop guilty of preaching what was called "the religion of the Lord of Heaven" in China after he had been ordered to leave the country, and of bringing in four more preachers for that purpose; the missionaries were condemned to be beheaded, and a Chinese catechist, Ambrose Ko, to be strangled. This sentence was in due course confirmed by the imperial court.

A Chinese priest hurried to bring the news to Bishop Sanz, and to bring him clothes suitable for his heavenly birthday. To the court that made the official announcement the bishop said, "I am going to Heaven, and there I will do all I can for the good of this empire of China." Followed by a large crowd, he was led through the south gate of Foochow, over

G

a bridge, to a spot where he was told to kneel. He did so and prayed for a few moments; then he turned to the executioner and said, "I am going to Heaven. I wish you were coming with me." "I want to go there with all my heart," was the reply. Then the executioner (he was lefthanded) removed the bishop's cap and beheaded him with one stroke.

A Chinese, known for his daring as a highway-robber, had been asked by the Christians to gather up the martyr's blood. He did so, and he did more: he took away the stone on which the bishop had knelt and set it up by his own house, carving on it the words: "This is the stone from which the honourable teacher named Peter went up to Heaven."

Bd Peter Sanz, who was about sixty-five years old, died on 26 May 1747. The execution of his companions was postponed, but in the meantime the mark of condemnation was branded on their faces. Their end was probably hastened by the arrival from Rome (where what had happened was not yet known) of a brief appointing Father Serrano coadjutor bishop to the vicar apostolic. The four Dominicans were strangled in private on 28 October 1748; whether or not the sentence on Ambrose Ko was carried out is apparently not known.

THE MARTYRS OF SEPTEMBER

IN PARIS, A.D. 1792

On 17 July 1794, during the last days of the period of the French Revolution called The Terror, sixteen nuns of the Carmel of Compiègne were guillotined in Paris; they mounted the scaffold singing Psalm 116, "Praise the Lord, all ye nations." In 1906 they were beatified, and this was the Church's first authoritative declaration that there had been true martyrs among the numberless victims of the Revolution. Others have been beatified since, individually and in groups, notably numerous victims of the massacres that took place during the first week of September 1792. Half a century earlier the French minister of state M. P. de Voyer d'Argenson had foretold a revolution in which priests would be slaughtered in the streets of Paris. These planned and deliberate killings had a political motive and were directed against "suspected" persons detained in prison; but few distinctions were made, and the 1400 who perished in Paris included many common criminals, as well as a number of women and of youths under eighteen. Such a situation obviously presents delicate problems from the point of view of martyrdom, and in fact eighteen names were rejected from the list presented in Rome; the remainder, 191 persons, who were beatified in 1926, were practically all priests who had refused the oath of recognition of the civil constitution of the clergy: three were bishops, and four were laymen.

The signal for the massacre was given at two in the afternoon of September 2. A large body of "executioners," by no means all drawn from the dregs of the people, led by one Maillard, first went to the town-hall, where a number of priests and others were detained. These were taken by carriage to the Abbaye prison; on the way the infuriated mob attacked the prisoners, and on reaching their destination some were killed on the spot as they got down from the carriages. The evidence is too confused to give a clear picture of what took place inside the Abbaye. But the prison had extended all over the buildings of the monastery of Saint-Germain-des-Prés, and it is known that killings went on at intervals in different parts of it until after midnight: of the eighty-three persons confined in the refectory, not one survived. As at *Les Carmes,* to give the proceedings an air of justice and legality, a sort of drum-head court martial was organized: a "court," complete with a president, Maillard, in a powdered wig, and with a green carpet on the floor. So far as the clergy were concerned each one was asked if he had taken the constitutional oath. At the answer "No," he was taken outside and butchered by the sword. Among the beatified victims here were two young Minim friars, brothers, too, according to the flesh, who had feared they would be spared because, not being priests, they were not required to take the oath. Their names were Charles and Louis Hurtrel.

The greater number of clergy, from many parts of France, were confined at the Carmelite friary in the Rue de Rennes, with the archbishop of Arles, John du Lau d'Alleman, at their head. They were taking their Sunday afternoon exercise in the garden when their assailants broke in. The archbishop and some others were at once slain, and the bishop of Beauvais had his leg broken by a bullet. Then the "court" took charge, sitting in the chapel: two by two priests had the oath tendered to them, and every one refused it. Each man then went out through a corridor, and as he came to the steps leading down into the garden he was killed by a sword stroke. Towards the end, the name of the bishop of Beauvais, Francis de La Rochefoucauld Maumont, was called. From the place where he lay helpless he answered, "Here I am at your disposal, gentlemen ready to die, but I cannot walk. Will you please be so kind as to carry me where you wish me to go." He was brought in on a mattress, refused the oath, and was carried out in the same way; with him died his brother, the bishop of Saintes.

The beatified martyrs *des Carmes* numbered ninety-one; some of the prisoners, here and elsewhere, were overlooked or allowed to escape. Before he was killed, James Galais, a priest of Saint-Sulpice, handed the "judge" a sum of money: he had been in charge of the catering, and owed this to the contractor. One of the martyrs here was a layman, the Count de Valfons, who was killed simply for saying, "I belong to the Catholic, Apostolic and Roman Church."*

At the prison of La Force in the Rue Saint-Antoine the massacre began about midnight, and here the best-known victim was the Princess de Lamballe, the devoted friend of Queen Marie-Antoinette; but she is not numbered among the martyrs. The Vincentian seminary of Saint-Firmin, which was being used as a prison, was attacked early in the morning of the next day, September 3. Here there were seventy victims who have been beatified, including the rector of the seminary, Louis François, who was offered an opportunity to escape, but refused to take it. Of the victims among those imprisoned elsewhere—the Châtelet, the Conciergerie, Bicêtre —none have been included among the martyrs, for lack of necessary evidence concerning the exact circumstances of their death.

* This is reminiscent of the Venerable Robert Price, who in 1644 was stopped by Parliamentarian soldiers in the streets of Lincoln and asked, "Are you Price the papist?" Upon his replying, "I am Price the Roman Catholic," he was shot dead.

BD JOHN DAT

Christianity made rapid headway in Indo-China from the time that missionaries of the Society of Jesus came there early in the seventeenth century, and this progress in due course provoked a century of persecution. Among the martyrs were Father Hyacinth Casteñeda and three other Dominicans, between 1745 and 1773, who were beatified, with other victims, in 1906. There are two accounts of the Indo-Chinese priest Bd John Dat, written by Christians closely associated with him: one by the physician Paul Huyen-Trang, the other by a catechist, Bernard Tang.

For a week after his arrest in the autumn of 1798, Father Dat was kept in custody, with a heavy *cang* round his neck, by a troop of soldiers, who tried to extort money from him and beat him because he had none. He had already refused to trample on a religious picture, representing the Last Judgement, and on the 22nd day of the seventh moon he was brought, with other people, before the governor, who asked him if he could read European books. He said he could.

GOVERNOR: "Read something then, and let these other Christians read with you."

DAT: "They cannot read these books."

GOVERNOR: "Very well. Then say some prayers in our language."

Father Dat and his fellows accordingly said the Ten Commandments. At the end, the governor asked the lay people, "If these are your religious principles, why do you forsake your parents for a teacher of Christianity?" However, they were all discharged except the priest and half-a-dozen catechists and other laymen, who were returned to custody and the brutalities of their guards. When Dr Huyen-Trang asked him why he did not try to convert these men, Father Dat answered with a laugh that it was forbidden to cast pearls before swine. He was always cheering up his fellow prisoners, though he was himself, he said, by nature nervous and fearful. After he had received the death-sentence, Bernard Tang asked him if he were afraid. "Not at the moment," was the reply, "but it may be a different matter when the time for execution comes. There is no greater happiness than to die for Jesus Christ. May God give us all strength for the contest." Another man said to him, "Father, remember me when you are happy in eternity." He answered, "I do not know yet what God destines for me. But why do you ask me this? The blessed in Heaven are always remembering us."

In the morning of the day of execution, all Christian prisoners, Father Dat at their head, were assembled before the governor, who addressed the priest. "Wretched man, why have you taken up with a foreign religion? Whose is the rice you eat? Who rules the country you live in? If you want to worship the Portuguese king,* why don't you go to Portugal? As for the rest of you Christians, go home, and do not dare to follow your religion; worhip as we do, or your death will be the penalty." "Christians!" exclaimed Father Dat in a loud voice. "Beware what you say! We must obey our ruler when his orders are just; but we must honour and obey God first." Then an image of our Lady of Sorrows was shown to him: "Who," he was asked, "is this woman with a dead man in her arms and swords in her heart?" "The woman you are looking at is the mother of the Saviour of the world," he replied.

The governor allowed Father Dat to sit down in the open, while the faithful crowded round for his blessing. Then he was given a meal, which he ate with good appetite. He walked to the place of execution (chewing *betel* leaves, we are told) through a storm of rain. A man in the crowd shouted, "Christians must die! They teach children to for-

* It is very significant that Jesus Christ should be referred to in this way.

sake their parents." Father Dat turned to him: "You are wrong," he said. "Our religion teaches children to have the greatest respect for their parents." Time was given him to compose himself; but even as he sat in prayer, hands folded, head bent, eyes shut, a soldier interrupted him to ask what the gall of the raven fish was good for. Father Dat raised his head: "Taken in wine, it cures colic," he said.

Huyen-Trang writes: "While Father John prayed, we stepped back three paces to salute the chief mandarin, who was there on his elephant, holding the signal flag in his hand. I watched for that flag to drop, and then turned to look at God's servant: his head was already severed; blood spurted out; his body had fallen backwards, hands still folded on his breast."

The mandarin shouted, "Christians, you can have the body and bury it." and rode quickly away. The faithful ran to soak cloths in the martyr's blood. It was about midday on Sunday, 28 October 1798, at a place called Trinh-ha. John Dat was thirty-four years old.

It seems not inappropriate to add here an English version of an account of a countrywoman and contemporary of Father Dat: one of those numberless anonymous patient sufferers of whom the history of humankind is so full. It was written in 1777 by a Dominican missionary at Fugan to the vicar apostolic of Fukien in China.

The woman in question was twenty-four years old, daughter of a heathen father and a Christian mother. Against her will, her father gave her in marriage to the only son of a widow, who had renounced Christianity years before. The wedding took place early in 1775, and it was the beginning of all her sufferings. As soon as she was taken, or rather, dragged to her husband's house, she was involved in the various superstitious observances associated with heathen wedding-rites; but she firmly refused to have anything to do with them whether privately or in public.

During the eighteen months that followed, her husband, and especially her mother-in-law, persecuted her with inconceivable malice and fury. Angered by her first refusal, they tried to force her at all costs to forswear her religion, to eat meat on fast-days, and to join in heathen worship, enforcing their pressure with blows and vile abuse. They took away everything associated with her faith, including her rosary; but that did not prevent her from praying, and using her ten fingers instead of beads. Sometimes they turned her from the house, and left her outside all night, in any weather; or else she was shut up in the kitchen, with only a bench to sleep on. Their cruelty went so far as to take away her clothes in the depths of winter and to refuse her enough food, so that she got weaker and weaker.

The end came in October 1776. She had been locked out for the night. In the morning her husband went to find her, knocked her about, and she died as the result. She was a quiet and gentle creature, and her husband's sole complaint about her was her religion. She bore her long and bitter martyrdom with the unshakable patience of a real Christian. All her neighbours testify to the truth of what I have written.

BD JOSEPH MARCHAND, BD JOHN CORNAY and BD PETER DUMOULIN BORIE

IN INDO-CHINA, A.D. 1835, 1837, 1838

There wa— a very violent renewal of persecution in Indo-China from 1820, when —he Annamite ruler Minh-Mang sought to stamp out the "foreign" r—igion; the storm abated considerably with Minh-Mang's death in 18—1, but rose again fiercely under Yu-Duk less than ten years later. Of the many hundreds of Indo-Chinese martyrs during the nineteen—th century, representatives of clergy and laity, native Indo-Chine— and foreign apostles, have been beatified at various times since 1900. The following three, who suffered under Minh-Mang, wer— all members of the Paris Society of Foreign Missions.

Joseph Marchand was born in France in 1803 and went to Indo-China immediately after his ordination to the priesthood in 1829. He served in various missions there, till in 1833 he was forced by persecution to take refuge in lower Cochin-China, where he was seized by rebels against Minh-Mang and kept a prisoner in the fort at Saigon. The rebels tried in vain to get him to encourage Christians to join their revolt. Nevertheless, when Minh-Mang's forces captured the fort in September 1835 Father Marchand was looked on as having added the crime of rebellion to his forbidden Christianity, and he suffered more than the usual unspeakable barbarities in consequence. No torment would induce him to admit guilt or to trample on the crucifix.

At Tho-duk, near Hue, on November 30, Father Marchand was brought out from his cage, bound, spreadeagled on a stretcher, practically naked. Five times his legs and thighs were torn with a pair of white-hot tongs. He cried out; and was asked why Christians tear the eyes from dying people. Five more applications of the tongs. "Why do people who are going to marry come before a priest at the altar?" Again five agonizing burns. "Why do Christians do such abominable things at their feasts? What is this magic bread they eat after going to confession?" Father Marchand was now incapable of answering even if he would. But the ritual required that he should take food, and he was asked what he would like to eat. He rallied and replied, "Thank you, I am not hungry now." A large pebble was forced into his mouth, and held there by a bamboo gag.

Then, replaced on the stretcher, he was carried at a run to the place of execution. His wounds were counted and recorded as correct. While one man pulled the skin of his eyebrows over his eyes, others with tongs tore two strips of flesh from his stomach, from his back, from his legs. But there was no need to do more: Joseph Marchand was dead.

In his twenty-fifth year John Charles Cornay, a native of Loudun, near Poitiers, was ordained priest in Tonking. He suffered so much from eye-strain and headaches that he wrote home, "I have to lead the life more of a contemplative hermit than of an active missionary," but in 1837 he was sent to minister in a partly Christian village. Here he was "framed," through the wiles of a brigand who had been driven out of the village: weapons were planted in the priest's food-plot, he was denounced for inciting to rebellion, and the weapons were found.

Father Cornay was kept in confinement for over three months, first in a big heavy wooden collar, called a *cang*, often without food and exposed to the direct rays of the fierce sun; then in a bamboo cage, too small for him to lie down properly. In an effort to make him confess to the sham plot and to implicate others, he was mercilessly beaten, and had to see some of his faithful Christians being tormented be-

fore his eyes. But Father Cornay bore his own miseries so
cheerfully that people, even his persecutors, would gather
round to hear him sing (he had a fine voice); once, when
asked if he was not afraid to die, he replied by singing a
verse of a hymn welcoming martyrdom.

At length he was sentenced to death by being cut to
pieces, because he was "a leader of a false religion, concealed in this country to stir up revolt." He wrote a last
letter to his parents, "from my cage": ". . . I weep when I
think of your grief; but the thought that by the time you get
this letter I shall be able to pray for you in Heaven comforts me, both for you and for myself. . . . I shall not be
tortured like Father Marchand, supposing they cut off my
limbs and head all at once. I [words illegible] not much to
suffer. So be comforted: soon it will all be over, and I shall
be waiting for you in Heaven."

The passion of John Charles Cornay took place on September 20, an ember-day, and here again, as with Bd
Gomidas Keumurgian, there is a reminiscence of St Fructuosus: for as he would not break the appointed fast, so
Father Cornay would not. Surrounded by a large crowd and
many guards, he walked firmly to execution, singing aloud as
he went. When writing to his father and mother he had not
understood the precise implications of his sentence (or perhaps had deliberately softened them out of consideration
for his parents): for "cut to pieces" meant that his limbs
would be hacked off *joint by joint,* and only then would he
be beheaded by the sword. But the presiding officer, apparently out of respect for a courageous man, ordered that
he be beheaded first, and the mutilation carried out afterwards. And so it was done.

Father Peter Dumoulin Borie suffered a year later. He was
the son of a miller near Beynat, in Corrèze, and had been a
missionary in Indo-China for six years, so enthusiastic and
enterprising that he had sometimes to be restrained. In this
time of persecution, when it was necessary for Christian

priests to efface themselves and often minister in secret, Father Borie was at a serious disadvantage in being "five or six inches taller than anyone else in the neighbourhood. . . . I am too long and they will shorten me," as he wrote in a letter to his sister that gives a vivid impression of the conditions in which he worked.

Father Borie was eventually captured through a member of his flock who, under stress of torture, betrayed the priest's hiding-place in a sand-dune. Stretched out on the ground, he was savagely beaten with bamboo sticks, and salt rubbed into the wounds, to make him give an account of his movements and disclose those who had sheltered him. But nothing could break his tough spirit. When asked if he would still keep silence when he was flogged, he replied, "We will wait and see. I don't like to flatter myself in advance"; and he coolly remarked to the official that, "In Europe we don't beat people to make them speak. That sort of treatment is for brute beasts that obey only from fear." With his back laid open in weals, the official taunted him with the question "Does it hurt?" and got the answer, "I'm made of skin and bone like other men: of course it hurts. But I was happy before, and I am happy now." Efforts to make such a man trample on the crucifix inevitably failed.

Father Borie wrote from prison to another missionary: "We must not hope to see one another again in this world. The tiger does not let his victim go, and I tell you plainly that I should be sorry to miss this good opportunity. . . . I am ready to appear before God's judgement-seat, trusting in the merits of our divine Redeemer and strengthened by the prayers of the good associates of the Society for the Propagation of the Faith. . . . I have no books here, and not even a rosary—only a bit of knotted string." The official in charge expressed his regret that Father Borie had to die. "I have not prostrated before anyone since I was a child," was the reply, "but to show how grateful I am for the privilege of dying thus, let me prostrate before the man who has brought it about"; he tried to suit the action to the word, but the officer would not allow it and burst into tears.

The execution took place at sundown, near Dong-hoi, on 24 November 1838. The headsman was drunk. The first stroke of his sword caught the martyr on the jaw-bone, the second on the nape of the neck, the third higher up: it took four more blows to sever the head, and even then not completely. . . . * With Father Borie there suffered, by strangulation, two Annamite priests, Vincent Diem and Peter Koa; they too have been beatified.

BD JOHN PERBOYRE

IN CHINA, A.D. 1840

Among the numerous martyrs in China during the nineteenth century one of the most outstanding was John Gabriel Perboyre: he was, indeed, the first martyr in that country to be beatified, in 1889. He was born into a farming family in France in 1802, and became a priest in St Vincent de Paul's Congregation of the Mission. When he was thirty-three he was sent to the Far East, for which, fired by the example of his brother, he had volunteered. Father Perboyre was quick in acquiring the Chinese language, and was in all respects, as his colleagues told him, "not a bad Chinaman." To his long pigtail and moustache, his tireless labours in all weathers soon added a tanned skin and prematurely grey beard. He worked in the provinces of Honan and Hupeh for something over four years, especially among children abandoned by their parents. Then, in the autumn of 1839, there was a sudden renewal of persecution.

* The official in charge was still repentant for what he had done: he now sentenced the executioner to forty stripes for being drunk on duty.

The missionaries at Chaokow in Hupeh, Father Perboyre among them, were warned to go into hiding, and he found a place of refuge in a large wood. But a traitor was soon found, a recent convert, who sold knowledge of his hiding-place for money; Father Perboyre was captured and was dragged from one foul place of confinement to another. He was questioned about his movements and those of his colleagues, beaten when he would say nothing, and sent from one official to another, till he was handed over to the authorities at Wuchangfu, opposite Hankow on the Yangtse river. Shortly before his death he wrote, in a letter of remarkable detachment and understatement:

The conditions of time and place do not allow me to go into lengthy details of my circumstances. You will learn them in abundance from other sources. I was arrested at Kucheng and was treated kindly enough all the time I was there, though I had to undergo questioning twice. At Siangyangfu I was questioned four times, and during one of these examinations I had to spend half a day hanging from a beam with my knees resting on the links of an iron chain. At Wuchangfu I was subjected to over twenty interrogatories, and was put to torture nearly every time. This was because I would not tell the mandarins what they wanted to know: had I spoken, persecution would certainly have been let loose throughout the whole empire. But my sufferings at Siangyangfu were directly on account of religion. At Wuchangfu I was given a hundred and ten strokes with a bamboo stick because I would not trample a cross underfoot. You will hear other details later on. Of the score or so other Christians who were captured and charged with me, two thirds have apostatized publicly.

"You will hear other details later on." Everybody knows that there are, among the inhabitants of the Far East, some people whose ingenuity in the devising of ways to inflict appalling physical agony is more properly called diabolical than brutal. These refinements of torment were exercised on Father Perboyre, so often and so effectively that a Chinese priest who saw him declared that his whole body was a mass of festering wounds, and that in places the bones themselves were laid bare.

A year elapsed between Father Perboyre's arrest and his execution for having brought a foreign religion into China. On 11 September 1840 he was led out to die, dressed in the red gown of a condemned criminal, barefooted, and with a brand on his face meaning "the teacher of a false religion." He was to be strangled, but in no simple fashion. His body was bound to a pillory, with the feet drawn back and fastened at the height of the buttocks. A cord was twisted round the neck and drawn tight, till the martyr nearly lost consciousness; then the pressure was relaxed till he came to. This torture was repeated twice, and only at the third time was he allowed to die.

Friends were able to obtain Father Perboyre's body, and twenty years later it was conveyed to the mother-house of the Vincentians (Lazarists) in Paris. There it lies beside that of another Vincentian marytr, Francis Regis Clet; he had been a missionary in China for nearly thirty years when, at the age of seventy-two, he was martyred in the same way as Father Perboyre and in the same place. This was on 17 February 1820, twenty years before, but Bd Francis Regis Clet was not beatified until eleven years after Bd John Gabriel Perboyre.

ST PETER CHANEL

ON FUTUNA, A.D. 1841

In 1836 the Holy See approved the religious congregation newly founded by the Venerable John Claud Colin, called the Society of Mary, and at the same time entrusted to it the great missionary area of Western Oceania. Soon afterwards, the first seven Marists were dispatched to this mission; among them, as superior, was Father Peter Louis Mary Chanel, destined to be the protomartyr of the South Seas and of the Society of Mary, which at that time numbered but a score of members. He had been born in France, son of a farmer, in 1803 and had ministered in parishes for four years before joining the Marists at the age of twenty-eight. Father Chanel was an outstanding example of the numerous priests, many of them now unknown or forgotten, who carried the Gospel to the heathen in remote places and were killed by those whom they had come to serve. He was canonized in 1954.

At the end of 1837 the vicar apostolic of Western Oceania, Bishop Pompallier, appointed Father Chanel to establish himself, with a lay-brother, on the island of Futuna in the New Hebrides, west of the Fijis. The people of the island, polytheistic animists by religion, were of a good Melanesian type, but had become so reduced in number, to barely 1000, that their ruler had forbidden the eating of human flesh. This man, Niuliki, was at first well-disposed towards the missionaries, and Father Chanel quietly set himself to learn the local language, with the help of an Englishman, Thomas Boog, whom he had met on the voyage out. In the meantime, he celebrated Mass in public on suitable occasions and with as much solemnity as was practicable, thereby making some impression on the people.

As well as inevitable difficulties with the language, food, and living conditions generally, Father Chanel suffered a good deal from bad health, and to these difficulties there was soon added worry about the attitude of Niuliki. Chanel had written: "This 'Prince' of ours maintains his authority by supporting idolatry and representing his god as the most powerful and to be feared. It will cost him a lot to tell his people that it is all nothing more than deception." But by the end of 1839 it was clear that he had no intention whatever of becoming a Christian. There had always been a party suspicious of the missionary and, led by Niuliki's adviser, Musumusu, it got the upper hand. Pressure was put on catechumens, to make the sign of the cross was decreed a crime, and it was forbidden to supply food to the missionaries, so that Father Chanel and Brother Nizier were in grave danger of starving to death.

During a long visit from two missionaries from New Zealand, on their way to Wallis Island, things looked rather brighter on Futuna; but they soon slipped back, and the crisis was reached in April 1841, when Father Chanel was able to baptize Niuliki's son, Meitala, and several other young men. The angry ruler failed to make Meitala repudiate his action, and the leading men advised that the missionary should be got rid of. On April 26 Father Chanel sent Brother Nizier and Mr Boog to look after a sick man at the other end of the island. This opportunity was not allowed to slip, and early in the morning of the 28th a messenger was sent to the priest to keep him engaged by a request for medicine. Meanwhile Musumusu and a gang drove the catechumens from their hut and set fire to it.

They then rushed to Father Chanel's hut, threw him to one side, and began to pillage it. Blows were aimed at him with clubs, one breaking his arm, another cutting open his head. Some catechumens tried to help him as he lay on the ground, while his assailants frantically looted what little they could find, taking no notice of Musumusu's bidding that they should finish the work of killing they had begun. So he did it himself, cleaving the martyr's head with an axe. Father

Chanel had said nothing but two words, in the island tongue: *Malie fuia,* "It is well with me."

The Futuna mission was abandoned for over a year; then missionaries came back at the request of the inhabitants; and within another year every one of them was a Christian, not excluding those who had murderously attacked St Peter Chanel. One of his catechumens said of him, when called on to justify his own conversion, "He loves us. He does what he teaches. He forgives his enemies. His teaching is true."

THE MARTYRS OF DAMASCUS

A.D. 1860

The mountains of Lebanon are chiefly populated by the Catholic Maronites and, less numerously, by the Druses, who by religion form an heretical sect of Islam. At the time with which we are concerned, Lebanon was part of the Turkish empire, but enjoyed a semi-independent status. In the early summer of 1860, in circumstances that need not here be gone into, a hideous massacre of Christians by their non-Christian neighbours began and went on for several weeks. It spread rapidly through Anti-Lebanon, and on July 9 reached Damascus. In this city the carnage would have been even more dreadful than it was had it not been for the noble Algerian patriot Abd al-Kader, who was living in exile there; himself, of course, a Mohammedan, he gave shelter to thousands of Christians and succeeded in thwarting more than one plot against them. Eleven victims of these massacres, eight European Franciscans and three Maronite laymen, were beatified as martyrs in 1926.

Most of the Catholics of Damascus were of Eastern rites; those of the Latin rite formed a parish in charge of the Franciscan Friars Minor, whose church and friary of St Paul was (and so in "the street that is called Straight" (Acts 9:11), within the eastern wall of the city. A number of Christians took refuge there, and when the mob reached that quarter the father guardian, Emmanuel Ruiz, brought them all together into the church. There he addressed them, not disguising their danger, and encouraged them to stand firm in the faith of Christ. Then the Blessed Sacrament was exposed, and together they all said the litany of the Saints; and afterwards they received absolution and holy communion. Hours went by, and it was not till after midnight that the mob tried to force an entrance; the building was a strong one and probably would have held out, but with the help of a traitor a way in was found through a back-door that had been forgotten and not barred. Even as it was, most of the refugees escaped with their lives; but not so the friars.

When the mob suddenly broke in, Father Emmanuel hurried to the church and consumed the Blessed Sacrament in the tabernacle. There he was found, and he asked and received a few minutes' grace. He knelt in prayer at the altar steps, amid shouts of "Testify! Testify!"* He rose to his feet and faced his threateners: "No!" he said. "I am a Christian and a Christian I will die." Then he went up the steps—Was he murmuring "Introibo ad altare Dei"?—and laid his head on the altar, uttering a single word, "Strike!" A blow from an axe caught him on the neck, and blood spurted over the altar and the gospel-book that lay thereon. Further blows showered on him, and he fell dead. Several men ran to the bells and pulled the ropes, yelling, "Come on! Mass has begun, the priest is waiting!"

Meantime, Father Nicanor Ascanio had been seized and ordered to testify. He did not understand Arabic very well

---

* That is to affirm that "there is no god but God, and Mohammed is the prophet of God"—the Islamic profession of faith.

and asked for the words to be repeated. He promptly refused, and was killed on the spot. Father Peter Soler was found in the parochial school next door. Two boys who were hiding there afterwards related what happened. Father Peter was asked, "Where is your money?" He replied quietly that he had none. "You are a Christian. If you want to go on living, renounce your infidelity." He answered firmly, choosing his words carefully, for his Arabic was poor, "I will not do this wicked thing. I am a Christian, and I will die a Christian." He was stabbed to death.

A layman who eventually escaped has left an account of the death of Father Carmel Volta, a man of patriarchal aspect who had endeared himself to all Damascus. "When the murderers broke in, Father Carmel and I took refuge in hiding-places near to one another. About two hours after midnight a Turk stumbled upon Father Carmel. 'Are you still alive?' exclaimed the man, and hit him violently on the head with a club. He then went away, and I came over to help Father Carmel. He told me to look after myself, and asked me to pray for him; his last words to me were, 'I am dying.' An hour later two other infidels found him; they were old friends of his and they offered to get him away and shelter him: 'But first,' they said, 'you must agree to testify.' 'Never will I do such a thing,' answered Father Carmel. 'Jesus Christ told us not to be afraid of those who can kill the body, but to fear Him who can chastise unfaithfulness with everlasting punishment.' Blinded by their fanaticism to all memory of kindness and friendship, the two men fell on Father Carmel with their clubs and killed him."

Two of these Franciscans were lay-brothers, Francis Pinzano and John Fernandez. They fled for refuge together to the top of the belfry of the church; but they were caught sight of, pursued and thrown from the window to the ground. Brother Francis died at once from the fall; but Brother John lingered in agony for the rest of the night, till he was found by a soldier in the early morning, who put an end to his life with a sword. Father Nicholas Alberca survived till the friary buildings were set on fire. Then, coming out into a passage, he was captured and, refusing to apostatize, shot. As he fell he was heard to say, "I will not betray my Redeemer."

All these martyrs were Spanish by nationality; the eighth, Father Engelbert Kolland, was an Austrian. With the exception of Father Nicholas, he was the youngest of them, thirty-three, and a man of both lively disposition and notable attainments, especially in languages. He was known among the people as *Abuna Maluk*, "Father Angel." Father Engelbert with several lay people was given shelter in an adjoining house, where a woman's large veil was thrown over him to conceal his habit. But the house was raided, and the friar was betrayed by his sandals, protruding from beneath the veil. A rifle was pointed at his breast, but he turned it gently aside, saying, "Friend, what harm have I done you that you should seek to kill me?"—"No harm at all, but you are a Christian." He was taken to the courtyard of the house, and knocked down with a ferocious blow: "Testify! acknowledge Mohammed!"—"Never!" was all the reply his assailants could get, and they hit him till he was dead.

The three beatified laymen, Maronites from Lebanon, who suffered at the same time and place, were brothers, Francis, Abdul-Muti and Raphael Masabki. The first was an old man, of some distinction in Damascus, and he lived with Abdul-Muti, who was also a retired merchant. All three were closely associated with the Franciscans in life as well as in martyrdom.

THE MARTYRS OF
UGANDA

AT NAMUGONGO, A.D. 1886

It was in 1878, ten years after its foundation by Cardinal Lavigerie, that the Society of Missionaries of Africa ("White Fathers") was entrusted with the evangelization of a large territory around Lake Victoria and Lake Tanganyika; and eight years later came the passion of the Uganda martyrs, far-off successors of those early African martyrs who had prompted Tertullian's famous saying that "the blood of martyrs is the seed of Christians." At that time the ruler of Uganda was the weak and debauched Mwanga, whom the British government eventually deported to the Seychelles. That he gave himself to sodomy was a principal factor in his becoming a persecutor, and some of his victims were martyrs of chastity no less than of the Christian faith. Twenty-two of them were beatified in 1920; of these, thirteen were burnt at Namugongo, and there suffered with them about eleven Protestants, as well as several non-Christians who appear to have been accused of being Christians.

The Christian community around Munyonyo numbered some two hundred souls, whose foremost member was Joseph Mukasa. He was only twenty-five years old, but an important man at King Mwanga's "court," being a sort of chief steward, and as such responsible for numerous royal "pages." These he watched over with a father's care, and time and again thwarted the king's designs against individuals among them. In October 1885 an Anglican missionary, Bishop James Hannington, with his escort was set upon and murdered by Mwanga's orders, and for this crime Joseph Mukasa rebuked his royal master; and shortly afterwards he rebuked him again, gently enough, for the general debauchery of his life. Mwanga, worked on by those who were jealous of Mukasa, began to regard him with a less favourable eye, and a few days later found a pretext for getting rid of him. Without any sort of trial, Mukasa was ordered to be burnt alive.

When it was attempted to bind his hands, Mukasa would have none of it: "I am going to die for my religion," he said. "Is it likely that I should resist? A Christian who gives his life for God is not afraid to die. Mwanga has condemned me without cause; but tell him I forgive him with all my heart. And tell him, too, that I advise him to repent of his wickedness, or else he will have to answer for my life before God's judgement-seat." Then he led the way to the place of execution, where the executioner, moved by respect, beheaded him before casting his body to the flames.

This happened on 15 November 1885, but it was not till six months later that persecution began in earnest, when Protestants as well as Catholics gladly gave their lives for Christ's sake. Meanwhile Mwanga became more and more enraged against Christians (two pages, a catechumen and a neophyte, were put to death for trifling misdemeanours), and the missionaries and their flock met together for instruction and worship in circumstances reminiscent of the Roman catacombs.

The storm broke in the evening of 25 May, when Mwanga sent for a fourteen-year-old page named Mwafu, and asked what he had been doing. "Denis Sebuggwawo has been teaching me religion," was the reply. Denis, an older page, agreed this was so, and the king rounded on him in a fury: "Wretched slave! You were doing what I have forbidden, and you dared to teach these things to my vassal's son!" Picking up a short spear, he struck Denis to the ground with it, and told a bystander to take him out and finish him off. He was killed with a butcher's knife (or, according to another account, was stabbed to death the next morning). That night the king gave orders for the death of every Christian in the royal enclosure, Catholic or not; precautions were taken to prevent their escape, and executioners were summoned. And while all this was going on Charles Lwanga, a young man who was master of the pages, baptized five of them, among them the thirteen-year-old Kizito, whom Lwanga had often saved from the king's vicious clutches. The neophytes kept a night-long vigil.

The next morning Charles Lwanga was told to muster the pages before the king. Mwanga looked at them, and said, "Those of you who do not pray, stand by me. Those who pray [*i.e.*, who are Christians], go over there." Charles Lwanga took the boy Kizito's hand, and together they led the way; others followed. They were nineteen in all,* and not one was much more than twenty years old. Mwanga turned to them: "Is it true that you are Christians?"

"Yes, master, we are."

"Do you mean to remain Christians?"

"Yes, master. If you want to pardon us you will do so of your own accord."

"Then you shall all be burnt! Away with you, and eat your cow in your Father's house in Heaven!"†

The chief executioner, who with his assistants had to bind the prisoners together, was the father of one of them, Mbaga. He quietly implored the boy to slip away home and hide, but Mbaga would not. At length the procession set out for Namugongo, the appointed place of execution. The superior of the White Fathers' mission, Father Lourdel, was present; he has left a description of the scene.

The heroic little band passed a few feet away from where I was standing. The young men were bound together in one group and the boys in another. They were tied so tightly to one another that it was difficult for them to walk. I saw little Kizito laughing as merrily at this as if it were a game. . . . As they passed me they looked their last farewell. I was so overcome that I had to lean against the palisade for support, while I prayed to the King of martyrs to give them strength

* Including two Protestants, who were afterwards set free, as were three others. Three more were released at the last moment at Namugongo, and one of them lived to be present at the beatification of his fellows in Rome in 1920.

† A sarcastic reference to local feasting on great occasions.

and asked the prayers of the Queen of sorrows, whose courage had held her erect at the foot of the cross. . . . I was not allowed even to say a word of encouragement to them, and I had to rest content with seeing the determination, the happiness, the manly courage depicted on their faces; and in the midst of my grief I thanked God that he had chosen these Negro children to bear the first witness by blood to the faith in Uganda.

Father Lourdel also tells of a young fighting-man, James Buzabaliawo, who was brought before the king at this time. Mwanga asked him if he were chief of the Kigowa Christians.

"I am a Christian, yes," said James, "but the title of chief does not belong to me."

"This young man gives himself airs. Anyone would think he was that conceited chief Kabunga."

James bowed low. "Thank you for bestowing so high an office on me," he said.

"And you are the man who dared to want me to join his religion," retorted Mwanga. "Take him away and kill him— I'll make a start with him."

"Goodbye, then I am going to Heaven, and I will pray to God for you.'

Amid the laughter that greeted this, a voice echoed down the centuries as someone was heard to say, "These Christians must be mad to talk like that."

"James passed close to where I stood, with a rope round his neck, led by the executioner," wrote Father Lourdel. "I raised my hand in absolution, and he responded by lifting his bound hands, pointing upwards to show me whither he was going and where he hoped we should meet again. He looked at me with smiling face, as if to say, 'Why are you sad? This is nothing to the joys you have taught us to look forward to.' " James Buzabaliawo was put with the others.

Father Lourdel made another attempt to soften Mwanga's heart; but all he could get was the contemptuous concession, "I won't kill all of them." But that same day saw the death

of Andrew Kaggwa, chief of Kigowa, who had converted two
of the sons of the chief counsellor (*katikiro*). Mwanga in fact
wanted to spare him, but seems to have been forced by fear to
leave the matter in the *katikiro's* hands. This man ordered
Kaggwa's immediate execution, adding, "I shall not eat till
you bring me his severed arm." When the executioners hesi-
tated, knowing the king's friendship for Kaggwa, their victim
hurried them on: "Didn't you hear your master say he was
hungry? Don't keep him waiting for his food—kill me!"

An eye-witness afterwards reported: "I saw Andrew
Kaggwa come out. He moved briskly and his face was happy;
there were eight executioners round him. They went behind
a palisade, and I stood waiting. In a few minutes an executioner came back; he was carrying Kaggwa's blood-stained
arm by a rope. He took it to the *katikiro*."

The oldest of these martyrs was Matthias Kalemba, a
middle-aged man who was a district judge at Mitiyana. When
he was brought before the *katikiro* the following dialogue
ensued.

THE KATIKIRO: "You are Kalemba the judge. Why has a
man of your position and age taken up with the white man's
religion?"

KALEMBA: "Because I chose to do so."

THE KATIKIRO: "Who cooks your meals now you have sent
your wives away?"

KALEMBA: "That is my business. Why have I been brought
here? Is it because I look thin and hungry, or because of my
religion?"

THE KATIKIRO: "Do you dare to ask me questions? Executioner, take him away and kill him."

KALEMBA: "Thank you; that is just what I want."

THE KATIKIRO: "Cut off his hands and feet. Tear bits off his
flesh and roast them before his eyes. No doubt his god will
rescue him."

KALEMBA: "Yes, God will rescue me. But you will not see

how he does it, because he will take my soul and leave you only my body."

With another martyr, Matthias Kalemba was hurried away to join the others at Namugongo. But on the way he asked to be put to death on the spot, refusing to go any further when he could quite well be buried there. The guards took him at his word, dismembering and butchering him in most appalling fashion, and leaving him lying in the bush. Three days later he was still not dead, for a passer-by heard him moaning for water: when the man drew near and saw that mutilated mass of human flesh, he ran away in a panic.

Meanwhile, the main body of the martyrs were on their agonizing way to Namugongo (three of them were slain on the road), a distance of over sixteen miles from Munyonyo. They stayed one night at Mengo, where they were confined in stocks and chains, so that the next day they could hardly walk; at Namugongo they were kept in somewhat similar fashion in various enclosures for seven whole days and nights. The day of their passion was the feast of the Ascension, 3 June 1886.

They were put to death by fire. While barbarously bedizened figures danced round singing "Today their mothers will weep,' the martyrs were brought out, and they greeted one another with such cheerfulness that it was remarked that they looked as if they were at a wedding, but, the speaker added, "We will give them something to laugh about!" Each one lay down on a reed mat, which was wrapped round him and bound fast. The chief executioner made a last effort to induce his son, Mbaga, to apostatize, but it was useless, and the father ordered that he should be killed quickly by a blow on the neck; but Charles Lwanga was put aside to be burned piecemeal by slow fire. A familiar taunt was heard: "Now we shall see whether the God you trust will deliver you." And from one of the sacrificial bundles there came the reply: "You can burn our bodies, but you cannot harm our souls!"

The martyrs were laid side by side on the great pyre of fuel. Fire was set to it at many places at once, and it roared into life. The executioners broke into ritual chants; but above them and above the noise of the flames could be heard the voices of the burnt-offerings, calling on the name of Jesus.

MARTYRS UNDER THE BOXERS

IN CHINA, A.D. 1900

The massacres of foreigners perpetrated in China in 1900, at the instigation of the secret society called in English "Boxers," were directed also against Christians as such, large numbers of whom perished, including very many Catholics. That the insurgents were actuated by hatred of Christianity, and not solely by hatred of foreign aggression, is shown, for example, by a proclamation of the dowager empress, Tzu-hsi: it called on Chinese Christians to repudiate their religion and so to gain immunity. "It is their religion we hate," said the governor of Shansi, Yu-hsien. The first group of martyrs in the Boxer rising to be beatified, in 1946, was made up of three bishops, four priests and a laybrother, all European Franciscan friars minor; seven nuns, Franciscan Missionaries of Mary, the protomartyrs of that congregation; five young Chinese church students; and nine Chinese laymen. All except three were massacred at Taiyuanfu on 9 July 1900.

This martyrdom was indeed literally a massacre—there were no interrogations, no imprisonment, no trial. Taiyuanfu was a Catholic centre, and when news of events reached there, a Christian mandarin wanted to organize resistance. The vicar apostolic, Bishop Gregory Grassi, who was sixty-seven years old, forbade it; but he closed the seminary and told the students to go home all save five succeeded in doing so. The nuns were recommended to put on Chinese clothes, to help their chances of escape, but they were more interested in trying to provide for the safety of their orphans and preparing themselves for martyrdom. Their superioress, Mother Hermina Grivot, was a Burgundian, of strong courage and power of leadership. The others were of various nationalities, and they all were in the prime of life.

An order came from the governor of Shansi, Yu-hsien, forbidding Christians to meet for prayer. Bishop Grassi rejected the order; and on July 5 he, with his coadjutor, Bishop Francis Fogolla, and the other clergy, together with the nuns, were carried off to a large building by Yu-hsien's house, where the five students already were. The name of this building was the Inn of Heavenly Peace. One student, John Chang of Taekuo, was playing a game so cheerfully in the courtyard that a friar quietly rebuked him. "What's the odds, Father?" was the reply. "If we die, to Heaven we go." In a separate part of the building were confined a number of Protestant Christians, including at least four American children and a doctor who was a great friend of the friars.

In the afternoon of July 9, Boxer soldiers slaughtered every one of these Protestants. At once Bishop Grassi called his flock together and gave them absolution. Then soldiers broke in, Yu-hsien himself at their head. First he took the bishops aside, and demanded why they had come to China and done so much harm. "We have done harm to no one, and good to many," replied Bishop Fogolla. "You lie!" retorted Yu-hsien and, shouting "Kill them all!", he struck him to the ground. First the clergy were hacked to pieces, and then the Chinese laymen, humble men on the staff of the mission, who could have walked away free at the price of a word. One of them had said to his wife the evening before, "Don't expect me back tomorrow"; an attempt was made to save another, who had been a soldier, by saying he was not a Christian: "I *am* a Christian," he declared, and died. There was a moment of unwillingness to kill the Chinese students, but they pressed forward and their heads were severed.

The nuns were left till later. They were led forward, singing the *Te Deum*; their hands were bound behind their backs, and they were then hoisted by ropes round their wrists to hooks on a beam, so that their heads hung forward. In this position they were stabbed in the throat, and they bled to death. The first to die was Mother Clare Nanetti; the last words heard to pass her lips were her motto: *Sempre avanti!*, "Always forward!"

The remaining three martyrs beatified in 1946 were Bishop Anthony Fantosati and two other Italian Franciscans; they were killed at Hengchowfu in Honan four days before those mentioned above.

MICHAEL PRO

IN MEXICO CITY, A.D. 1927

Michael Augustine Pro-Juárez was born in 1891 at Concepción del Oro in the Mexican state of Zacatecas and was partly of Indian descent; his father was a wealthy mining director. In due course young Michael entered the noviceship of the Society of Jesus at El Llano in Michoacán, but his years of training were not destined to be passed in quietness. The revolutionary ferment that had begun in Mexico in 1911 was rising to a climax, and in October 1914 a group of Jesuits that included Michael Pro crossed their country's border into California. For the next eleven years he pursued his studies and training in Spain, in Nicaragua, in Spain again, and finally at Enghien in Belgium, where in 1925 he was ordained priest. The effect of his contacts at this time with the Young Christian Workers movement was to be-

come apparent in his work that followed; a less happy factor was a serious breakdown in health.

Religious persecution in Mexico had reached a high pitch after the coming to the presidency of P. E. Calles in 1924. All foreign clergy had been expelled, religious orders were outlawed, and there was a shortage of clergy. His superiors recalled Father Pro to Mexico.

During the first week of May 1926 seventeen priests were put to death in Mexico City; six gentlewomen were publicly hanged at Colima; women and girls were flogged and tortured for helping priests and demonstrating; in July, a stone-deaf old man, priest at Purificación in Guadalajara, was shot. In the midst of such happenings, Father Michael Pro arrived in his native land on July 7, and joined his family in Mexico City. Rather than submit the Church to state administration and control, the Mexican bishops had issued an interdict: all churches were to be left open, but assemblies therein for *public* worship and ministrations were forbidden; Mass, baptisms, confessions, weddings, reservation of the Blessed Sacrament, all had to be in private. The care of church buildings was entrusted to the laity, and the faithful were forbidden to resort to violence. It was the life of the catacombs over again; and Father Pro flung himself into it. One of his first activities was to organize "what I call 'eucharistic stations.' I have assigned to the faithful various places where I give holy communion every day, with extra places for the first Friday of the month. Last Friday I gave communion to twelve hundred people." One day when this was taking place the police beat on the door. Father Pro dispersed the people over the large house, hid the Blessed Sacrament about his person, lit a cigarette in an enormously long holder (he was dressed in a shabby light grey suit),* and went to meet the visitors. "Public worship is going on here," said the police-inspector.

* There exists a snapshot of Father Pro in those days: he wears a lounge suit and a straw hat, one hand elegantly in his pocket, the other holding a cigarette in a long holder. It was taken outside President Calles' house, and "his attitude is one of complete and unconcerned ease."

PRO: "Oh no, it is not."

THE INSPECTOR: "Yes, it is."

PRO: "Someone has pulled your leg this time."

THE INSPECTOR: "What do you mean? We saw the priest come in. In any case we have orders to search this house. Come with me!"

PRO: "What next! Come with you? What right have you to make me?—show me your warrant. You can go all over the house if you like, and if you find public worship going on, tell me, so that I can come to Mass."

The police had to go away disappointed, but this was only one of many close shaves, some of which, as it has been put, had "quite an Edgar Wallace atmosphere" about them. Father Pro laboured in the prisons, among the poor, and especially for men and boys, from professional men and students to taxi-drivers; "I am at home with all of them," he wrote, "whatever their class or occupation. I am only sorry I can't give them all the time I should like." "Pious ladies adore me," he added mischievously, "drunks call me 'mate,' pedlars wink at me, to the flower and cream rascals I am a pal." A League of Young Christians was organized, in which Father Pro had the training of the leaders and speakers; they were a most devoted band, and one of its leaders was executed with his teacher. A colleague writes: "I cannot tell you how energetically Father Pro 'multiplied himself' for the welfare of others. Orders were often given for his arrest, but he always succeeded in escaping, and he did so without any slowing-down of his activities. . . . I could see for myself the great danger he was running; but he wanted only one thing for himself—to die for Jesus Christ. . . . He was in prison several times, but was always released just when it seemed he was going to get his wish."

On 15 November 1927 an attempt, which failed, was made on the life of the candidate for the Mexican presidency, General Obrégon. Obrégon himself suspected Calles, but the opportunity was taken by the government to get rid of two specially active Christians, Father Pro and his brother Hum-

H

bert. Three nights after the attempt, they were arrested at
their father's house and lodged in underground cells. Every
day for a week they were questioned and bullied by the police;
interviewed by a newspaper reporter, Father Pro said: "I do
not wish to make any statement. I will only say that I have
had nothing whatever to do with this business—I am a law-
abiding man. My mind is quite at ease, and I am confident that
justice will be done. I absolutely deny having had any part in
this plot." They were not allowed to see a lawyer, all provisions of Mexican law respecting criminal prosecutions were
disregarded, there was no trial.*

On the morning of 23 November 1927 a policeman called
Father Pro from his cell. "You are wanted," he said; then,
seeing how he was dressed, in coat and trousers, "you had
better put on a waistcoat." Father Pro complied, and it seems
it was at that moment that he realized that he was going to his
death and not, as he had supposed, to his trial. He turned to
the other prisoners and said, "Goodbye, my sons. Goodbye,
my brothers." The embarrassed policeman asked his forgiveness. Father Pro put his arm around his shoulders and answered, "I do more than forgive you, I thank you." He then,
with three companions, walked out into the bright sunlight
of the courtyard of the police-headquarters: it was lined with
soldiers, with general officers and others sitting on a platform,
smoking and chatting. As the prisoners approached they were
stopped, in order that the newspaper men could take
photographs.

Then an officer signed to Father Pro to stand against a
stockade of wooden logs. He was asked if he had a last request. "I wish to pray," he said. He knelt down, arms folded
across his breast, eyes closed; after two minutes he got up and
faced the firing-squad, raising one arm in a wide gesture and
saying, "May God have mercy on you! May God bless you!
You, Lord, know that I am innocent. I forgive my enemies

---

* In any case, the legal penalty for attempted murder was a long
term of imprisonment, not death.

with all my heart." He stretched out his arms crosswise, holding in his right hand a small crucifix, in his left a rosary. The officer gave a word of command. Father Pro, in a low but very distinct voice, uttered three words, *Viva Cristo rey!* "Hail, Christ, our King!" Then he fell dead.

His three companions, whose execution followed, were his brother Humbert, a young engineer and leader of the youth group named Luis Segura Vilchis, and a nineteen-year-old creole workman named Tirado. This youth was so ill with pneumonia that he could not stand upright; his last request was to see his mother: it was ignored. All three were as innocent as Michael Pro.

THEODORE ROMZA

AT MUKACEVO, A.D. 1947

George Theodore Romza was a native of that little-known land, below the Carpathian mountains and beyond eastern Slovakia, that has sometimes been called in English "Ruthenia," but is better called Podkarpatska Rus. He was born at Veliky Bočkov in 1911 and, aspiring to the priesthood, was sent to do his studies in Rome. The Rusin Catholics are of Slav-Byzantine rite, and in due course young Romza entered the Russian College (Russicum), where he made a deep impression: one who knew him there remarks on his manliness and solidity, "there was nothing soft, showy or affected about him." He returned to his homeland, a priest, in 1938, and was quickly appointed spiritual father in the seminary at Uzhorod. The political situation was such that little is known of Father Theodore in those days, but nobody was surprised when, in 1944, at the age of thirty-three, he was made bishop. He became responsible for the large and populous eparchy of Mukačevo at the time when the Soviet troops drove out the Germans and Hungarians and occupied Uzhorod, the capital of Podkarpatska Rus and the bishop's place of residence.

For three years Bishop Theodore stood up to the occupying authorities. Soviet policy in ecclesiastical affairs was to endeavour to detach the Catholic majority from Rome and to strengthen the hand of the minority of dissidents; charitable and educational institutions under religious auspices were expropriated, the seminary was closed, religious instruction in schools forbidden, youth groups secularized, and attempts made to force the clergy to preach the glories of Communism (some of them were jailed). The set-up was a familiar one, and Bishop Theodore fought it doggedly and fearlessly. He was called on publicly to deny that there had been religious persecution in Russia; he refused. He was asked to speak at an anniversary celebration of the Russian revolution; he agreed—but said the "wrong" things, talking about peace and God's mercies. When he found he could come to no satisfactory understanding with the occupying forces, he concentrated on fortifying his flock, and made a visitation of every parish of his scattered territory. A heavy tax was put on pilgrimages, the archimandrite and an abbot of the Basilian monks were interned, and still the bishop was coaxed and threatened to make him break with Rome; the secret police several times sent for him for questioning, and lectured him on the iniquities of the Church, the pope, and bishops in general. Writing to the rector of the *Russicum* soon after the beginning of the war, Romza had said, "To die for Christ means to live for ever"; when he came to an *impasse* with Soviet generals and N.K.V.D. men, and they urged him to schism, he would tell them, "I would rather suffer and die than betray the Church."

In 1947, soon after Easter, Bishop Theodore made another visitation of his eparchy and found the people standing firm, and not only his own welcomed him—many dissident Orthodox too were looking to him for leadership. In the most difficult conditions, extraordinary numbers of people flocked to any church where he was, especially on a great feast. It seems that it was the failure of an anti-Catholic demonstration, staged by the Soviet authorities for the feast of the Assumption in that year, that decided them that the bishop must be somehow got rid of. An account of what happened eventually was drawn up by a responsible person, and it may be taken as trustworthy.

On 27 October 1947 Bishop Theodore was returning from Lavky, where a large number of people had been reconciled with the Church; he was driving in a horse-drawn carriage, with two priests and two clerics. A lorry loaded with Soviet soldiers and police crashed into the carriage, it would seem deliberately, with the intention of producing an appearance of accident. The carriage was smashed and the horses killed, but the passengers were not seriously hurt. Thereupon the soldiers struck at them with metal levers, and quickly drove off, leaving them lying there. Passers-by conveyed the victims to hospital at Mukačevo, where the doctors reported that none of them was in danger; the bishop was most seriously hurt— his jaw broken in two places and most of his teeth gone—but he would recover.

Two days later the nuns in charge of the hospital were withdrawn from the ward where Bishop Theodore lay, and replaced by a nurse brought in from outside. On the morning of October 31, speaking with great difficulty, he made his confession and sent a message of encouragement and hope to his people. He was being given nourishment through a tube, and was progressing favourably. But by half an hour after midnight Theodore Romza was dead.

It was given out officially that he, and one of his companions, had "died as the result of a carriage accident." Stringent police measures were taken to prevent any demonstration at his funeral, but they were not successful. A huge crowd gathered and filed in orderly fashion past the coffin, to imprint a last kiss on the body of a faithful shepherd who had given his life for his sheep.

JOHN TUNG CHI-SHIH

CONTEMPORARY

It is not certain that Father Tung Chi-shih has paid the extreme penalty for his faithfulness, but it is fitting here to include the substance of the profession of faith that deprived him of his liberty, for it is a characteristic example in our own day of the timeless Christian answer to a demand that the things of God should be handed over to Caesar.

Father Tung was born in 1906 at Kunming in the Chinese province of Yunnan, and he ministered as a priest at Chungking in the province of Szechwan. In June 1951 the civil authorities of Chungking (as elsewhere) organized a demonstration to demand the expulsion from China of the internuncio of the Holy See, Archbishop Antony Riberi. The pretext was that Mgr Riberi had interfered in the internal affairs of the Chinese government, by advising the bishops of China that the so-called "three-autonomies" movement was schismatic. This movement covered the state-sponsored scheme for the Catholic Church in China to be administered quite independently of the Holy See, and is the movement referred to by Father Tung in his address. Catholics were forced to attend this demonstration; it was hoped to induce at least some of them openly to support the agitation for Mgr Riberi's expulsion, and Father Tung was put up to speak. The greater part of what he said is set out below; it completely upset the official programme.

A month later, early in the morning of July 2, while vesting for Mass, Father Tung was arrested and carried off to prison. Since then nothing has been seen or heard of him. There have been repeated rumours that he has been put to death, or has died from ill-treatment; these reports have not been confirmed, and if they are true the civil authorities are unlikely to admit it. One thing is certain, however: many Christians have been put to death in communist China for being far less outspoken than Father Tung.

. . . I am going to speak to you about offering myself as a sacrifice to two supreme powers [my religion and my country].

People who do not believe that God or the soul exists, who

do not recognize the Pope as representing Christ on earth, or the authority of the bishops of the Catholic Church, tell us that the three-autonomies movement is simply a matter of patriotism. At the same time they admit that we are free to profess the Catholic faith, and that there can be purely religious relations between the faithful and the Holy See. But today this movement calls on us to attack the Pope's representative, Archbishop Riberi. Tomorrow, it may perhaps call on us to attack Christ's representative, the Pope. And the day after tomorrow, why should it not call upon us to attack Jesus Christ himself, our Lord and our God?

No doubt it is always possible in theory to make distinctions in an object of attack. But in fact God is one; the Pope is one; and the Pope's representative is one. No distinction or division can be admitted. Under this movement, which we are told is purely a matter of patriotism, I should cease to be a Catholic, for it is incompatible with the Church's own essential autonomy.

I have one single soul, and it cannot be divided; but I have also a body, and that can be broken apart. It therefore seems best to me to give my soul, whole and entire, to God and his holy Church, and my body to my country. If my country wants it, I do not refuse it. Consistent materialists will be satisfied with this offering of my body, for they deny that there is any such thing as a soul. . . . Since I am powerless to remedy the present situation, I can do nothing better than to offer my soul to one side and my body to the other, as a sacrifice in the hope of helping them to understand one another. Until that understanding is brought about, there is nothing else I can do. So be it. I only ask God to be merciful to my natural weakness and give me courage above nature: then I shall be unshakable till death. . . .

But in case at some future time I should lose control of myself and, in a moment of weakness, utter words of surrender, I use this opportunity now, when my mind is perfectly clear, solemnly to disclaim them in advance and declare them of no effect whatever.

The [civil] authorities have often told us that they do not mean to force our hand but only to rouse us to thought and action. It is therefore my duty to speak frankly and never to say what I do not mean: if I approve a declaration, to sign it in all sincerity; if I do not approve it, not to subscribe to it dishonestly. The authorities have recognized our freedom to speak and our freedom to be silent: why should we not trust that declaration?

Suppose that, moved by fear, I should act against my conscience, speak against my thoughts, and sign what I do not approve. Then I am openly deceiving the authorities. And if in private I admit that I said what I did not mean because I was forced, then I have been deceiving the bishops of the Church. That, surely, is the way to sow discord between the government and the Church. If I stifle my conscience, deny God, forsake the Church and deceive the government, then I am simply an opportunist and a coward, one of those miserable creatures whom no one can trust and who is no use to anybody. . .

I am a Catholic. But that does not prevent me from greatly admiring the communists for more than one quality. [Firstly, their readiness to die.] Am I then shamefully to cling to life on the pretext of protecting myself to serve the Church later on? A Christian who betrays God is fit for nothing but to betray his fellows in the Church and his country. Communists like to repeat that "For one man who falls dead, ten thousand rise up." Shall a Catholic forget that the blood of martyrs is the seed of Christians?

[Secondly, communists' indifference to what is said about them.] And is a Christian to fear being an object of wicked, intolerable accusations? Is he to refuse an unjust death as something without value or meaning, when he knows that he will be judged by Almighty God, who is all wisdom and goodness, majesty and justness itself?

[Thirdly, communists' belief and trust in their own principles.] Can a Christian forget that his faith comes to him from God? Why should he give up simply because he himself is unable to convince others? Is he to suppose the whole Church is beaten in his own person? That would be to falsify the Church's teaching and to overturn her discipline, to betray God and his own soul.

If I were to betray God and my own soul, what guarantee is there that I would not also be a traitor to my country and her people? That is why I refuse to falter in my faith, and still more refuse to shake the faith of other Christians—and abuse my position as a priest in order to do it.

The communists and the government they control have a real regard for the Church, and they seek to gain Christian support. I say that I am greatly honoured thereby. How then can I fail to redouble my efforts to be an unshakable Christian, one fit to respond to the government's worthy intentions? . . . But over and above this, I want so much in my turn to offer them something—the Catholic Church, which is so dear to me: to bring them to God and to make them our brothers in the faith. Please do not take me for a raving lunatic, or think that I am insincere. I say that, on the day when communists with such ideals truly recognize the Catholic Church, they will give themselves so entirely to the faith that they will be a thousand times better Christians than such a man as I am.

Therefore I pray God that there may be in the heart of the Communist Party many Sauls who will become Pauls, who will far outdistance the poor priest now speaking to you. That is my most fervent prayer, and I implore that it may soon be heard. For this I will withhold no sacrifice, praying in the hope that the earthly life I offer today may be the purchase price of the conversion of the generation to come. . . .

I am a Chinese and I am a Catholic. I love my country and I love my Church. I categorically reject all that is contrary to the laws of that country and to the laws of that Church. Above all, I will not take part in anything that might give rise

H*

to discord. But if Church and government cannot reach agreement, then sooner or later no Chinese Catholic will have any alternative but to die.

Why, then, should I not offer up my life here and now to hasten the mutual understanding of the two parties? . . .

Please forgive all the shortcomings of this poor speech.

In the name of the Father and of the Son and of the Holy Spirit. Amen.

APPENDIX:

ST CYPRIAN'S EXHORTATION TO MARTYRDOM

The Exhortation to Martyrdom of St Cyprian, whose own passion is related on pages 36-40 herein, was addressed to one Fortunatus, probably the bishop of that name who was at the Council of Carthage in the year 256. It consists for the most part of a collection of texts from the writings of the Old and New Testaments in support of twelve considerations relative to the martyrs' destiny. One or more examples from each of these heads is given below, together with the beginning and end of the "treatise."

At this time when the burden of persecution and trouble is lying heavy upon us, when the time of the enemy Antichrist at the end of the world is near, you, my dear Fortunatus, have asked me to bring together some passages from the sacred

Scriptures for the instruction and strengthening of the minds of the brethren, that Christ's soldiers may be in good heart for their spiritual warfare. That is a very natural request, and I must comply with it, so far as my poor abilities allow and divine help is forthcoming. . . . It is not enough to encourage God's people with the sound of *our* voice: we must strengthen the faith of believers, and their courage must be dedicated and devoted to God, by the divine words of the Scriptures. There can be no more fitting part of my responsibility and duty than by continual exhortation to prepare the congregation committed by God to my charge, that it may be a garrison of the heavenly camp against the Devil's slings and arrows. It is no use a soldier going into battle unless he has first been trained, and no athlete will win a crown in the stadium unless he has first learned his own strength and how to use it.

Our adversary is an old one: it is now nearly six thousand years since the Devil became man's enemy. During those long ages he has found out all the temptations, all the deceptions and tricks, by which we can be overcome. If he finds Christ's soldier unprepared, untrained, lacking enthusiasm and sufficient watchfulness, he takes advantage of his ignorance, want of thought and inexperience. But he must needs be overcome by anyone who withstands him in faithfulness to the Lord's words, strong in the Lord's footsteps, for the Christ whom we confess cannot be vanquished.

In order, dear brother, not to make my discourse too long and so to tire the hearer or reader, I have arranged my matter thus: first, a list of those things which everyone ought to know and remember; then, those passages from God's written word that confirm, with the authority of divine Scripture, the truth of what I have said. In this way, I do not so much send you a treatise of my own as supply others with the means for making one. This will be more useful to people. For were I to give someone a coat all ready made, he would simply be wearing my coat, and it might not fit him. As it is, I send you the materials, the wool and the purple thread, from the Lamb who has redeemed us and given us life; from it you can make a coat to suit yourself, and be more pleased with it because it will be your very own. You will, too, put what I send at the disposal of others, so that they also may use it according to their own choice. Thus they may all cover their old nakedness and stand forth in the garments of Christ, girt with the sanctification of heavenly grace.

Another rule that seems to me useful and salutary, dear brother, is this: in so serious an exhortation as one which invites men to be martyrs, no time must be wasted in being eloquent, there is no room for the elaboration of our human speech. We must say only what God says, the words which Christ uses to stir his servants to martyrdom. The divine precepts must be put into the hands of the fighters as their arms, those precepts must be the notes sounded by the war trumpet. It is those precepts that must strike the ear, put the mind on the alert, strengthen body and soul to endure any hardship. We, by the Lord's permission, have conferred their first baptism on the faithful: it is for us also to prepare them for the next, teaching them that this second baptism is yet greater in grace, more mighty in power and more exalted in dignity. This is the baptism the angels use; God and his Anointed One rejoice in it; after it, no one sins again; it is the full flower of our faith; it takes us out of this world and joins us with God. Baptism of water obtains forgiveness of sin; baptism of blood earns the crown of righteousness. That baptism we have to desire and welcome, to ask for with the most earnest prayer, that, being God's servants, we may become his friends.

* * *

So, in encouraging and training our brethren to confess the Lord in the strength of faith and virtue, and in arming them for the warfare of persecution and suffering, we must affirm that the idols which man makes for himself are not gods. Things made cannot be greater than their maker; they cannot protect or help anybody—they themselves perish in their temples if man does not look after them. Nor, again, are the natural elements to be worshipped as divine: they serve man in accordance with God's providence and will.

Having thrown down the idols and shown the truth about the natural elements, we have to show that the Lord alone is to be worshipped. Then we must show God's warning to those who sacrifice to idols; that he does not easily forgive idolaters; and that he even ordered them to be put to death, such is his wrath against idolatry.

Then we must add that, since Christ has redeemed us and given us life through his blood, we ought to let nothing stand between him and us: for he dealt so with us, preferring hardship to comfort, poverty to wealth, servitude to power, death to life—all for our sakes. But we, when we accept suffering, make our choice of the joys of Heaven rather than this world's misery, an everlasting kingdom rather than the slavery of the present time, life rather than death, God and Christ rather than the Devil and Antichrist.

It must be emphasized that when those who have been snatched from the Devil's jaws and freed from the world's fetters meet trials and tribulations, they must not allow themselves to slip back into worldly ways and so lose what they have gained. Rather must we persevere in faith and righteousness, striving to be perfected in Heaven's grace, that we may attain the palm and the crown; for troubles and persecutions happen so that we may be tried and tested. Nor should these trials and oppressions make us afraid, because God is mightier as our protector than the Devil is as our attacker.

In order that no one shall be frightened in this way, we ought to make clear that it was foretold that the world would hate and persecute us, and the fact that these things come to pass confirms the truth of the divine promise of the rewards that are to follow. What happens to faithful Christians is nothing new, for the good have suffered, and been oppressed and killed by wicked men, since the beginning of the world. Lastly, we have to show the hope and reward that await

martyrs and other righteous men and women after the suffering and struggles of this life. The recompense for patient
suffering that we shall receive in Heaven is immeasurably
greater than the pain and sorrow that we endure here.

*   *   *

[Idols and the powers of nature are not divine.] It is shown
in Psalm 1:3: "The heathen have silver idols and golden,
gods which the hands of men have fashioned. They have
mouths, and yet are silent; eyes they have, and yet are sightless;
ears they have, and want all hearing; noses, and yet no smell
can reach them; hands unfeeling, feet unstirring; never a sound
their throats may utter. Such be the end of all who make
them, such the reward of all who trust them." . . . And in
Exodus: "Thou shalt not carve images or fashion the likeness
of anything . . . to bow down and worship it." And in the
Wisdom of Solomon, concerning the elements: " . . . Or was
it power, and power's exercise, that awoke their wonder-
ment? Why then, how many times greater must he be, who
contrived it!"

[Only God is to be worshipped.] It is written in Deuteronomy: "Thou shalt worship the Lord thy God, to him only
shalt thou do service." And in Exodus: "Thou shalt not defy
me by making other gods thy own." . . . The Lord in the
Gospel refers to the first and second commandment, when
he says: "Listen, Israel; there is no God but the Lord thy
God; and thou shalt love the Lord thy God with the love
of thy whole heart, and thy whole soul, and thy whole mind,
and thy whole strength. This is the first commandment, and
the second, its like, is this, Thou shalt love thy neighbour as
thyself. There is no other commandment greater than these."
And again: "Eternal life is knowing thee, who art the only
true God, and Jesus Christ, whom thou hast sent."

[God's warning to idolaters.] In Exodus: "Sacrifice is for
the Lord alone; he who offers it to other gods must be put
to death." . . .

[God's strictness towards idolaters.] In Exodus, Moses prays and God replies: "Thy people have sinned heinously, in making themselves gods of gold. I entreat thee, pardon this offence of theirs; or else blot out my name too from the record thou hast written. Whoever sins against me, the Lord answered, shall be blotted out from my record." . . . And in the first Book of Kings: "If man does wrong to man, God's justice may yet be satisfied; if man sins against the Lord, who shall plead his cause for him?"

[Men might even be put to death for idolatry: Deuteronomy 13:6-18.] If these commandments about the worship of God and the rejection of idols were kept during the old dispensation, how much more must they be kept since the Christ has come. For he did not speak to us in words alone, but by deeds as well: he accepted injury and abuse, he suffered and was crucified, so that he might teach us to suffer and die, following his example. Therefore, since he suffered for us, man is bound to suffer for him; and as he suffered for the sins of others, each of us ought to be the more ready to bear suffering because of his own sins. Accordingly, Christ warns us in the Gospel: "Whoever acknowledges me before men, I too will acknowledge him before my Father who is in Heaven; and whoever disowns me before men, before my Father in Heaven I too will disown him." . . .

[Nothing must come between us and Christ.] The Lord says in the Gospel: "He is not worthy of me, that loves father or mother more; he is not worthy of me, that loves son or daughter more; he is not worthy of me, that does not take up his cross and follow me." . . . And the apostle Paul writes: "Who will separate us from the love of Christ? Will affliction, or distress, or persecution, or hunger, or nakedness, or peril, or the sword? For thy sake, says the scripture, we face death at every moment, reckoned no better than sheep marked down for slaughter. Yet in all this we are conquerors, through him who has granted us his love." . . .

[There must be no backsliding.] We learn from Exodus

that, after God had delivered them from slavery to Pharaoh in Egypt (that is, to the Devil and the world), the Jews, prefiguring us people, were disbelieving and thankless, and murmured against Moses because of their hardships in the wilderness. They did not appreciate God's gifts of freedom and salvation, they tried to return to their old state of slavery to the Egyptians (that is, to the world), instead of putting their faith and trust in God, who protects his people whom he has delivered from the Devil and the world. . . . The Lord says in the Gospel, "No one who looks behind him, when he has once put his hand to the plough, is fitted for the kingdom of God," thus warning us against going back to the Devil and the world which we have put behind us. Again, "If a man is in the fields, he too must beware of turning back. Remember Lot's wife." And, lest our natural affections and the things of the world make us dilatory in following Christ, he says further: "None of you can be my disciple if he does not take leave of all that he possesses."

[Perseverance in righteousness.] In the Gospel the Lord says: . . . "That man will be saved, who endures to the last." And again: "If you continue faithful to my word, you are my disciples in earnest; so you will come to know the truth, and the truth will set you free." . . . The same lesson is taught in the Apocalypse, when it says, "Hold what is in thy grasp, so that none may rob thee of thy crown." An example of perseverance is shown forth in Exodus, when Moses, for the overcoming of Amalek (a type of the Devil), held up his hands in sign and sacrament of the Cross: the enemy was overcome only so long as Moses persevered in holding up his hands in that sign [Exodus 17:11-14].

[Persecution is a test.] . . . Peter in his [first] Letter says: "Do not be surprised, beloved, that this fiery ordeal should have befallen you, to test your quality; there is nothing strange in what is happening to you. Rather rejoice, when you share in some measure the sufferings of Christ; so joy will be yours, and triumph, when his glory is revealed. Your lot will be a blessed one, if you are reproached for the name of Christ; it means that the virtue of God's honour and glory and power, it means that his own Spirit, is resting upon you."

[God is all-powerful.] As John says in his [first] Letter, "There is a stronger power at work in you, than in the world." And Psalm 117: "With the Lord at my side, I have no fear of the worst man can do." . . . God is able to open the mouth of a man devoted to him, giving that man strength and courage in speech (did he not make even a she-ass speak, against the prophet Balaam?) Therefore, when persecution is abroad, no one should fear the Devil's threats, but rather have trust in God's help. Do not cower under attack, but stand upright beneath God's protecting hand. Every man receives as much divine help as his faith, trusting in God's promises, enables him to expect; unless that faith be wavering and weak, Almighty God cannot withhold his aid.

[Persecution is not a new or unforeseen thing.] The Lord has forewarned us in the Gospel: "If the world hates you, be sure that it hated me before it learned to hate you. . . . They will persecute you just as they have persecuted me." Again: "The time is coming when anyone who puts you to death will claim that he is performing an act of worship to God. . . ." And again: "In the world, you will only find tribulation; but take courage, I have overcome the world." . . . These things that are happening to Christians are nothing new. Good and virtuous people, those who are dedicated to God in innocence, awe and true religion, always have to tread a narrow path, beset by many hardships and tribulations and injustices. In the earliest days of the world, righteous Abel was killed by his brother, Jacob was exiled, Joseph sold into slavery; King Saul persecuted the gentle David, and King Ahab tried to oppress Elias, who boldly and unfailingly upheld God's majesty; the priest Zacharias was slain between the Temple and the altar, being thus made a victim in the very place where he had offered sacrifice to God. . . . The three young men, Ananias, Azarias and Misael, were of one age and one in love, steadfast in faith, constant in virtue, and they were stronger than the flames that encompassed them, so that they cried aloud in testimony that they served none other, knew none other and worshipped none other but God only [Daniel 3:16-18]. Daniel, a man devoted to God and full of the Holy Spirit, declared that idols he had none, but that he worshipped "that living God that made heaven and earth." Tobias [the elder] while in captivity yet remained free in mind and spirit; he would not forsake his religion, and gloriously praised God's power and goodness: "I, at least, in this land of exile, will be the spokesman of his praise, tell the story of his dread dealings with a sinful race." And in the Book of Maccabees we read of seven brothers, equals in quality and goodness, filling up the number seven by the sacrament of a full perfection, martyrs every one. . . .

[The palm and crown.] . . . The fruit and reward of suffering is made manifest by the Holy Spirit in Psalm 115: "Dear in the Lord's sight is the death of those who love him." And in Psalm 125: "The men who are sowing in tears will reap, one day, with joy. Mournful enough they go, but with seed to scatter; trust me, they will come back rejoicing, as they carry their sheaves with them." . . . The Lord is the avenger and the rewarder, and he says in his Gospel: "Blessed are those who suffer persecution in the cause of right; the kingdom of Heaven is theirs." . . . The divine promises are not made to the oppressed and slain alone: even though he is not put to death, the faithful Christian whose faith remains true and unconquered, who prefers his religion above everything and approves himself a follower of Christ, he also is numbered among the martyrs, according to Christ's word: "I promise you, everyone who has forsaken home, or parents, or brethren, or wife, or children for the sake of the kingdom of God, will receive, in this present world, many times their worth, and in the world to come, everlasting life."

God willed that the blessed apostle Paul should be carried into the third heaven and Paradise, where, he tells us, he heard hidden things that man may not utter; he glories that he saw Jesus Christ by a faith that was not wholly blind; and he says what he learned from that assurance: that he does not count "present sufferings as the measure of that glory which is to be revealed to us." Who, then, will not endeavour with all his strength to reap the harvest of divine reward after the trials and sufferings of this life, to be made God's friend and be in happiness with Christ? It is a fine thing for the world's soldiers to defeat the foe and to return home in triumph: but how much better and greater is the glory, after overcoming the Devil, of coming home in triumph to Paradise, of carrying the trophies of victory over the Adversary into the very place where Adam failed and was cast out. How much greater is the glory of offering to God the gifts that are the most acceptable to him—a pure faith, unfailing goodness of spirit, praise and honour and unalloyed devotedness; of standing with him when he sits in judgement and brings retribution upon his adversaries; of being made joint heir with Christ, of being equal with the angels, patriarchs, prophets and apostles, of rejoicing in possession of the heavenly kingdom. What persecution can nullify, what sufferings dispel, such thoughts as these? The spirit that is grounded in religious contemplation confronts the Devil's terrors with confidence and steadfastness, it is unshaken by the world's threats, because its strength is in a sure and certain faith in that which is to come.

In time of persecution, earth closes in on us, but Heaven opens; Antichrist threatens, but Christ defends; death comes, but everlasting life follows; we are destroyed and lose the world, but we are renewed and gain Paradise; the life of time is ended, the life of eternity begins. It is fitting and salutary to go hence cheerfully, to glory in leaving adversity and oppression. At one moment human eyes close upon men and earth, at the next they open upon God and his Christ. How swift is the passage into happiness! We find ourselves in the heavenly courts as suddenly as we are snatched from the world. These things should occupy our mind, we ought to think about them constantly. If when persecution comes God's soldier is found thus employed, his eager strength will be invincible. If he is called away before persecution strikes, his faith, all ready for martyrdom, will have its reward. God, the Judge of all, will not be slow to make his award: in persecution, the crown goes to the fighting-man; in peace, it goes to the true of heart.

BIBLIOGRAPHY OF SOURCES

ST STEPHEN

The Acts of the Apostles, chs. 6 and 7. The translation on pp. 1-3 herein is from the Westminster Version of the Sacred Scriptures, by permission of Fr. Philip Caraman, s.j.

ST POLYCARP

Kirsopp Lake, *The Apostolic Fathers,* vol. ii (London and New York, 1917), gives a Greek text and translation of the Martyrdom of Polycarp. The account on pp. 3-8 herein follows the original closely. For a translation of the letters of Ignatius, see J. A. Kliest, *The Epistles of St Clement of Rome and St Ignatius of Antioch* (London and Westminster, Md., 1946).

ST JUSTIN

A text of Justin's *acta* is printed in the *Acta Sanctorum,* June, vol. i, and elsewhere. The narrative on pp. 9-11 herein is a translation of the "acts."

ST CARPUS

Three texts of the *acta,* two Greek and one Latin, are printed in *Analecta Bollandiana,* vol. lviii (1940), pp. 142-176. The account on pp. 12-14 herein follows the "acts."

ST BLANDINA

Eusebius gives the letter about the Lyons martyrs in his *Ecclesiastical History,* bk.v, ch. 1. There is a text and translation of Eusebius, by Kirsopp Lake and J. E. L. Oulton, in the Loeb Classical Library (2 vols. 1926-32). Several pages of extracts from the letter are given by Walter Pater in his *Marius the Epicurean,* ch. 26. The account of Blandina on pp. 15-18 herein is extracted from the letter.

THE SCILLITAN MARTYRS

The text is edited by J. Armitage Robinson in *Texts and Studies*, vol. i, pt. 2 (Cambridge, 1891), pp. 112-116. The narrative on pp. 19-21 herein is a translation of the *acta*.

ST PERPETUA AND ST FELICITY

In *The Passion of SS. Perpetua and Felicity* (London, 1931) W. H. Shrewing gives a Latin text, which is probably the original language, with a translation. There are several other editions and translations. The narrative on pp. 21-30 herein is a close paraphrase of the *passio*.

ST PIONIUS

The Greek text is in O. von Gebhardt, *Acta martyrum selecta* (1902). The account herein, pp. 30-33, is considerably abbreviated; for a fuller English version, see A. J. Mason, *Historic Martyrs of the Primitive Church* (London, 1905), pp. 123-135.

ST LAWRENCE

In the Loeb series *Prudentius*, vol. ii (London, 1953), pp. 108-143, there is a text of the poem on St Lawrence, with translation by Dr H. J. Thomson.

ST CYPRIAN

The text is printed in the *Acta Sanctorum*, September, vol. iv, and elsewhere. The narrative on pp. 36-40 herein is a translation of the *passio*.

ST FRUCTUOSUS

Text in R. Knopf and G. Krüger, *Ausgewählte Märtyrerakten* (3rd edn., 1929) and elsewhere. The account on pp. 40-43 herein follows the "acts" with some small omissions.

ST MARIAN AND ST JAMES

Text in O. von Gebhardt, *op. cit.* There is a full English translation in E. C. E. Owen, *Some Authentic Acts of the Early Martyrs* (Oxford, 1927), pp. 105-118.

MARTYRS OF THE ALEXANDRIAN PLAGUE

The passage on pp. 48-49 is from the *Ecclesiastical History* of Eusebius, bk. vii, ch. 22, where the Greek text can be found, and also in C. L. Feltoe, *Letters . . . of Dionysius of Alexandria* (Cambridge, 1904), pp. 79-84.

ST ALBAN

The passage of Gildas is from *De excidio Britanniae*, x and xi, and that of Bede from his *Ecclesiastical History*, i, 7. See "St Alban and Saint Albans," by W. Levison, in *Antiquity*, vol. xv (1941), pp. 337-359.

ST MARCELLUS

Text in *Analecta Bollandiana*, vol. xli (1923), pp. 257-287. The account herein, pp. 54-56, is a translation of the *passio*.

ST PROCOPIUS AND ST PAMPHILUS

The Passion of St Procopius given herein on pp. 56-58 follows the Latin text. H. Delehaye gives an account of the development of the Procopius legends in *Legends of the Saints* (London and New York, 1907), ch. 5. The account of St Pamphilus and his companions herein (pp. 58-60) is abridged; the full account may be read in N. J. Lawlor's and J. E. L. Oulton's translation of the *Ecclesiastical History and Martyrs of Palestine* of Eusebius, vol. ii (London, 1928).

ST AGAPE

The Greek text of the *acta* was published by P. Franchi de' Cavalieri in *Studi e Testi*, no. ix (Rome, 1902). The account on pp. 60-63 herein is an abridgement of these "acts."

ST PHILIP AND ST HERMES

The Latin text of the *acta* is given in the *Acta Sanctorum*, October, vol. ix, and elsewhere. The account herein, pp. 63-66, is shortened.

ST JONAN AND ST BERIKJESU

A Latin translation was printed with the Syriac text by S. E. Assemani in *Acta sanctorum martyrum orientalium*; the embellished Greek text, also with a Latin version, is in *Patrologia Orientalis*, vol. ii, pp. 421-439.

ST SABAS THE GOTH

The Greek text of the letter to the churches may be found in *Analecta Bollandiana*, vol. xxxi (1912), pp. 216-221, and elsewhere. The account on pp. 68-70 herein follows this letter.

MARTYRS UNDER THE VANDALS

The *Historia persecutionis africanae* of Victor of Vita is printed in Migne, P. L., vol. lviii, cc. 180 ff. The excerpts herein on pp. 71-73 are paraphrased.

ST MARTIN I

Martin's letters and the narrative of a companion are printed in Migne, P. L., vol. lxxxvii, cc. 197-204 and cxxix, 585-604. Other sources are the *Liber Pontificalis*, ed. Duchesne, vol. i, pp. 336-340, and a Greek life in *Analecta Bollandiana*, vol. li (1933), pp. 225-262.

THE TWO HEWALDS

The passage is from Bede's *Ecclesiastical History*, bk v, ch. 10.

ST BONIFACE

The text of Willibald's Life of Boniface can be found in the *Acta Sanctorum*, June, vol. i, and elsewhere. There is a translation by C. H. Talbot in *The Anglo-Saxon Missionaries in Germany* (London and New York, 1954); the passages on pp. 79-82 herein are taken from this, by kind permission of Messrs Sheed & Ward.

ST STEPHEN THE YOUNGER

Text of a life in Migne, P. G., vol. c, cc. 1069-1085, written about forty-four years after the martyr's death.

ST EULOGIUS AND OTHERS

A short life of Eulogius by his friend Alvarus is printed in Migne, P. L., vol. cxv, where also his own writings on the other martyrs can be found.

ST THOMAS OF CANTERBURY

Contemporary and near-contemporary accounts of the murder of Thomas Becket are numerous. Four of them are by writers who claim to have been eye-witnesses, including Edward Grim and William FitzStephen; the French account in verse by Guernes of Pont-Saint-Maxence, though not by an eye-witness, is of particular interest. Dean Stanley, in his *Historical Memorials of Canterbury* (1st edn., 1885; reprinted several times) worked these into a vivid detailed narrative, complete with references, which in the main is followed herein. It must be remembered that the happenings that are recorded by various writers with such particularity took place almost in darkness and amid wild confusion. E. A. Abbott in the first volume of his *St Thomas of Canterbury* (London, 1898. A rather acrimonious work) examines the evidence concering the marytrdom in yet more detail. See David Knowles's character-study, *Archbishop Thomas Becket* (Oxford, 1950).

ST BERARD AND ST DANIEL

See the *Acta Sanctorum*, January 16, and October, vol. vi; and H. Koehler, *L'Église chrétienne du Maroc* . . . (Paris, 1934).

BD ANTONY OF RIVOLI

Text of contemporary accounts are printed in the *Acta Sanctorum*, August, vol. vi, and in *Analecta Bollandiana*, vol. xxiv (1905), pp. 357-374.

ST JOHN OF ROCHESTER

The Life of Fisher from B. M. MS. Harleian 6382 is printed in the E. E. T. S. Extra Series no. cxvii (1921, for 1915); a version in modernized spelling, edited by Father Philip Hughes, was published in 1935.

BD CUTHBERT MAYNE

The manuscript referred to is printed in J. Morris, *The Troubles of Our Catholic Forefathers*, vol. i (London, 1872), pp. 65-140. The best general account of Mayne is in B. Camm, *Lives of the English Martyrs*, vol. ii (London, 1905), pp. 204-221.

BD RICHARD GWYN

The evidence of the sources for Gwyn is well summarized in E. H. Burton and J. H. Pollen, *Lives of the English Martyrs* (London, 1914), pp. 127-144; and in T. P. Ellis, *The Catholic Martyrs of Wales* (London, 1933), pp. 18-33.

BD MARGARET CLITHEROW

Mrs Clitherow's confessor, John Mush, left a manuscript memoir of her, which is printed in J. Morris, *op. cit.*, vol. iii, pp. 360-440. An abridgement of this by an unkown hand, *An abstract of the life and martirdome of Mistres Margaret Clitherowe*, was published at Mechlin in 1619; it was addressed to the martyr's daughter, Ann, a member of the community of English canonesses of St Augustine at Louvain. This community is now at St Augustine's Priory, Newton Abbot, which possesses a copy of the 1619 edition of the Abstract; it was reprinted some years ago. The account herein on pp. 115-123 is taken from this contemporary source, through the kindness of the Mother Prioress at Newton Abbot.

BD EDMUND GENINGS AND BD SWITHIN WELLS

See Bishop Richard Challoner's *Memoirs of Missionary Priests* (1924 edn.), pp. 169-182, 591-592.

BD ALEXANDER RAWLINS AND BD HENRY WALPOLE

The particulars herein on pp. 128-130 follow Challoner, *op. cit.*, pp. 217-227.

BD JOHN OGILVIE

There exists an account in Latin of Ogilvie's imprisonment and examinations, written by himself in jail at Glasgow and completed by other hands. A translation is given, with other documents and a connected narrative, in W. E. Brown's *John Ogilvie* (London, 1925).

FOUR JAPANESE

A translation into French of Fray Diego de San Francisco's report is printed in H. Leclercq, *Les Martyrs*, vol. ix (Paris, 1910), pp. 26-68.

THE GREAT MARTYRDOM IN JAPAN

There are many works on the martyrs in Japan, e.g., G. Boero, *Les 205 martyrs du Japon* (Paris, 1868; translated from Italian).

ST. JOSAPHAT OF POLOTSK

The only full treatment of Josaphat Kunsevich in a Western language is A. Guépin's *Un apôtre de l'union des églises . . . St Josaphat . . .* (2 vols., Paris, 1898). Two volumes of the beatification documents have been published by the Basilian monks of St Josaphat in Rome.

BD ALBAN ROE

The narrative on pp. 144-146 follows Challoner (*op. cit.*, pp. 404-411), who uses a contemporary manuscript now at Oscott. There is a full account of Roe in B. Camm, *Nine Martyr Monks* (London, 1931), and see T. Horner, *Ampleforth and Its Origins* (London, 1952).

THE NORTH AMERICAN MARTYRS

See Francis Parkman, *The Jesuits in North America* (Boston, 1868), passim. There have been many books about these martyrs published in recent years.

BD PETER WRIGHT

Challoner, *op. cit.*, pp. 499-504, uses a life of Father Wright written by an eye-witness of his martyrdom, and published at Antwerp in the same year.

BD JOHN WALL

See Challoner, *op. cit.*, pp. 550-555.

BD OLIVER PLUNKET

Plunket's trial and execution are set out at length from the sources in Alice Curtayne's *The Trial of Oliver Plunkett* (London and New York, 1953).

ST JOHN DE BRITTO

A French translation of a report from the superior of the

Madura mission, written six days after John de Britto's death, is printed in H. Leclercq, *op. cit.*, vol. ix, pp. 337-357.

BD GOMIDAS KEUMURGIAN

Father Matthew's Armenian biography (Venice, *c.* 1710) of this martyr is summarized in Minas Nuikhan's *Life and Times of . . . Abbot Mechitar* (trans. by John McQuillan; Venice, 1915), pp. 162-183. There are further particulars of Bd Gomidas in D. Attwater's *Book of Eastern Saints* (Milwaukee, 1938).

BD PETER SANZ

There is a contemporary account of this and other martyrs in China printed in H. Leclercq, *op. cit.*, vol. x, pp. 153-202.

THE MARTYRS OF SEPTEMBER

Because of the circumstances and the destruction of records, information about these massacres is not as clear and detailed as could be wished; but there are several works on the subject, *e.g.*, J. Grente, *Les martyrs de Septembre* (Paris, 1919), and P. Caron, *Les massacres de Septembre* (Paris, 1935).

BD JOHN DAT

Translations into French of the three documents referred to may be found in H. Leclercq, *op. cit.*, pp. 358-359, 388-409.

BD JOSEPH MARCHAND AND OTHERS

There is a life of Father Marchand by J. Chauvin (Paris, 1936), of Father Cornay by R. Plus (Paris, 1947) and of Father Borie by M. Vermeil (Brive, 1897), and several general works on the martyrs of Indo-China.

BD JOHN PERBOYRE

There are several books in French about this martyr; the latest is by A. Chatelet *J.-G. Perboyre . . . martyr* (Paris, 1943).

ST PETER CHANEL

There is a full life by C. Nicolet, *Vie du bx. P. M. Chanel* (Lyons, 1935).

THE DAMASCUS MARTYRS

In 1926 books were published in Rome by P. Paoli, *Il b. Emmanuele Ruiz e i suoi sette compagni,* and by C. Salotti, *L'eroismo di tre martiri maroniti.*

THE UGANDA MARTYRS

There are full accounts in several languages, notably J. P. Thoonen's *Black Martyrs* (London, 1942).

MARTYRS UNDER THE BOXERS

There is an account of these martyrs in English, *Franciscan Martyrs of the Boxer Rising,* by Father Jerome, o.f.m., and a recent one in French by M. T. de Blarer.

MICHAEL PRO

There is a biography by Mrs George Norman, *The Life and Martyrdom of Father Michael Pro* (London, 1938), based on Father A. Dragon's *Le Père Pro.* Francis McCullagh's *Red Mexico* contains a detailed account of the execution, of which the author was an eye-witness.

THEODORE ROMZA

There are some particulars of Bishop Romza in a Ukrainian publication, *First Victims of Communism* (English trans., Rome, 1953). Other details on pp. 209-211 herein were kindly supplied by the rector of the Russian College, Father Theophil Horaček, and by Father Stanislaus Tyszkiewicz, s.j.

JOHN TUNG

An English translation of Father Tung's speech in full was printed in the *China Missionary Bulletin* (C. T. S., Hongkong) for 8 October 1951, and most of it appeared also in *The Ensign* (Montreal) for 29 March 1952. For further information I am indebted to Mgr René Boisguérin, of the Paris Foreign Missions, and to the Maryknoll Information Bureau, N. Y. There is a relevant article in *Études* (Paris) for October 1951. At the time of going to press there seems reason to believe that Father Tung is still alive.

APPENDIX

There is a full translation of St Cyprian's exhortation in, *e.g.*, the Library of the Fathers, vol. iii (Oxford, 1846); text in Migne, P. L., and elsewhere. The biblical passages on pp. 220 ff. herein are in Mgr Knox's version.